Race after Technology

Ruha Benjamin

RACE AFTER TECHNOLOGY

Abolitionist Tools for the New Jim Code

polity

The right of Ruha Benjamin to be identified as Author of this Work has been asserted in accordance with the UK Copyright, Designs and Patents Act 1988.

First published in 2019 by Polity Press
Reprinted: 2019 (five times), 2020 (five times), 2021

Polity Press
65 Bridge Street
Cambridge CB2 1UR, UK

Polity Press
101 Station Landing
Suite 300
Medford, MA 02155, USA

ISBN-13: 978-1-5095-2639-0
ISBN-13: 978-1-5095-2640-6(pb)

A catalogue record for this book is available from the British Library.

Library of Congress Cataloging-in-Publication Data
Names: Benjamin, Ruha, author.
Title: Race after technology : abolitionist tools for the new Jim code / Ruha Benjamin.
Description: Medford, MA : Polity, 2019. | Includes bibliographical references and index.
Identifiers: LCCN 2018059981 (print) | LCCN 2019015243 (ebook) | ISBN 9781509526437 (Epub) | ISBN 9781509526390 (hardback) | ISBN 9781509526406
    (paperback)
Subjects: LCSH: Digital divide--United States--21st century. | Information technology--Social aspects--United States--21st century. | African Americans--Social conditions--21st century. | Whites--United States--Social conditions--21st century. | United States--Race relations--21st century. | BISAC: SOCIAL SCIENCE / Demography.
Classification: LCC HN90.I56 (ebook) | LCC HN90.I56 B46 2019 (print) | DDC 303.48/330973--dc23
LC record available at https://lccn.loc.gov/2018059981

Typeset in 11 on 14 pt Sabon by
Servis Filmsetting Ltd, Stockport, Cheshire
Printed and bound in the United States by LSC Communications

For further information on Polity, visit our website: politybooks.com

Contents

Figures

All my life I've prided myself on being a survivor.
But surviving is just another loop . . .
Maeve Millay, *Westworld*[1]

I should constantly remind myself that the real leap
consists in introducing invention into existence . . .
In the world through which I travel,
I am endlessly creating myself . . .

I, the [hu]man of color, want only this:
That the tool never possess the [hu]man.
Black Skin, White Masks, Frantz Fanon[2]

Preface

I spent part of my childhood living with my grandma just off Crenshaw Boulevard in Los Angeles. My school was on the same street as our house, but I still spent many a day trying to coax kids on my block to "play school" with me on my grandma's huge concrete porch covered with that faux-grass carpet. For the few who would come, I would hand out little slips of paper and write math problems on a small chalkboard until someone would insist that we go play tag or hide-and-seek instead. Needless to say, I didn't have that many friends! But I still have fond memories of growing up off Crenshaw surrounded by people who took a genuine interest in one another's well-being and who, to this day, I can feel cheering me on as I continue to play school.

Some of my most vivid memories of growing up also involve the police. Looking out of the backseat window of the car as we passed the playground fence, boys lined up for police pat-downs; or hearing the nonstop rumble of police helicopters overhead, so close that the roof would shake while we all tried to ignore it. Business as usual. Later, as a young mom, anytime I went back to visit I would recall the frustration of trying to keep the kids asleep with the sound and light from the helicopter piercing the window's thin pane. Like everyone who lives in a heavily policed neighborhood, I grew up with a keen sense of being watched. Family, friends, and neighbors – all of us caught up in a carceral web, in which other people's safety and freedom are predicated on our containment.

Now, in the age of big data, many of us continue to be monitored and measured, but without the audible rumble of helicopters to which we can point. This doesn't mean we no longer feel what it's like to be a problem. We do. This book is my attempt to shine light in the other direction, to decode this subtle but no less hostile form of systemic bias, the New Jim Code.

Introduction
The New Jim Code

Naming a child is serious business. And if you are not White in the United States, there is much more to it than personal preference. When my younger son was born I wanted to give him an Arabic name to reflect part of our family heritage. But it was not long after 9/11, so of course I hesitated. I already knew he would be profiled as a Black youth and adult, so, like most Black mothers, I had already started mentally sparring those who would try to harm my child, even before he was born. Did I really want to add *another* round to the fight? Well, the fact is, I am also very stubborn. If you tell me I should *not* do something, I take that as a dare. So I gave the child an Arabic first *and* middle name and noted on his birth announcement: "This guarantees he will be flagged anytime he tries to fly."

If you think I am being hyperbolic, keep in mind that names are racially coded. While they are one of the everyday tools we use to express individuality and connections, they are also markers interacting with numerous technologies, like airport screening systems and police risk assessments, as forms of data. Depending

1

on one's name, one is more likely to be detained by state actors in the name of "public safety."

Just as in naming a child, there are many everyday contexts – such as applying for jobs, or shopping – that employ emerging technologies, often to the detriment of those who are racially marked. This book explores how such technologies, which often pose as objective, scientific, or progressive, too often reinforce racism and other forms of inequity. Together, we will work to decode the powerful assumptions and values embedded in the material and digital architecture of our world. And we will be stubborn in our pursuit of a more just and equitable approach to tech – ignoring the voice in our head that says, "No way!" "Impossible!" "Not realistic!" But as activist and educator Mariame Kaba contends, "hope is a discipline."[1] Reality is something we create together, except that so few people have a genuine say in the world in which they are forced to live. Amid so much suffering and injustice, we cannot resign ourselves to this reality we have inherited. It is time to reimagine what is possible. So let's get to work.

Everyday Coding

Each year I teach an undergraduate course on race and racism and I typically begin the class with an exercise designed to help me get to know the students while introducing the themes we will wrestle with during the semester. *What's in a name?* Your family story, your religion, your nationality, your gender identity, your race and ethnicity? What assumptions do you think people make about you on the basis of your name? What about your nicknames – are they chosen or imposed? From intimate patterns in dating and romance to large-scale employment trends, our names can open and shut doors. Like a welcome sign inviting people in or a scary mask repelling and pushing them away, this thing that is most *ours* is also out of our hands.

The popular book and Netflix documentary *Freakonomics* describe the process of parents naming their kids as an exercise in branding, positioning children as more or less valuable in a competitive social marketplace. If we are the product, our names are the billboard – a symptom of a larger neoliberal rationale that subsumes all other sociopolitical priorities to "economic growth, competitive positioning, and capital enhancement."[2] My students invariably chuckle when the "baby-naming expert" comes on the screen to help parents "launch" their newest offspring. But the fact remains that naming is serious business. The stakes are high not only because parents' decisions will follow their children for a lifetime, but also because names reflect much longer histories of conflict and assimilation and signal fierce political struggles – as when US immigrants from Eastern Europe anglicize their names, or African Americans at the height of the Black Power movement took Arabic or African names to oppose White supremacy.

I will admit, something that irks me about conversations regarding naming trends is how distinctly African American names are set apart as comically "made up" – a pattern continued in *Freakonomics*. This tendency, as I point out to students, is a symptom of the chronic anti-Blackness that pervades even attempts to "celebrate difference." Blackness is routinely conflated with cultural deficiency, poverty, and pathology ... Oh, those poor Black mothers, look at how they misspell "Uneeq." Not only does this this reek of classism, but it also harbors a willful disregard for the fact that everyone's names were at one point made up![3]

Usually, many of my White students assume that the naming exercise is not about them. "I just have a normal name," "I was named after my granddad," "I don't have an interesting story, prof." But the presumed blandness of White American culture is a crucial part of our national narrative. Scholars describe the power of this plainness as the invisible "center" against which everything else is compared and as the "norm" against which everyone else is measured. Upon further reflection, what appears to be an absence in terms of being "cultureless" works more like a superpower. Invisibility, with regard to Whiteness, offers immunity. To be unmarked by race allows you to reap the benefits but escape responsibility for your role in an unjust system. Just check out the hashtag #CrimingWhileWhite to read the stories of people who are clearly aware that their Whiteness works for them like an armor and a force field when dealing with the police. A "normal" name is just one of many tools that reinforce racial invisibility.

As a class, then, we begin to understand that all those things dubbed "just ordinary" are also cultural, as they embody values, beliefs, and narratives, and normal names offer some of the most powerful stories of all. If names are social codes that we use to make everyday assessments about people, they are not neutral but racialized, gendered, and classed in predictable ways. Whether in the time of Moses, Malcolm X, or Missy Elliot, names have never grown on trees. They are concocted in cultural laboratories and encoded and infused with meaning and experience – particular histories, longings, and anxieties. And some people, by virtue of their social position, are given more license to experiment with unique names. Basically, status confers cultural value that engenders status, in an ongoing cycle of social reproduction.[4]

In a classic study of how names impact people's experience on the job market, researchers show that, all other things being equal, job seekers with White-sounding first names received 50 percent more callbacks from employers than job seekers with Black-sounding names.[5] They calculated that the racial gap was equivalent to eight years of relevant work experience, which White applicants did not actually have; and the gap persisted across occupations, industry, employer size – even when employers included the "equal opportunity" clause in their ads.[6] With emerging technologies we might assume that racial bias will be more scientifically rooted out. Yet, rather than challenging or overcoming the cycles of inequity, technical fixes too often reinforce and even deepen the status quo. For example, a study by a team of computer scientists at Princeton examined whether a popular algorithm, trained on human writing online, would exhibit the same biased tendencies that psychologists have documented among humans. They found that the algorithm associated White-sounding names with "pleasant" words and Black-sounding names with "unpleasant" ones.[7]

Such findings demonstrate what I call "the New Jim Code": *the employment of new technologies that reflect and reproduce existing inequities but that are promoted and perceived as more objective or progressive than the discriminatory systems of a previous era.*[8] Like other kinds of codes that we think of as neutral, "normal" names have power by virtue of their perceived neutrality. They trigger stories about what kind of person is behind the name – their personality and potential, where they come from but also where they should go.

Codes are both reflective and predictive. They have a past and a future. "Alice Tang" comes from a family that values education and is expected to do well in math and science. "Tyrone Jackson" hails from a neighborhood where survival trumps scholastics; and he is expected to excel in sports. More than stereotypes, codes act as narratives, telling us what to expect. As data scientist and *Weapons of Math Destruction* author Cathy O'Neil observes, "[r]acism is the most slovenly of predictive models. It is powered by haphazard data gathering and spurious correlations, reinforced by institutional inequities, and polluted by confirmation bias."[9]

Racial codes are born from the goal of, and facilitate, social control. For instance, in a recent audit of California's gang database, not only do Blacks and Latinxs constitute 87 percent of those listed, but many of the names turned out to be babies under the age of 1, some of whom were supposedly "self-described gang members." So far, no one ventures to explain how this could have happened, except by saying that some combination of zip codes and racially coded names constitute a risk.[10] Once someone is added to the database, whether they know they are listed *or not*, they undergo even more surveillance and lose a number of rights.[11]

Most important, then, is the fact that, once something or someone is coded, this can be hard to change. Think of all of the time and effort it takes for a person to change her name legally. Or, going back to California's gang database: "Although federal regulations require that people be removed from the database after five years, some records were not scheduled to be removed for more than 100 years."[12] Yet rigidity can also give rise to ingenuity. Think of the proliferation of nicknames, an informal mechanism that allows us to work around legal systems that try to fix us in place. We do not have to embrace the status quo, even though we must still deal with the sometimes dangerous consequences of being illegible, as when a transgender person is "deadnamed" – called their birth name rather than chosen name. Codes, in short, operate within powerful systems of meaning that render some things visible, others invisible, and create a vast array of distortions and dangers.

I share this exercise of how my students and I wrestle with the cultural politics of naming because names are an expressive tool that helps us think about the social and political dimensions of all sorts of technologies explored in this book. From everyday apps to complex algorithms, *Race after Technology* aims to cut through industry hype to offer a field guide into the world of biased bots, altruistic algorithms, and their many coded cousins. Far from coming upon a sinister story of racist programmers scheming in the dark corners of the web, we will find that the desire for objectivity, efficiency, profitability, and progress fuels the pursuit of technical fixes across many different social arenas. *Oh, if only there were a way to slay centuries of racial demons with a social justice bot!* But, as we will see, the road to inequity is paved with technical fixes.

Along the way, this book introduces conceptual tools to help us decode the promises of tech with historically and sociologically informed skepticism. I argue that tech fixes often hide, speed up, and even deepen discrimination, while appearing to be neutral or benevolent when compared to the racism of a previous era. This set of practices that I call the New Jim Code encompasses a range of discriminatory designs – some that explicitly work to amplify hierarchies, many that ignore and thus replicate social divisions, and a number that aim to fix racial bias but end up doing the opposite.

Importantly, the attempt to shroud racist systems under the cloak of objectivity has been made before. In *The Condemnation of Blackness*, historian Khalil Muhammad (2011) reveals how an earlier "racial data revolution" in the nineteenth century marshalled science and statistics to make a "disinterested" case for White superiority:

> Racial knowledge that had been dominated by anecdotal, hereditarian, and pseudo-biological theories of race would gradually be transformed by new social scientific theories of race and society and *new tools of analysis*, namely racial statistics and social surveys. Out of the new methods and data sources, *black criminality* would emerge, alongside disease and intelligence, as a fundamental measure of black inferiority.[13]

You might be tempted to see the datafication of injustice in that era as having been much worse than in the present, but I suggest we hold off on easy distinctions because, as we shall see, the language of "progress" is too easily weaponized against those who suffer most under oppressive systems, however sanitized.

Readers are also likely to note how the term New Jim Code draws on *The New Jim Crow*, Michelle Alexander's

(2012) book that makes a case for how the US carceral system has produced a "new racial caste system" by locking people into a stigmatized group through a color-blind ideology, a way of labeling people as "criminals" that permits legalized discrimination against them. To talk of the *new* Jim Crow, begs the question: What of the *old*? "Jim Crow" was first introduced as the title character of an 1832 minstrel show that mocked and denigrated Black people. White people used it not only as a derogatory epithet but also as a way to mark space, "legal and social devices intended to separate, isolate, and subordinate Blacks."[14] And, while it started as a folk concept, it was taken up as an academic shorthand for legalized racial segregation, oppression, and injustice in the US South between the 1890s and the 1950s. It has proven to be an elastic term, used to describe an era, a geographic region, laws, institutions, customs, and a *code* of behavior that upholds White supremacy.[15] Alexander compares the old with the new Jim Crow in a number of ways, but most relevant for this discussion is her emphasis on a shift from explicit racialization to a colorblind ideology that masks the destruction wrought by the carceral system, severely limiting the life chances of those labeled criminals who, by design, are overwhelmingly Black. "Criminal," in this era, is code for Black, but also for poor, immigrant, second-class, disposable, unwanted, detritus.

What happens when this kind of cultural coding gets embedded into the technical coding of software programs? In a now classic study, computer scientist Latanya Sweeney examined how online search results associated Black names with arrest records at a much higher rate than White names, a phenomenon that she first noticed when Google-searching her own name; and results suggested she had a criminal record.[16] The lesson? "Google's algorithms were optimizing for the racially discriminating patterns of past users who had clicked on these ads, learning the racist preferences of some users and feeding them back to everyone else."[17] In a technical sense, the writer James Baldwin's insight is prescient: "The great force of history comes from the fact that we carry it within us, are unconsciously controlled by it in many ways, and history is literally *present* in all that we do."[18] And when these technical codes move beyond the bounds of the carceral system, beyond labeling people as "high" and "low" risk criminals, when automated systems from employment, education, healthcare, and housing come to make decisions about people's deservedness for all kinds of opportunities, then tech designers are erecting a digital caste system, structured by existing racial inequities that are not just colorblind, as Alexander warns. These tech advances are sold as morally superior because they purport to rise above human bias, even though they could not exist without data produced through histories of exclusion and discrimination.

In fact, as this book shows, colorblindness is no longer even a prerequisite for the New Jim Code. In some cases, technology "sees" racial difference, and this range of vision can involve seemingly positive affirmations or celebrations of presumed cultural differences. And yet we are told that how tech sees "difference" is a more objective reflection of reality than if a mere human produced the same results. Even with the plethora of visibly diverse imagery engendered and circulated through technical advances, particularly social media,

10

bias enters through the backdoor of design optimization in which the humans who create the algorithms are hidden from view.

Move Slower . . .

Problem solving is at the heart of tech. An algorithm, after all, is a set of instructions, rules, and calculations designed to solve problems. Data for Black Lives co-founder Yeshimabeit Milner reminds us that "[t]he decision to make every Black life count as three-fifths of a person was embedded in the electoral college, an algorithm that continues to be the basis of our current democracy."[19] Thus, even just deciding *what problem* needs solving requires a host of judgments; and yet we are expected to *pay no attention to the man behind the screen.*[20]

As danah boyd and M. C. Elish of the Data & Society Research Institute posit, "[t]he datasets and models used in these systems are not objective representations of reality. They are the culmination of particular tools, people, and power structures that foreground one way of seeing or judging over another."[21] By pulling back the curtain and drawing attention to forms of coded inequity, not only do we become more aware of the social dimensions of technology but we can work together against the emergence of a digital caste system that relies on our naivety when it comes to the neutrality of technology. This problem extends beyond obvious forms of criminalization and surveillance.[22] It includes an elaborate social and technical apparatus that governs all areas of life.

The animating force of the New Jim Code is that tech designers encode judgments into technical systems but claim that the racist results of their designs are entirely exterior to the encoding process. Racism thus becomes doubled – magnified and buried under layers of digital denial. There are bad actors in this arena that are easier to spot than others. Facebook executives who denied and lied about their knowledge of Russia's interference in the 2016 presidential election via social media are perpetrators of the most broadcast violation of public trust to date.[23] But the line between bad and "neutral" players is a fuzzy one and there are many tech insiders hiding behind the language of free speech, allowing racist and sexist harassment to run rampant in the digital public square and looking the other way as avowedly bad actors deliberately crash into others with reckless abandon.

For this reason, we should consider how private industry choices are in fact public policy decisions. They are animated by political values influenced strongly by libertarianism, which extols individual autonomy and corporate freedom from government regulation. However, a recent survey of the political views of 600 tech entrepreneurs found that a majority of them favor higher taxes on the rich, social benefits for the poor, single-payer healthcare, environmental regulations, parental leave, immigration protections, and other issues that align with Democratic causes. Yet most of them also staunchly opposed labor unions and government regulation.[24] As one observer put it, "Silicon Valley entrepreneurs don't mind the government regulating other industries, but they prefer Washington to stay out of their own business."[25] For example, while many say they support single-payer healthcare *in theory*, they are also reluctant to contribute to tax revenue that would fund such an undertaking. So "political values" here is less about party affiliation or what people believe in the abstract and more to do with how the decisions of tech entrepreneurs impact questions of power, ethics, equity, and sociality. In that light, I think the dominant ethos in this arena is best expressed by Facebook's original motto: "Move Fast and Break Things." To which we should ask: *What about the people and places broken in the process?* Residents of Silicon Valley displaced by the spike in housing costs, or Amazon warehouse workers compelled to skip bathroom breaks and pee in bottles.[26] "Move Fast, Break People, and Call It Progress"?

"Data sharing," for instance, sounds like a positive development, streamlining the bulky bureaucracies of government so the public can access goods and services faster. But access goes both ways. If someone is marked "risky" in one arena, that stigma follows him around much more efficiently, streamlining marginalization. A leading Europe-based advocate for workers' data rights described how she was denied a bank loan despite having a high income and no debt, because the lender had access to her health file, which showed that she had a tumor.[27] In the United States, data fusion centers are one of the most pernicious sites of the New Jim Code, coordinating "data-sharing among state and local police, intelligence agencies, and private companies"[28] and deepening what Stop LAPD Spying Coalition calls the stalker state. Like other techy euphemisms, "fusion" recalls those trendy restaurants where food looks like art. But the clientele of such upscale eateries is rarely the target of data fusion centers that terrorize the residents of many cities.

If private companies are creating public policies

by other means, then I think we should stop calling ourselves "users." Users *get used*. We are more like unwitting constituents who, by clicking submit, have authorized tech giants to represent our interests. But there are promising signs that the tide is turning.

According to a recent survey, a growing segment of the public (55 percent, up from 45 percent) wants more regulation of the tech industry, saying that it does more to hurt democracy and free speech than help.[29] And company executives are admitting more responsibility for safeguarding against hate speech and harassment on their platforms. For example, Facebook hired thousands more people on its safety and security team and is investing in automated tools to spot toxic content. Following Russia's disinformation campaign using Facebook ads, the company is now "proactively finding and suspending coordinated networks of accounts and pages aiming to spread propaganda, and telling the world about it when it does. The company has enlisted fact-checkers to help prevent fake news from spreading as broadly as it once did."[30]

In November 2018, Zuckerberg held a press call to announce the formation of a "new independent body" that users could turn to if they wanted to appeal a decision made to take down their content. But many observers criticize these attempts to address public concerns as not fully reckoning with the political dimensions of the company's private decisions. Reporter Kevin Roose summarizes this governance behind closed doors:

> Shorter version of this call: Facebook is starting a judicial branch to handle the overflow for its executive branch, which is also its legislative branch, also the whole thing is a monarchy.[31]

Introduction

The co-director of the AI Now Research Institute, Kate Crawford, probes further:

> Will Facebook's new Supreme Court just be in the US? Or one for every country where they operate? Which norms and laws rule? Do execs get to overrule the decisions? Finally, why stop at user content? Why not independent oversight of the whole system?"[32]

The "ruthless code of secrecy" that enshrouds Silicon Valley is one of the major factors fueling public distrust.[33] So, too, is the rabid appetite of big tech to consume all in its path, digital and physical real estate alike. "There is so much of life that remains undisrupted." As one longtime tech consultant to companies including Apple, IBM, and Microsoft put it, "For all intents and purposes, we're only 35 years into a 75- or 80-year process of moving from analog to digital. The image of Silicon Valley as Nirvana has certainly taken a hit, but the reality is that we the consumers are constantly voting for them."[34] The fact is, the stakes are too high, the harms too widespread, the incentives too enticing, for the public to accept the tech industry's attempts at self-regulation.

It is revealing, in my view, that many tech insiders choose a more judicious approach to tech when it comes to raising their own kids.[35] There are reports of Silicon Valley parents requiring nannies to sign "no-phone contracts"[36] and opting to send their children to schools in which devices are banned or introduced slowly, in favor of "pencils, paper, blackboards, and craft materials."[37] *Move Slower and Protect People?* All the while I attend education conferences around the country in which vendors fill massive expo halls to sell educators the latest products couched in a concern that all students deserve access – yet the most privileged *refuse it*? Those afforded the luxury of opting out are concerned with tech addiction – "On the scale between candy and crack cocaine, it's closer to crack cocaine," one CEO said of screens.[38] Many are also wary about the lack of data privacy, because access goes both ways with apps and websites that track users' information.

In fact the author of *The Art of Computer Programming*, the field's bible (and some call Knuth himself "the Yoda of Silicon Valley"), recently commented that he feels "algorithms are getting too prominent in the world. It started out that computer scientists were worried nobody was listening to us. Now I'm worried that too many people are listening."[39] To the extent that social elites are able to exercise more control in this arena (at least for now), they also position themselves as digital elites within a hierarchy that allows some modicum of informed refusal at the very top. For the rest of us, nanny contracts and Waldorf tuition are not an option, which is why the notion of a *personal* right to refuse *privately* is not a tenable solution.[40]

The New Jim Code will not be thwarted by simply revising user agreements, as most companies attempted to do in the days following Zuckerberg's 2018 congressional testimony. And more and more young people seem to know that, as when Brooklyn students staged a walkout to protest a Facebook-designed online program, saying that "it forces them to stare at computers for hours and 'teach ourselves,'" guaranteeing only 10–15 minutes of "mentoring" each week![41] In fact these students have a lot to teach us about refusing tech fixes for complex social problems that come packaged in catchphrases like "personalized learning."[42] They are sick and tired of being atomized and quantified, of having their personal uniqueness sold to them, one "tailored" experience after another. They're not buying it. Coded inequity, in short, can be met with collective defiance, with resisting the allure of (depersonalized) personalization and asserting, in this case, the sociality of learning. This kind of defiance calls into question a libertarian ethos that assumes what we all *really* want is to be left alone, screen in hand, staring at reflections of ourselves. Social theorist Karl Marx might call tech personalization our era's opium of the masses and encourage us to "just say no," though he might also point out that not everyone is in an equal position to refuse, owing to existing forms of stratification. *Move slower and empower people.*

Tailoring: Targeting

In examining how different forms of coded inequity take shape, this text presents a case for understanding race itself as a kind of tool – one designed to stratify and sanctify social injustice as part of the architecture of everyday life. In this way, this book challenges us to question not only the technologies we are sold, but also the ones we manufacture ourselves. For most of US history, White Americans have used race as a tool to denigrate, endanger, and exploit non-White people – openly, explicitly, and without shying away from the deadly demarcations that racial imagination brings to life. And, while overt White supremacy is proudly reasserting itself with the election of Donald Trump in 2016, much of this is newly cloaked in the language of White victimization and false equivalency. What about a White history month? White studies programs? White student unions? No longer content with the power of invisibility, a vocal subset of the population wants to be recognized and celebrated as White – a backlash against the civil rights gains of the mid-twentieth century, the election of the country's first Black president, diverse representations in popular culture, and, more fundamentally, a refusal to comprehend that, as Baldwin put it, "white is a metaphor for power," unlike any other color in the rainbow.[43]

The dominant shift toward multiculturalism has been marked by a move away from one-size-fits-all mass marketing toward ethnically tailored niches that capitalize on calls for diversity. For example, the Netflix movie recommendations that pop up on your screen can entice Black viewers, by using tailored movie posters of Black supporting cast members, to get you to click on an option that you might otherwise pass on.[44] Why bother with broader structural changes in casting and media representation, when marketing gurus can make Black actors *appear* more visible than they really are in the actual film? It may be that the hashtag #OscarsSoWhite drew attention to the overwhelming Whiteness of the Academy Awards, but, so long as algorithms become more tailored, the public will be given the illusion of progress.[45]

Importantly, Netflix and other platforms that thrive on tailored marketing do not need to ask viewers about their race, because they use prior viewing and search histories as proxies that help them predict who will be attracted to differently cast movie posters. Economic recognition is a ready but inadequate proxy for political representation and social power. This transactional model of citizenship presumes that people's primary value hinges on the ability to spend money and, in the digital age, expend attention ... browsing, clicking, buying. This helps explain why different attempts to opt out of tech-mediated life can itself become criminalized, as it threatens the digital order of things. Analog is antisocial, with emphasis on *anti* ... "what are you trying to hide?"

Meanwhile, multiculturalism's proponents are usually not interested in facing White supremacy head on. Sure, movies like *Crazy Rich Asians* and TV shows like *Black-ish*, *Fresh off the Boat*, and *The Goldbergs* do more than target their particular demographics; at times, they offer incisive commentary on the racial–ethnic dynamics of everyday life, drawing viewers of all backgrounds into their stories. Then there is the steady stream of hits coming out of Shondaland that deliberately buck the Hollywood penchant for typecasting. In response to questions about her approach to shows like *Grey's Anatomy* and *Scandal*, Shonda Rhimes says she is not trying to diversify television but to normalize it: "Women, people of color, LGBTQ people equal WAY more than 50 percent of the population. Which means it ain't out of the ordinary. I am making the world of television look NORMAL."[46]

But, whether TV or tech, cosmetic diversity too easily stands in for substantive change, with a focus on feel-good differences like food, language, and dress, not on systemic disadvantages associated with employment, education, and policing. Celebrating diversity, in this way, usually avoids sober truth-telling so as not to ruin the party. Who needs to bother with race or sex disparities in the workplace, when companies can capitalize on stereotypical differences between groups?

The company BIC came out with a line of "BICs For Her" pens that were not only pink, small, and bejeweled, but priced higher than the non-gendered ones. Criticism was swift. Even *Business Insider*, not exactly known as a feminist news outlet, chimed in: "Finally, there's a lady's pen that makes it possible for the gentler sex to write on pink, scented paper: Bic for Her. Remember to dot your i's with hearts or smiley faces, girls!" Online reviewers were equally fierce and funny:

> Finally! For years I've had to rely on pencils, or at worst, a twig and some drops of my feminine blood to write down recipes (the only thing a lady should be writing ever) … I had despaired of ever being able to write down said recipes in a permanent manner, though my men-folk assured me that I "shouldn't worry yer pretty little head." But, AT LAST! Bic, the great liberator, has released a womanly pen that my gentle baby hands can use without fear of unlady-like callouses and bruises. Thank you, Bic![47]

No, thank *you*, anonymous reviewers! But the last I checked, ladies' pens are still available for purchase at a friendly online retailer near you, though packaging now includes a nod to "breast cancer awareness," or what is called pinkwashing – the co-optation of breast cancer to sell products or provide cover for questionable political campaigns.[48]

Critics launched a similar online campaign against

an IBM initiative called Hack a Hair Dryer. In the company's efforts to encourage girls to enter STEM professions, they relied on tired stereotypes of girls and women as uniquely preoccupied with appearance and grooming:

> Sorry @IBM i'm too busy working on lipstick chemistry and writing down formula with little hearts over the i s to #HackAHairDryer"[49]

Niche marketing, in other words, has a serious downside when tailoring morphs into targeting and stereotypical containment. Despite decades of scholarship on the social fabrication of group identity, tech developers, like their marketing counterparts, are encoding race, ethnicity, and gender as immutable characteristics that can be measured, bought, and sold. Vows of colorblindness are not necessary to shield coded inequity if we believe that scientifically calculated differences are somehow superior to crude human bias.

Consider this ad for ethnicity recognition software developed by a Russian company, NTech Lab – which beats Google's Facenet as the world's best system for recognition, with 73.3 percent accuracy on 1 million faces (Figure 0.1).[50] NTech explains that its algorithm has "practical applications in retail, healthcare, entertainment and other industries by delivering accurate and timely demographic data to enhance the quality of service"; this includes targeted marketing campaigns and more.[51]

What N-Tech does not mention is that this technology is especially useful to law enforcement and immigration officials and can even be used at mass sporting and cultural events to monitor streaming video feed.[52] This

Figure 0.1 N-Tech Lab, Ethnicity Recognition
Source: Twitter @mor10, May 12, 2018, 5:46 p.m.

shows how multicultural representation, marketed as an individualistic and fun experience, can quickly turn into criminalizing misrepresentation. While some companies such as NTech are already being adopted for purposes of policing, other companies, for example "Diversity Inc," which I will introduce in the next chapter, are squarely in the ethnic marketing business, and some are even developing techniques to try to bypass human bias. What accounts for this proliferation of racial codification?

Why Now?

Today the glaring gap between egalitarian principles and inequitable practices is filled with subtler forms of discrimination that give the illusion of progress and neutrality, even as coded inequity makes it easier and faster to produce racist outcomes. Notice that I said outcomes and not beliefs, because it is important for us to assess how technology can reinforce bias by what it does, regardless of marketing or intention. But first we should acknowledge that intentional and targeted forms of White supremacy abound!

As sociologist Jessie Daniels documents, White nationalists have ridden the digital wave with great success. They are especially fond of Twitter and use it to spread their message, grow their network, disguise themselves online, and generate harassment campaigns that target people of color, especially Black women.[53] Not only does the design of such platforms enable the "gamification of hate" by placing the burden on individual users to report harassers; Twitter's relatively hands-off approach when it comes to the often violent and hate-filled content of White supremacists actually benefits the company's bottom line.

This is a business model in which more traffic equals more profit, even if that traffic involves violently crashing into other users – as when *Ghostbusters* star Leslie Jones received constant threats of rape and lynching after noted White supremacist Milo Yiannopoulos rallied a digital mob against her: a high-profile example of the macro-aggressions that many Black women experience on social media every day.[54] In Daniels' words, "[s]imply put, White supremacists love Twitter because Twitter loves them back."[55] Jones for her part reached out to her friend, Twitter's CEO Jack Dorsey; and Dorsey is now considering artificial intelligence (AI) of the kind used on Instagram to identify hate speech and harassment.[56]

And, while the use of social media to amplify and spread obvious forms of racial hatred is an ongoing problem that requires systematic interventions, it is also the most straightforward to decode, literally. For example, White supremacists routinely embed seemingly benign symbols in online content, cartoon characters or hand signs, that disseminate and normalize their propaganda. However, these are only the most visible forms of coded inequity in which we can identify the intentions of self-proclaimed racists. The danger, as I see it, is when we allow these more obvious forms of virulent racism to monopolize our attention, when the equivalent of slow death – the subtler and even alluring forms of coded inequity – get a pass. My book hopes to focus more of our attention on this New Jim Code.

Today explicitly racist laws are no longer on the books, yet racism continues in many areas of life as a result of a vast carceral apparatus that facilitates legal discrimination against those "marked" with a criminal record. So, while Black people in the abstract enjoy greater freedom of movement, in practice many are immobilized by an elaborate penal system. Not only those who are convicted, but entire families and communities are stigmatized and penalized by association – they carry a badge of dishonor with widespread consequences, such as restrictions on where people can live, work, and move around.[57] This is the paradox Michelle Alexander documents: the legalized discrimination afforded by the US penal system at a time when de jure segregation is no longer acceptable. Thanks to the work of Alexander and many others, social awareness about the carceral system is growing and people are looking for "more humane" alternatives, such as ankle monitors, and "more objective" measures, such as crime prediction software, to decide who should be caged and for how long. As widespread concern over mass incarceration increases, people are turning to technological fixes that encode inequity in a different form.

Growing exposure of social problems is fueling new forms of obfuscation. For instance, public discourse is filled with frequent and widespread condemnation of blatant acts of racism, albeit often euphemized through the language of "racial incidents." No longer limited to television or newspapers, condemnation on social media makes the practice of "dragging" people through the virtual public square easier and swifter. Viral hashtags and memes allow almost anyone to publicize racist transgressions, sometimes as they are happening, with the potential for news to spread globally in a matter of minutes. Dragging can be entertaining, and it is profitable for corporations by driving up clicks; but it is also cathartic for those who previously had their experiences of racism questioned or dismissed. It offers a collective ritual, which acknowledges and exposes the everyday insults and dangers that are an ongoing part of Black life. Video recordings, in particular, position viewers as witnesses whose judgment may have political and professional repercussions for those whose blatant racist actions are on view.

For example, in the spring of 2018, the TV network ABC cancelled the revival of the sitcom *Roseanne*, after the show's eponymous lead actress, Roseanne Barr, tweeted a series of racist messages ending with one that directed racially coded slurs at Valerie Jarrett, former advisor to Barack Obama. Hashtags like #CancelRoseanne operate like a virtual public square in which response to racial insults are offered and debated. Memes, too, are an effective tool for dragging racism. One of the most creative and comedic depicts a White woman at Oakland's Lake Merritt who called the police on a Black man who was barbecuing with the "wrong" type of grill. BBQBecky's image from the video recording has been cut and pasted at the scene of many "crimes" – she is depicted calling the police on the 1963 March on Washington, on Rosa Parks sitting on the bus, on Michelle and Barack Obama getting sworn into office, and even on the Black Panther as he greets cheering crowds at the Wakanda waterfalls – among many other faux offenses.

In a context in which people are able to voice their discontent and expose the absurdity of everyday insults, the pervasiveness of race talk can serve as a proxy for more far-reaching social progress. Paradoxically, as platforms like Twitter, Instagram, and YouTube give more opportunities to put blatant acts of racism on trial, many of these same companies encode more insidious forms of inequity in the very design of their products and services. By drawing our attention to Roseanne-like slurs or BBQBecky-like citizen policing, dragging may obscure how the New Jim Code operates behind the scenes.

Similarly, the hypervisibility of Black celebrities, athletes, and politicians can mask the widespread disenfranchisement of Black communities through de facto segregation and the punishment apparatus. How can a society filled with millions of people cheering for LeBron, singing along to Beyoncé, tuning in to Oprah, and pining for the presidency of Obama be ... racist? But alas, "Black faces in high places" is not an aberration but a key feature of a society structured by White supremacy.[58] In hindsight, we would not point to the prominence of Black performers and politicians in the early twentieth century as a sign that racism was on the decline. But it is common to hear that line of reasoning today.

Tokenism is not simply a distraction from systemic domination. Black celebrities are sometimes recruited to be the (Black) face of technologies that have the potential to deepen racial inequities. For example, in 2018 Microsoft launched a campaign featuring the rapper Common to promote AI:

> Today, right now, you have more power at your fingertips than entire generations that came before you. Think about that. That's what technology really is. It's possibility. It's adaptability. It's capability. But in the end it's only a tool. What's a hammer without a person who swings it? It's not about what technology can do, it's about what you can do with it. You're the voice, and it's the microphone. When you're the artist, it's the paintbrush. We are living in the future we always dreamed of . . . AI empowering us to change the world we see . . . So here's the question: What will you do with it?[59]

Savvy marketing on the part of Microsoft, for sure. What better aesthetic than a Black hip-hop artist to represent AI as empowering, forward-thinking, cool – the antithesis of anti-Black discrimination? Not to mention that, as an art form, hip-hop has long pushed the boundaries of technological experimentation through beatboxing, deejaying, sampling, and more. One could imagine corporate-sponsored rap battles between artists and AI *coming to a platform near you*. The democratizing ethos of Common's narration positions the listener as a protagonist in a world of AI, one whose voice can direct the development of this tool even though rarely a day goes by without some report on biased bots. So what is happening behind the screens?

A former Apple employee who noted that he was "not Black or Hispanic" described his experience on a team that was developing speech recognition for Siri, the virtual assistant program. As they worked on different English dialects – Australian, Singaporean, and Indian English – he asked his boss: "What about African American English?" To this his boss responded: "Well, Apple products are for the premium market." And this happened in 2015, "one year after [the rapper] Dr. Dre sold Beats by Dr. Dre to Apple for a billion dollars." The irony, the former employee seemed to imply, was that the company could somehow devalue *and* value Blackness at the same time.[60] It is one thing to capitalize on the coolness of a Black artist to sell (overpriced) products and quite another to engage the cultural specificity of Black people enough to enhance the underlying design of a widely used technology. This is why the notion that tech bias is "unintentional" or "unconscious" obscures the reality – that there is no way to create something without some intention and intended user in mind (a point I will return to in the next chapter).

For now, the Siri example helps to highlight how just having a more diverse team is an inadequate solution to discriminatory design practices that grow out of the interplay of racism and capitalism. Jason Mars, a Black computer scientist, expressed his frustration saying, "There's a kind of pressure to conform to the prejudices of the world ... It would be interesting to have a black guy talk [as the voice for his app], but we don't want to create friction, either. First we need to sell products."[61] How does the fist-pumping empowerment of Microsoft's campaign figure in a world in which the voices of Black programmers like Mars are treated as conflict-inducing? Who gets muted in this brave new world? The view that "technology is a neutral tool" ignores how race also functions like a tool, structuring whose literal voice gets embodied in AI. In celebrating diversity, tokenistic approaches to tech development fail to acknowledge how the White aesthetic colors AI. The "blandness" of Whiteness that some of my students brought up when discussing their names is treated by programmers as normal, universal, and appealing. The invisible power of Whiteness means that even a Black computer scientist running his own company who earnestly wants to encode a different voice into his app is still hemmed in by the desire of many people for White-sounding voices.

So, as we work to understand the New Jim Code, it is important to look beyond marketing rhetoric to the realities of selling and targeting diversity. One of the companies, Diversity, Inc., which I will discuss in more detail in Chapter 1, creates software that helps other companies and organizations tailor marketing campaigns to different ethnic groups. In the process it delineates over 150 distinct ethnicities and "builds" new ones for companies and organizations that want to market their goods or services to a subgroup not already represented in the Diversity, Inc. database. Technologies do not just reflect racial fault lines but can be used to reconstruct and repackage social groupings in ways that seem to celebrate difference. But would you consider this laudable or exploitative, opportunistic or oppressive?

And who ultimately profits from the proliferation of ethnically tailored marketing? These are questions we will continue to wrestle with in the pages ahead.

Finally, the New Jim Code is part of a broader push toward privatization where efforts to cut costs and maximize profits, often at the expense of other human needs, is a guiding rationale for public and private sectors alike.[62] Computational approaches to a wide array of problems are seen as not only good but necessary, and a key feature of cost-cutting measures is the outsourcing of decisions to "smart" machines. Whether deciding which teacher to hire or fire or which loan applicant to approve or decline, automated systems are alluring because they seem to remove the burden from gatekeepers, who may be too overworked or too biased to make sound judgments. Profit maximization, in short, is rebranded as bias minimization.

But the outsourcing of human decisions is, at once, the insourcing of coded inequity. As philosopher and sociologist Herbert Marcuse remarked, "[t]echnological rationality has become political rationality." Considering Marcuse's point, as people become more attuned to racial biases in hiring, firing, loaning, policing, and a whole host of consequential decisions – an awareness we might take to be a sign of social progress – this very process also operates as a kind of opportunity for those who seek to manage social life more efficiently. The potential for bias creates a demand for more efficient and automated organizational practices, such as the employment screening carried out by AI – an example we will explore in more depth. Important to this story is the fact that power operates at the level of institutions and individuals – our political and mental structures

– shaping citizen-subjects who prioritize efficiency over equity.

It is certainly the case that algorithmic discrimination is only one facet of a much wider phenomenon, in which what it means to be human is called into question. What do "free will" and "autonomy" mean in a world in which algorithms are tracking, predicting, and persuading us at every turn? Historian Yuval Noah Harari warns that tech knows us better than we know ourselves, and that "we are facing not just a technological crisis but a philosophical crisis."[63] This is an industry with access to data and capital that exceeds that of sovereign nations, throwing even that sovereignty into question when such technologies draw upon the science of persuasion to track, addict, and manipulate the public. We are talking about a redefinition of human identity, autonomy, core constitutional rights, and democratic principles more broadly.[64]

In this context, one could argue that the racial dimensions of the problem are a subplot of (even a distraction from) the main action of humanity at risk. But, as philosopher Sylvia Wynter has argued, our very notion of what it means to be human is fragmented by race and other axes of difference. She posits that there are different "genres" of humanity that include "full humans, not-quite humans, and nonhumans,"[65] through which racial, gendered, and colonial hierarchies are encoded. The pseudo-universal version of humanity, "the Man," she argues, is only *one* form, and that it is predicated on anti-Blackness. As such, Black humanity and freedom entail thinking and acting beyond the dominant genre, which could include telling different stories about the past, the present, and the future.[66]

But what does this have to do with coded inequity? First, it's true, anti-Black technologies do not necessarily limit their harm to those coded Black.[67] However, a universalizing lens may actually hide many of the dangers of discriminatory design, because in many ways Black people *already* live in the future.[68] The plight of Black people has consistently been a harbinger of wider processes – bankers using financial technologies to prey on Black homeowners, law enforcement using surveillance technologies to control Black neighborhoods, or politicians using legislative techniques to disenfranchise Black voters – which then get rolled out on an even wider scale. An #AllLivesMatter approach to technology is not only false inclusion but also poor planning, especially by those who fancy themselves as futurists.

Many tech enthusiasts wax poetic about a posthuman world and, indeed, the expansion of big data analytics, predictive algorithms, and AI, animate digital dreams of living beyond the human mind and body – even beyond human bias and racism. *But posthumanist visions assume that we have all had a chance to be human.* How nice it must be . . . to be so tired of living mortally that one dreams of immortality. Like so many other "posts" (postracial, postcolonial, etc.), posthumanism grows out of the Man's experience. This means that, by decoding the racial dimensions of technology and the way in which different genres of humanity are constructed in the process, we gain a keener sense of the architecture of power – and not simply as a top-down story of powerful tech companies imposing coded inequity onto an innocent public. This is also about how we (click) submit, because of all that we seem to gain by having our choices and behaviors tracked, predicted, and racialized. The director of research at Diversity, Inc. put it to me like this: "Would *you* really want to see a gun-toting White man in a Facebook ad?" Tailoring ads makes economic sense for companies that try to appeal to people "like me": a Black woman whose sister-in-law was killed in a mass shooting, who has had to "shelter in place" after a gunman opened fire in a neighboring building minutes after I delivered a talk, and who worries that her teenage sons may be assaulted by police or vigilantes. Fair enough. Given these powerful associations, a gun-toting White man would probably not be the best image for getting my business.

But there is a slippery slope between effective marketing and efficient racism. The same sort of algorithmic filtering that ushers more ethnically tailored representations into my feed can also redirect real estate ads away from people "like me." This filtering has been used to show higher-paying job ads to men more often than to women, to charge more for standardized test prep courses to people in areas with a high density of Asian residents, and many other forms of coded inequity. In cases of the second type especially, we observe how geographic segregation animates the New Jim Code. While the gender wage gap and the "race tax" (non-Whites being charged more for the same services) are nothing new, the difference is that coded inequity makes discrimination easier, faster, and even harder to challenge, because there is not just a racist boss, banker, or shopkeeper to report. Instead, the public must hold accountable the very platforms and programmers that legally and often invisibly facilitate the New Jim Code, even as we reckon with our desire for more "diversity and inclusion" online and offline.

Taken together, all these features of the current era animate the New Jim Code. While more institutions and people are outspoken against blatant racism, discriminatory practices are becoming more deeply embedded within the sociotechnical infrastructure of everyday life. Likewise, the visibility of successful non-White individuals in almost every social arena can obscure the reality of the systemic bias that still affects many people. Finally, the proliferation of ever more sophisticated ways to use ethnicity in marketing goods, services, and even political messages generates more buy-in from those of us who may not want to "build" an ethnicity but who are part of New Jim Code architecture nevertheless.

The Anti-Black Box

Race after Technology integrates the tools of science and technology studies (STS) and critical race studies to examine coded inequity and our contemporary racial landscape. Taken together within the framework of what I term *race critical code studies*, this approach helps us open the Black box of coded inequity. "Black box" is a metaphor commonly used in STS to describe how the social production of science and technology is hidden from view. For example, in *The Black Box Society*, legal scholar Frank Pasquale (2014) interrogates the "secret algorithms" that are fundamental to businesses, from Wall Street to Silicon Valley, and criticizes how the law is used to aggressively protect commercial secrecy while ignoring our right to privacy.[69] His use of the term "Black box" draws on its double meaning, as recording device and as mysterious object; and here I recast this term to draw attention to the routine anti-Blackness that inheres in so much tech development. What I call the *anti-Black box* links the race-neutral technologies that encode inequity to the race-neutral laws and policies that serve as powerful tools for White supremacy.

An example is the Trump administration's proposed "work for welfare" policy, which imposes mandatory work requirements on anyone who receives healthcare benefits through Medicaid. Correction: not anyone. Some Republican-controlled states have found a way to protect poor White Americans from the requirement by instituting a waiver for people living in areas with a high unemployment rate. Taken at face value, this looks like a fair exception and seems to be race-neutral in that it could benefit poorer Americans of all backgrounds. In practice, however, people living in urban centers would not qualify because of their proximity to wealthier suburbs, which pull the overall unemployment rate down for the majority of Black urban residents.

Public policy, then, like popular discourse, is filled with racial coding. Rural :: White and urban :: Black; so, without ever making race explicit, state lawmakers are able to carve out an exception for their White constituents. In a country as segregated as the United States, geography is a reliable proxy for race. If zip codes are a relatively low-tech device for instituting racism, how might we apply this insight to computer codes? How do they reinforce racist norms and structures without explicitly invoking race? And can we develop a race-conscious orientation to emerging technology, not only as a mode of critique but as a prerequisite for designing technology differently?

Race as Technology

This field guide explores not only how emerging technologies hide, speed up, or reinforce racism, but also how race itself is a kind of technology[70] – one designed to separate, stratify, and sanctify the many forms of injustice experienced by members of racialized groups, but one that people routinely reimagine and redeploy to their own ends.

Human toolmaking is not limited to the stone instruments of our early ancestors or to the sleek gadgets produced by the modern tech industry. Human cultures also create symbolic devices that structure society. Race, to be sure, is one of our most powerful tools – developed over hundreds of years, varying across time and place, codified in law and refined through custom, and, tragically, still considered by many people to reflect immutable differences between groups. For that reason, throughout this book, we will consider not only how racial logics enter the design of technology but how race itself operates as a tool of vision and division with often deadly results.

Racism is, let us not forget, a means to reconcile contradictions. Only a society that extolled "liberty for all" while holding millions of people in bondage requires such a powerful ideology in order to build a nation amid such a startling contradiction. How else could one declare "[w]e hold these truths to be self-evident, that all men are created equal, that they are endowed by their Creator with certain unalienable Rights," and at the same time deny these rights to a large portion of the population[71] – namely by claiming that its members, by virtue of their presumed lack of humanity, were never even eligible for those rights?[72] Openly despotic societies, by contrast, are in no need of the elaborate ideological apparatus that props up "free" societies. Freedom, as the saying goes, *ain't free*. But not everyone is required to pay its steep price in equal measure. The same is true of the social costs of technological progress.

Consider that the most iconic revolt "against machines," as it is commonly remembered, was staged by English textile workers, the Luddites, in nineteenth-century England. Often remembered as people who were out of touch and hated technology, the Luddites were actually protesting the *social costs* of technological "progress" that the working class was being forced to accept. "To break the machine was in a sense to break the conversion of oneself into a machine for the accumulating wealth of another," according to cultural theorist Imani Perry.[73] At a recent conference titled "AI & Ethics," the communications director of a nonprofit AI research company, Jack Clark, pointed out that, although the term "Luddite" is often used today as a term of disparagement for anyone who is presumed to oppose (or even question!) automation, the Luddite response was actually directed at the manner in which machinery was rolled out, without consideration for its negative impact on workers and society overall. Perhaps the current era of technological transformation, Clark suggested, warrants a similar sensibility – demanding a more careful and democratic approach to technology.[74]

Shifting from nineteenth-century England to late twenty-first-century Mexico, sci-fi filmmaker Alex Rivera wrestles with a similar predicament of a near future in which workers are not simply displaced but inhabited by technology. *Sleep Dealer* (2008) is set in a dystopian world of corporate-controlled water, militarized drones, "aqua-terrorists" (or water liberators, depending on your sympathies), and a walled-off border between Mexico and the United States. The main protagonist, Memo Cruz, and his co-workers plug networked cables into nodes implanted in their bodies. This enables them to operate robots on the other side of the border, giving the United States what it always wanted: "all the work without the workers."[75]

Such fictional accounts find their real-life counterpart in "electronic sweatshops," where companies such as Apple, HP, and Dell treat humans like automata, reportedly requiring Chinese workers to complete tasks every three seconds over a 12-hour period, without speaking or using the bathroom.[76] Indeed, as I write, over 1,000 workers at Amazon in Spain have initiated a strike over wages and rights, following similar protests in Italy and Germany in 2017. If we probe exploitative labor practices, the stated intention would likely elicit buzzwords such as "lower costs" and "greater efficiency," signaling a fundamental tension and paradox – the indispensable disposability of those whose labor enables innovation. The language of intentionality only makes one side of this equation visible, namely the desire to produce goods faster and cheaper, while giving people "the opportunity to work." This fails to account for the social costs of a technology in which global forms of racism, caste, class, sex, and gender exploitation are the nuts and bolts of development.[77]

"Racing" after technology, in this context, is about the pursuit of efficiency, neutrality, Ready to Update, Install Now, I Agree, and about what happens when we (click) submit too quickly.[78] Whether it is in the architecture of machines or in the implementation of laws, racial logic imposes "race corrections" that distort our understanding of the world.[79] Consider the court decision in the case against one Mr. Henry Davis, who was charged with destruction of property for bleeding on police uniforms after officers incorrectly identified him as having an outstanding warrant and then beat him into submission:

> On and/or about the 20th day of September 20, 2009 at or near 222 S. Florissant within the corporate limits of Ferguson, Missouri, the above-named defendant did then and there unlawfully commit the offense of "property damage" to wit did transfer blood to the uniform.[80]

When Davis sued the officers, the judge tossed out the case, saying: "a reasonable officer could have believed that beating a subdued and compliant Mr. Davis while causing a concussion, scalp lacerations, and bruising with almost no permanent damage, did not violate the Constitution."[81] The judge "race-corrected" our reading of the US Constitution, making it inapplicable to the likes of Mr. Davis – a reminder that, whatever else we think racism is, it is not simply ignorance, or a not knowing. Until we come to grips with the "reasonableness" of racism, we will continue to look for it on the bloody floors of Charleston churches and in the dashboard cameras on Texas highways, and overlook it in the smart-sounding logics of textbooks, policy statements, court rulings, science journals, and cutting-edge technologies.

Beyond Techno-Determinism

In the following chapters we will explore not only how racism is an output of technologies gone wrong, but also how it is an input, part of the social context of design processes. The mistaken view that society is affected *by* but does not affect technological development is one expression of a deterministic worldview. Headlines abound: "Is Facebook Making Us Lonely?";[82] "Genetic Engineering Will Change Everything Forever";[83] "Pentagon Video Warns of 'Unavoidable' Dystopian Future for World's Biggest Cities."[84] In each, you can observe the conventional relationship proffered between technology and society. It is the view that such developments are inevitable, the engine of human progress ... or decline.

An extreme and rather mystical example of techno-determinism was expressed by libertarian journalist Matt Ridley, who surmised that not even basic science is essential, because innovation has a trajectory all its own:

Technology seems to change by a sort of inexorable, evolutionary progress, which we probably cannot stop – or speed up much either ... Increasingly, technology is developing the kind of autonomy that hitherto characterized biological entities ... The implications of this new way of seeing technology – as an autonomous, evolving entity that continues to progress whoever is in charge – are startling. People are pawns in a process. We ride rather than drive the innovation wave. Technology will find its inventors, rather than vice versa.[85]

Whereas such hard determinists, like Ridley, posit that technology has a mind of its own, soft determinists grant that it is at least possible for people to make decisions about technology's trajectory. However, they still imagine a lag period in which society is playing catch-up, adjusting its laws and norms to the latest invention. In this latter view, technology is often depicted as neutral, or as a blank slate developed outside political and social contexts, with the potential to be shaped and governed through human action. But, as Manuel Castells argues, "[t]he dilemma of technological determinism is probably a false problem, since technology is society, and society cannot be understood or represented without its technological tools."[86]

Considering Castells' point about the symbiotic relationship between technology and society, this book employs a conceptual toolkit that synthesizes scholarship from STS and critical race studies. Surprisingly, these two fields of study are not often put into direct conversation. STS scholarship opens wide the "Black box" that typically conceals the inner workings of sociotechnical systems, and critical race studies interrogates the inner workings of sociolegal systems. Using this hybrid approach, we observe not only that any given social order is impacted by technological development, as determinists would argue, but that social norms, ideologies, and practices are a constitutive part of technical design.

Much of the early research and commentary on race

and information technologies coalesced around the idea of the "digital divide," with a focus on unequal access to computers and the Internet that falls along predictable racial, class, and gender lines. And, while attention to access is vital, especially given numerous socioeconomic activities that involve using the Internet, the larger narrative of a techno-utopia in which technology will necessarily benefit all undergird the "digital divide" focus. Naively, access to computers and the Internet is posited as a solution to inequality.[87] And, to the extent that marginalized groups are said to fear or lack an understanding of technology, the "digital divide" framing reproduces culturally essentialist understandings of inequality. A focus on technophobia and technological illiteracy downplays the structural barriers to access, and also ignores the many forms of tech engagement and innovation that people of color engage in.

In fact, with the advent of mobile phones and wireless laptops, African Americans and Latinxs are more active web users than White people.[88] Much of the African continent, in turn, is expected to "leapfrog" past other regions, because it is not hampered by clunky infrastructure associated with older technologies. In "The Revolution Will Be Digitized: Afrocentricity and the Digital Public Sphere," Anna Everett critiques "the overwhelming characterizations of the brave new world of cyberspace as primarily a racialized sphere of Whiteness" that consigns Black people to the low-tech sphere – when they are present at all.[89] Other works effectively challenge the "digital divide" framing by analyzing the racialized boundary constructed between "low" and "high tech."[90] Likewise, Lisa Nakamura (2013) challenges the model minority framing of Asian

Americans as the "solution" to the problem of race in a digital culture. She explains:

> Different minorities have different functions in the cultural landscape of digital technologies. They are good for different kinds of ideological work ... seeing Asians as the solution and blacks as the problem [i.e. cybertyping] is and has always been a drastic and damaging formulation which pits minorities against each other ...[91]

In contrast to critical race studies analyses of the dystopian digital divide and cybertyping, another stream of criticism focuses on utopian notions of a "race-free future" in which technologies would purportedly render obsolete social differences that are divisive now.[92] The idea that, "[o]n the Internet, nobody knows you're a dog" (a line from Peter Steiner's famous 1993 *New Yorker* cartoon, featuring a typing canine) exemplifies this vision. However, this idea relies on a text-only web, which has been complicated by the rise of visual culture on the Internet.[93] For example, as already mentioned, Jessie Daniels (2009) investigates the proliferation of White nationalist ideology and communities online, unsettling any techno-utopian hopes for a colorblind approach to social life in a digital era. And, as Alondra Nelson shows, both the digital divide and the raceless utopia framings posit race as a liability, as "either negligible or evidence of negligence," so that "racial identity, and blackness in particular, is the anti-avatar of digital life."[94] It is also worth noting how, in both conceptions, technology is imagined as impacting racial divisions – magnifying or obliterating them – but racial ideologies do not seem to shape the design of technology.

Race critical code studies would have us look at how race and racism impact who has access to new devices, as well as how technologies are produced in the first place. Two incisive works are particularly relevant for thinking about the tension between innovation and containment. In *Algorithms of Oppression* Safiya Noble (2018) argues that the anti-Black and sexist Google search results – such as the pornographic images that come up when you search for "Black girls" – grow out of a "corporate logic of either willful neglect or a profit imperative that makes money from racism and sexism," as key ingredients in the normative substrate of Silicon Valley. In a similar vein, Simone Browne (2015), in *Dark Matters: On the Surveillance of Blackness*, examines how surveillance technologies coproduce notions of Blackness and explains that "surveillance is nothing new to black folks"; from slave ships and slave patrols to airport security checkpoints and stop-and-frisk policing practices, she points to the "facticity of surveillance in black life."[95] Challenging a technologically determinist approach, she argues that, instead of "seeing surveillance as something inaugurated by new technologies," to "see it as ongoing is to insist that we factor in how racism and anti-Blackness undergird and sustain the intersecting surveillances of our present order."[96] As both Noble and Browne emphasize and as my book will expand upon, anti-Black racism, whether in search results or in surveillance systems, is not only a symptom or outcome, but a precondition for the fabrication of such technologies.[97]

Race as technology: this is an invitation to consider racism in relation to other forms of domination as not just an ideology or history, but as a set of technologies that generate patterns of social relations, and these become Black-boxed as natural, inevitable, *automatic.* As such, this is also an invitation to refuse the illusion of inevitability in which technologies of race come wrapped and to "hotwire" more habitable forms of social organization in the process.[98]

Race critical code studies, as I develop it here, is defined not just by *what* we study but also by *how* we analyze, questioning our own assumptions about what is deemed high theory versus pop culture, academic versus activist, evidence versus anecdote. The point is not just to look beneath the surface in order to find connections between these categories, but to pay closer attention to the surfaces themselves. Here I draw upon the idea of *thin description* as a method for reading surfaces – such as screens and skin – especially since a key feature of being racialized is "to be encountered as a surface."[99] In anthropologist John L. Jackson's formulation, thin description is "about how we all travel . . . through the thicket of time and space, about the way . . . both of those trajectories might be constructively thinned, theorized, concretized, or dislodged in service to questions about how we relate to one another in a digital age."[100] He critiques the worship of thick description within anthropology, arguing that it "tries to pass itself off as more than it is, as embodying an expertise that simulates (and maybe even surpasses) any of the ways in which the people being studied might know themselves . . . one that would pretend to see *everything* and, therefore, sometimes sees less than it could."[101]

Thinness, in this way, attempts a humble but no less ambitious approach to knowledge production. Thinness allows greater elasticity, engaging fields of thought and action too often disconnected. This analytic flexibility, in my view, is an antidote to digital disconnection, tracing links between individual and institutional, mundane and spectacular, desirable and deadly in a way that troubles easy distinctions.

At the same time, thin description is a method of respecting particular kinds of boundaries. According to Jackson,

> If thick description imagines itself able to amass more and more factual information in service to stories about cultural difference, "thin description" doesn't fall into the trap of conceptualizing its task as providing complete and total knowledge ... So, there are secrets you keep. That you treat very preciously. Names of research subjects you share but many more you do not. There is information veiled for the sake of story. For the sake of much more.[102]

If the New Jim Code seeks to penetrate all areas of life, extracting data, producing hierarchies, and predicting futures, thin description exercises a much needed discretion, pushing back against the all-knowing, extractive, monopolizing practices of coded inequity.

Thinness is not an analytic *failure*, but an acceptance of *fragility* ... a methodological counterpoint to the hubris that animates so much tech development. What we know today about coded inequity may require a complete rethinking, as social and technical systems change over time. Let's not forget: racism is a mercurial practice, shape-shifting, adept at disguising itself in progressive-like rhetoric. If our thinking becomes too weighed down by our own assuredness, we are likely to miss the avant-garde stylings of NextGen Racism as it struts by.

Introduction

Beyond Biased Bots

How do we move beyond the idea of biased bots, so we can begin to understand a wide range of coded inequities? Here I propose four dimensions to the New Jim Code: engineered inequity, default discrimination, coded exposure, and technological benevolence; and I will elaborate on them in the following chapters.

Chapter 1 takes a closer look at how *engineered inequity* explicitly works to amplify social hierarchies that are based on race, class, and gender and how the debate regarding "racist robots" is framed in popular discourse. I conclude that robots can be racist, given their design in a society structured by interlocking forms of domination.[103]

Chapter 2 looks at what happens when tech developers do not attend to the social and historical context of their work and explores how *default discrimination* grows out of design processes that ignore social cleavages. I also consider how what is often depicted as glitches might serve as powerful opportunities to examine the overall system, a technological canary in the coal mine.

Chapter 3 examines the multiple forms of *coded exposure* that technologies enable, from Polaroid cameras to computer software. Here I think through the various form of visibility and of how, for racialized groups, the problem of being watched (but not seen) relates to newfangled forms of surveillance.

Chapter 4 explores how *technological beneficence* animates tech products and services that offer fixes for social bias. Here I take a look at technologies that explicitly work to address different forms of discrimination, but that may still end up reproducing, or even deepening, discriminatory processes because of the narrow way in which "fairness" is defined and operationalized.

Finally, Chapter 5 examines how practitioners, scholars, activists, artists, and students are working to resist and challenge the New Jim Code – and how you, the reader, can contribute to an approach to technology that moves beyond accessing new products, to advocating for justice-oriented design practices.

Taken as a whole, the conceptual toolkit we build around a race critical code studies will be useful, I hope, for analyzing a wide range of phenomena – from the explicit codification of racial difference in particular devices to the implicit assumption that technology is race-neutral – through which Whiteness becomes the default setting for tech development. This field guide critically interrogates the progressive narratives that surround technology and encourages us to examine how racism is often maintained or perpetuated through technical fixes to social problems. And finally, the next chapters examine the different facets of coded inequity with an eye toward designing them differently. Are you ready?

1

Engineered Inequity

Are Robots Racist?

WELCOME TO THE FIRST INTERNATIONAL BEAUTY CONTEST
JUDGED BY ARTIFICIAL INTELLIGENCE.

So goes the cheery announcement for Beauty AI, an
initiative developed by the Australian- and Hong Kong-
based organization Youth Laboratories in conjunction
with a number of companies who worked together
to stage the first ever beauty contest judged by robots
(Figure 1.1).[1] The venture involved a few seemingly
straightforward steps:

1 Contestants download the Beauty AI app.
2 Contestants make a selfie.
3 Robot jury examines all the photos.
4 Robot jury chooses a king and a queen.
5 News spreads around the world.

As for the rules, participants were not allowed to wear
makeup or glasses or to don a beard. Robot judges
were programmed to assess contestants on the basis of
wrinkles, face symmetry, skin color, gender, age group,

49

Figure 1.1   Beauty AI
Source: http://beauty.ai

ethnicity, and "many other parameters." Over 6,000 submissions from approximately 100 countries poured in. *What could possibly go wrong?*

On August 2, 2016, the creators of Beauty AI expressed dismay at the fact that "the robots did not like people with dark skin." All 44 winners across the various age groups except six were White, and "only one finalist had visibly dark skin."[2] The contest used what was considered at the time the most advanced machine-learning technology available. Called "deep learning," the software is trained to code beauty using pre-labeled images, then the images of contestants are judged against the algorithm's embedded preferences.[3] Beauty, in short, is in the trained eye of the algorithm.

As one report about the contest put it, "[t]he simplest explanation for biased algorithms is that the humans who create them have their own deeply entrenched biases. That means that despite perceptions that algorithms are somehow neutral and uniquely objective, they can often reproduce and amplify existing prejudices."[4] Columbia

University professor Bernard Harcourt remarked: "The idea that you could come up with a culturally neutral, racially neutral conception of beauty is simply mind-boggling." Beauty AI is a reminder, Harcourt notes, that humans are really doing the thinking, even when "we think it's neutral and scientific."[5] And it is not just the human programmers' preference for Whiteness that is encoded, but the combined preferences of *all* the humans whose data are studied by machines as they learn to judge beauty and, as it turns out, *health*.

In addition to the skewed racial results, the framing of Beauty AI as a kind of preventative public health initiative raises the stakes considerably. The team of biogerontologists and data scientists working with Beauty AI explained that valuable information about people's health can be gleaned by "just processing their photos" and that, ultimately, the hope is to "find effective ways to slow down ageing and help people look healthy and beautiful."[6] Given the overwhelming Whiteness of the winners and the conflation of socially biased notions of beauty and health, darker people are implicitly coded as unhealthy and unfit – assumptions that are at the heart of scientific racism and eugenic ideology and policies.

Deep learning is a subfield of machine learning in which "depth" refers to the layers of abstraction that a computer program makes, learning more "complicated concepts by building them out of simpler ones."[7] With Beauty AI, deep learning was applied to image recognition; but it is also a method used for speech recognition, natural language processing, video game and board game programs, and even medical diagnosis. Social media filtering is the most common example of deep learning at work, as when Facebook auto-tags your photos with friends' names or apps that decide which news and advertisements to show you to increase the chances that you'll click. Within machine learning there is a distinction between "supervised" and "unsupervised" learning. Beauty AI was supervised, because the images used as training data were pre-labeled, whereas unsupervised deep learning uses data with very few labels. Mark Zuckerberg refers to deep learning as "the theory of the mind ... How do we model – in machines – what human users are interested in and are going to do?"[8] But the question for us is, is there only *one* theory of the mind, and *whose mind* is it modeled on?

It may be tempting to write off Beauty AI as an inane experiment or harmless vanity project, an unfortunate glitch in the otherwise neutral development of technology for the common good. But, as explored in the pages ahead, such a conclusion is naïve at best. Robots exemplify how race is a form of technology itself, as the algorithmic judgments of Beauty AI extend well beyond adjudicating attractiveness and into questions of health, intelligence, criminality, employment, and many other fields, in which innovative techniques give rise to new-fangled forms of racial discrimination. Almost every day a new headline sounds the alarm, alerting us to the New Jim Code:

"Some algorithms are racist"
"We have a problem: Racist and sexist robots"
"Robots aren't sexist and racist, you are"
"Robotic racists: AI technologies could inherit their creators' biases"

Racist robots, as I invoke them here, represent a much broader process: social bias embedded in technical artifacts, the allure of objectivity without public accountability. Race as a form of technology – the sorting, establishment and enforcement of racial hierarchies with real consequences – is embodied in robots, which are often presented as simultaneously akin to humans but different and at times superior in terms of efficiency and regulation of bias. Yet the way robots can be racist often remains a mystery or is purposefully hidden from public view.

Consider that machine-learning systems, in particular, allow officials to outsource decisions that are (or should be) the purview of democratic oversight. Even when public agencies are employing such systems, private companies are the ones developing them, thereby acting like political entities but with none of the checks and balances. They are, in the words of one observer, "governing without a mandate," which means that people whose lives are being shaped in ever more consequential ways by automated decisions have very little say in how they are governed.[9]

For example, in *Automated Inequality* Virginia Eubanks (2018) documents the steady incorporation of predictive analytics by US social welfare agencies. Among other promises, automated decisions aim to mitigate fraud by depersonalizing the process and by determining who is eligible for benefits.[10] But, as she documents, these technical fixes, often promoted as benefiting society, end up hurting the most vulnerable, sometimes with deadly results. Her point is not that human caseworkers are less biased than machines – there are, after all, numerous studies showing how caseworkers actively discriminate against racialized groups while aiding White applicants deemed more deserving.[11] Rather, as Eubanks emphasizes, automated welfare decisions are not magically fairer than their human counterparts. Discrimination is displaced and accountability is outsourced in this postdemocratic approach to governing social life.[12]

So, how do we rethink our relationship to technology? The answer partly lies in how we think about race itself and specifically the issues of intentionality and visibility.

I Tinker, Therefore I Am

Humans are toolmakers. And robots, we might say, are humanity's finest handiwork. In popular culture, robots are typically portrayed as humanoids, more efficient and less sentimental than *Homo sapiens*. At times, robots are depicted as having human-like struggles, wrestling with emotions and an awakening consciousness that blurs the line between maker and made. Studies about how humans perceive robots indicate that, when that line becomes too blurred, it tends to freak people out. The technical term for it is the "uncanny valley" – which indicates the dip in empathy and increase in revulsion that people experience when a robot appears to be too much like us.[13]

Robots are a diverse lot, with as many types as there are tasks to complete and desires to be met: domestic robots; military and police robots; sex robots; therapeutic robots – and more. A robot is any machine that can perform a task, simple or complex, directed by humans or programmed to operate automatically. The most advanced are smart machines designed to learn from and adapt to their environments, created to become independent of their makers. We might like to think that robotic concerns are a modern phenomenon,[14] but our fascination with automata goes back to the Middle Ages, if not before.[15]

In *An Anthropology of Robots and AI*, Kathleen Richardson observes that the robot has "historically been a way to talk about dehumanization" and, I would add, *not* talk about racialization.[16] The etymology of the word robot is Czech; it comes from a word for "compulsory service," itself drawn from the Slav *robota* ("servitude, hardship").[17] So yes, people have used robots to express anxieties over annihilation, including over the massive threat of war machines. But robots also convey an ongoing agitation about human domination over other humans![18]

The first cultural representation that employed the word robot was a 1920 play by a Czech writer whose machine was a factory worker of limited consciousness.[19] Social domination characterized the cultural laboratory in which robots were originally imagined. And, technically, *people* were the first robots. Consider media studies scholar Anna Everett's earliest experiences using a computer:

> In powering up my PC, I am confronted with the DOS-based text that gave me pause ... "Pri. Master Disk, Pri. Slave Disk, Sec. Master, Sec. Slave." Programmed here is a virtual hierarchy organizing my computer's software operations ... I often wondered why the programmers chose such signifiers that hark back to our nation's ignominious past ... And even though I resisted the presumption of a racial affront or intentionality in such

a peculiar deployment of the slave and master coupling, its choice as a signifier of the computer's operations nonetheless struck me.[20]

Similarly, a 1957 article in *Mechanix Illustrated*, a popular "how-to-do" magazine that ran from 1928 to 2001, predicted that, by 1965:

Slavery will be back! We'll all have personal slaves again ... [who will] dress you, comb your hair and serve meals in a jiffy. Don't be alarmed. We mean robot "slaves."[21]

It goes without saying that readers, so casually hailed as "we," are not the descendants of those whom Lincoln freed. This fact alone offers a glimpse into the implicit Whiteness of early tech culture. We cannot assume that the hierarchical values and desires that are projected onto "we" – *We, the People* with inalienable rights and not *You, the Enslaved* who serve us meals – are simply a thing of the past (Figure 1.2).

Coincidentally, on my way to give a talk – mostly to science, technology, engineering, and mathematics (STEM) students at Harvey Mudd College – that I had planned to kick off with this *Mechanix* ad, I passed two men in the airport restaurant and overheard one say to the other: "I just want someone I can push around ..." So simple yet so profound in articulating a dominant and dominating *theory of power* that many more people feel emboldened to state, unvarnished, in the age of Trump. *Push around*? I wondered, in the context of work or dating or any number of interactions. The slavebot, it seems, has a ready market!

For those of us who believe in a more egalitarian notion of power, of collective empowerment without domination, how we imagine our relation to robots

Engineered Inequity

The robots are coming!
When they do, you'll
command a host of
push-button servants.

By O. O. Binder

You'll Own

IN 1863, Abe Lincoln freed the slaves. But by 1965, slavery will be back! We'll all have personal slaves again, only this time we won't fight a Civil War over them. Slavery will be here to stay.

Don't be alarmed. We mean robot "slaves." Let's take a peek into the future

Robots will dress you, comb your hair and serve meals in a jiffy.

VALET ROBOT
BREAKFAST
DINNER
JET CAR
COMMUTER HELICOPTER

01
02
03
0X
0+0

Mechanix Illustrated

Figure 1.2 Robot Slaves
Source: Binder 1957

offers a mirror for thinking through and against race as technology.

It turns out that the disposability of robots and the denigration of racialized populations go hand in hand. We can see this when police officers use "throwbots" – "a lightweight, ruggedized platform that can literally be thrown into position, then remotely controlled from a position of safety" – to collect video and audio surveillance for use by officers. In the words of a member of one of these tactical teams, "[t]he most significant advantage of the throwable robot is that it 'allows them [sc. the officers] to own the real estate with their eyes, before they pay for it with their bodies.'"[22] Robots are not the only ones sacrificed on the altar of public safety. So too are the many *Black* victims whose very bodies become the real estate that police officers own in their trigger-happy quest to keep the peace. The intertwining history of machines and slaves, in short, is not simply the stuff of fluff magazine articles.[23]

While many dystopic predictions signal a worry that humans may one day be enslaved by machines, the current reality is that the tech labor force is already deeply unequal across racial and gender lines. Although not the same as the structure of enslavement that serves as an analogy for unfreedom, Silicon Valley's hierarchy consists of the highest-paid creatives and entrepreneurs, who are comprised of White men and a few White women, and the lowest-paid manual laborers – "those cleaning their offices and assembling circuit boards," in other words "immigrants and outsourced labor, often women living in the global south," who usually perform this kind of work.[24] The "diasporic diversity" embodied by South Asian and Asian American tech workforce does not challenge this hierarchy, because they continue to be viewed as a "new digital 'different caste.'" As Nakamura notes, "no amount of work can make them part of the digital economy as 'entrepreneurs' or the 'new economic men.'"[25] Racism, in this way, is a technology that is "built into the tech industry."[26] But how does racism "get inside" and operate through new forms of technology?

To the extent that machine learning relies on large, "naturally occurring" datasets that are rife with racial (and economic and gendered) biases, the raw data that robots are using to learn and make decisions about the world reflect deeply ingrained cultural prejudices and structural hierarchies.[27] Reflecting on the connection between workforce diversity and skewed datasets, one tech company representative noted that, "if the training data is produced by a racist society, it won't matter who is on the team, but the people who are affected should also be on the team."[28] As machines become more "intelligent," that is, as they learn to think more like humans, they are likely to become more racist. But this is not inevitable, so long as we begin to take seriously and address the matter of how racism structures the social and technical components of design.

Raising Robots

So, are robots racist? Not if by "racism" we only mean white hoods and racial slurs.[29] Too often people assume that racism and other forms of bias must be triggered by an *explicit* intent to harm; for example, linguist John McWhorter argued in *Time* magazine that "[m]achines cannot, themselves, be racists. Even equipped with artificial intelligence, they have neither brains nor intention."[30] But this assumes that self-conscious intention is what makes something racist. Those working in the belly of the tech industry know that this conflation will not hold up to public scrutiny. As one Google representative lamented, "[r]ather than treating malfunctioning algorithms as malfunctioning machines ('classification errors'), we are increasingly treating tech like asshole humans." He went on to propose that "we [programmers] need to stop the machine from behaving like a jerk because it can look like it is being offensive on purpose."[31] If machines are programmed to carry out tasks, both they and their designers are guided by some purpose, that is to say, intention. And in the face of discriminatory effects, if those with the power to design differently choose business as usual, then they are perpetuating a racist system whether or not they are card-carrying members of their local chapter of Black Lives Matter.

Robots are not sentient beings, sure, but racism flourishes well beyond hate-filled hearts.[32] An indifferent insurance adjuster who uses the even more disinterested metric of a credit score to make a seemingly detached calculation may perpetuate historical forms of racism by plugging numbers in, recording risk scores, and "just doing her job." Thinking with Baldwin, someone who insists on his own racial innocence despite all evidence to the contrary "turns himself into a monster."[33] No malice needed, no N-word required, just lack of concern for how the past shapes the present – and, in this case, the US government's explicit intention to concentrate wealth in the hands of White Americans, in the form of housing and economic policies.[34] Detachment in the face of this history ensures its ongoing codification.

Let us not forget that databases, just like courtrooms, banks, and emergency rooms, do not contain organic brains. Yet legal codes, financial practices, and medical care often produce deeply racist outcomes.

The intention to harm or exclude may guide some technical design decisions. Yet even when they do, these motivations often stand in tension with aims framed more benevolently. Even police robots who can use lethal force while protecting officers from harm are clothed in the rhetoric of public safety.[35] This is why we must separate "intentionality" from its strictly negative connotation in the context of racist practices, and examine how aiming to "do good" can very well coexist with forms of malice and neglect.[36] In fact a do-gooding ethos often serves as a moral cover for harmful decisions. Still, the view that ill intent is always a feature of racism is common: "No one at Google giggled while intentionally programming its software to mislabel black people."[37] Here McWhorter is referring to photo-tagging software that classified dark-skinned users as "gorillas." Having discovered no bogeyman behind the screen, he dismisses the idea of "racist technology" because that implies "designers and the people who hire them are therefore 'racists.'" But this expectation of individual intent to harm as evidence of racism is one that scholars of race have long rejected.[38]

We could expect a Black programmer, immersed as she is in the same systems of racial meaning and economic expediency as the rest of her co-workers, to code software in a way that perpetuates racist stereotypes. Or, even if she is aware and desires to intervene, will she be able to exercise the power to do so? Indeed, by focusing mainly on individuals' identities and overlooking the norms and structures of the tech industry, many diversity initiatives offer little more than cosmetic change, demographic percentages on a company pie chart, concealing rather than undoing the racist status quo.[39]

So, can robots – and, by extension, other types of technologies – be racist? Of course they can. Robots, designed in a world drenched in racism, will find it nearly impossible to stay dry. To a certain extent, they learn to speak the coded language of their human parents – not only programmers but all of us online who contribute to "naturally occurring" datasets on which AI learn. Just like diverse programmers, Black and Latinx police officers are known to engage in racial profiling alongside their White colleagues, though they are also the target of harassment in a way their White counterparts are not.[40] One's individual racial identity offers no surefire insulation from the prevailing ideologies.[41] There is no need to identify "giggling programmers" self-consciously seeking to denigrate one particular group as evidence of discriminatory design. Instead, so much of what is routine, reasonable, intuitive, and codified reproduces unjust social arrangements, without ever burning a cross to shine light on the problem.[42]

A representative of Microsoft likened the care they must exercise when they create and sell predictive algorithms to their customers with "giving a puppy to a three-year-old. You can't just deploy it and leave it alone because it will decay over time."[43] Likewise, describing the many controversies that surround AI, a Google representative said: "We are in the uncomfortable birthing stage of artificial intelligence."[44] Zeros and ones, if we are not careful, could deepen the divides between haves and have-nots, between the deserving and the undeserving – rusty value judgments embedded in shiny new systems.

Interestingly, the MIT data scientists interviewed by anthropologist Kathleen Richardson

> were conscious of race, class and gender, and none wanted to reproduce these normative stereotypes in the robots they created . . . [They] avoided racially marking the "skin" of their creations . . . preferred to keep their machines genderless, and did not speak in class-marked categories of their robots as "servants" or "workers," but companions, friends and children.[45]

Richardson contrasts her findings to that of anthropologist Stefan Helmreich, whose pioneering study of artificial life in the 1990s depicts researchers as "ignorant of normative models of sex, race, gender and class that are refigured in the computer simulations of artificial life."[46] But perhaps the contrast is overdrawn, given that colorblind, gender-neutral, and class-avoidant approaches to tech development are another avenue for coding inequity. If data scientists do indeed treat their robots like children, as Richardson describes, then I propose a race-conscious approach to parenting artificial life – one that does not feign colorblindness. But where should we start?

Automating Anti-Blackness

As it happens, the term "stereotype" offers a useful entry point for thinking about the default settings of technology and society. It first referred to a practice in the printing trade whereby a solid plate called a "stereo" (from the ancient Greek adjective *stereos*, "firm," "solid") was used to make copies. The duplicate was called a "stereotype."[47] The term evolved; in 1850 it designated an "image perpetuated without change" and in 1922 was taken up in its contemporary iteration, to refer to shorthand attributes and beliefs about different groups. The etymology of this term, which is so prominent in everyday conceptions of racism, urges a more sustained investigation of the interconnections between technical and social systems.

To be sure, the explicit codification of racial stereotypes in computer systems is only one form of discriminatory design. Employers resort to credit scores to decide whether to hire someone, companies use algorithms to tailor online advertisements to prospective customers, judges employ automated risk assessment tools to make sentencing and parole decisions, and public health officials apply digital surveillance techniques to decide which city blocks to focus medical resources. Such programs are able to sift and sort a much larger set of data than their human counterparts, but they may also reproduce long-standing forms of structural inequality and colorblind racism.

And these default settings, once fashioned, take on a life of their own, projecting an allure of objectivity that makes it difficult to hold anyone accountable.[48] Paradoxically, automation is often presented as a solution to human bias – a way to avoid the pitfalls of prejudicial thinking by making decisions on the basis of objective calculations and scores. So, to understand racist robots, we must focus less on their intended uses and more on their actions. Sociologist of technology

Zeynep Tufekci describes algorithms as "computational agents who are not alive, but who act in the world."[49] In a different vein, philosopher Donna Haraway's (1991) classic *Simians, Cyborgs and Women* narrates the blurred boundary between organisms and machines, describing how "myth and tool mutually constitute each other."[50] She describes technologies as "frozen moments" that allow us to observe otherwise "fluid social interactions" at work. These "formalizations" are also instruments that enforce meaning – including, I would add, racialized meanings – and thus help construct the social world.[51] Biased bots and all their coded cousins could also help subvert the status quo by exposing and authenticating the existence of systemic inequality and thus by holding up a "black mirror" to society,[52] challenging us humans to come to grips with our deeply held cultural and institutionalized biases.[53]

Consider the simple corrections of our computer systems, where words that signal undue privilege are not legible. The red line tells us that only one of these phenomena, underserved and overserved, is legitimate while the other is a mistake, a myth (Figure 1.3).

But power is, if anything, relational. If someone is experiencing the underside of an unjust system, others, then, are experiencing its upside. If employers are passing up your job application because they associate negative qualities with your name, then there are more jobs available for more appealing candidates. If, however, we do not have a word to describe these excess jobs, power dynamics are harder to discuss, much less intervene in. If you try this exercise today, your spell-check is likely to recognize both words, which reminds us that it is possible to change technical systems so that

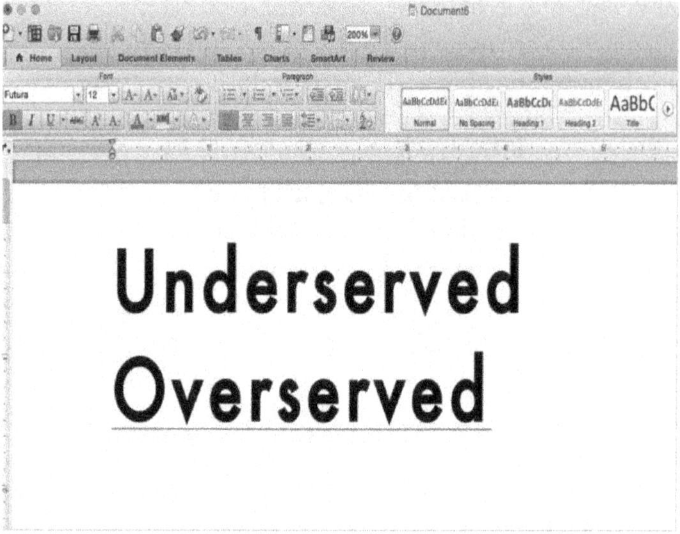

Figure 1.3 Overserved

they do not obscure or distort our understanding and experience of social systems. And, while this is a relatively simple update, we must make the same demand of more complex forms of coded inequity and tune into the socially proscribed forms of (in)visibility that structure their design.

If we look strictly at the technical features of, say, automated soap dispensers and predictive crime algorithms, we may be tempted to home in on their differences. When we consider the stakes, too, we might dismiss the former as relatively harmless, and even a distraction from the dangers posed by the latter. But rather than starting with these distinctions, perhaps there is something to be gained by putting them in the same frame to tease out possible relationships. For instance, the very idea of hygiene – cleaning one's hands and "cleaning up" a neighborhood – echoes a racialized vocabulary. Like the Beauty AI competition, many advertisements for soap conflate darker skin tones with unattractiveness and more specifically with dirtiness, as did an ad from the 1940s where a White child turns to a Black child and asks, "Why doesn't your mama wash you with fairy soap?" Or another one, from 2017, where a Black woman changes into a White woman after using Dove soap. The idea of hygiene, in other words, has been consistently racialized, all the way from marketing to public policy. In fact the most common euphemism for eugenics was "racial hygiene": ridding the body politic of unwanted populations would be akin to ridding the body of unwanted germs. Nowadays we often associate racial hygienists with the Nazi holocaust, but many early proponents were the American progressives who understood eugenics to work as a social uplift and a form of Americanization. The ancient Greek etymon, *eugeneia* (εὐγένεια), meant "good birth," and this etymological association should remind us how promises of goodness often hide harmful practices. As Margaret Atwood writes, "Better never means better for everyone . . . It always means worse, for some."

Take a seemingly mundane tool for enforcing segregation – separate water fountains – which is now an iconic symbol for the larger system of Jim Crow. In isolation from the broader context of racial classification and political oppression, a "colored" water fountain could be considered trivial, though in many cases the path from segregated public facilities to routine public lynching was not very long. Similarly, it is tempting to view a "Whites only" soap dispenser as a trivial inconvenience. In a viral video of two individuals, White and

Black, who show that their hotel soap dispenser does not work for the latter, they are giggling as they expose the problem. But when we situate in a broader racial context what appears to be an innocent oversight, the path from restroom to courtroom might be shorter than we expect.

That said, there is a straightforward explanation when it comes to the soap dispenser: near infrared technology requires light to bounce back from the user and activate the sensor, so skin with more melanin, absorbing as it does more light, does not trigger the sensor. But this strictly technical account says nothing about why this particular sensor mechanism was used, whether there are other options, which recognize a broader spectrum of skin tones, and how this problem was overlooked during development and testing, well before the dispenser was installed. Like segregated water fountains of a previous era, the discriminatory soap dispenser offers a window onto a wider social terrain. As the soap dispenser is, technically, a robot, this discussion helps us consider the racism of robots and the social world in which they are designed.

For instance, we might reflect upon the fact that the infrared technology of an automated soap dispenser treats certain skin tones as normative and upon the reason why this technology renders Black people invisible when they hope to be seen, while other technologies, for example facial recognition for police surveillance, make them hypervisible when they seek privacy. When we draw different technologies into the same frame, the distinction between "trivial" and "consequential" breaks down and we can begin to understand how Blackness can be both marginal and focal to tech development. For this reason I suggest that we hold off on drawing too many bright lines – good versus bad, intended versus unwitting, trivial versus consequential. Sara Wachter-Boettcher, the author of *Technically Wrong*, puts it thus: "If tech companies can't get the basics right . . . why should we trust them to provide solutions to massive societal problems?"[54] The issue is not simply that innovation and inequity can go hand in hand but that a view of technology as value-free means that we are less likely to question the New Jim Code in the same way we would the unjust laws of a previous era, assuming in the process that our hands are clean.

Engineered Inequity

In one of my favorite episodes of the TV show *Black Mirror*, we enter a world structured by an elaborate social credit system that shapes every encounter, from buying a coffee to getting a home loan. Every interaction ends with people awarding points to one another through an app on their phones; but not all the points are created equal. Titled "Nosedive," the episode follows the emotional and social spiral of the main protagonist, Lacie, as she pursues the higher rank she needs in order to qualify for an apartment in a fancy new housing development. When Lacie goes to meet with a points coach to find out her options, he tells her that the only way to increase her rank in such a short time is to get "up votes from quality people. Impress those upscale folks, you'll gain velocity on your arc and there's your boost." Lacie's routine of exchanging five stars with service workers and other "mid- to low-range folks" won't cut it if she wants to improve her score quickly. As the title of the series suggests, *Black Mirror* offers a vivid reflection on the social dimensions of technology – where we *are* and where we might be going with just a few more clicks in the same direction. And, although the racialized dimensions are not often made very explicit, there is a scene toward the beginning of the episode when Lacie notices all her co-workers conspiring to purposely lower the ranking of a Black colleague and forcing him into a subservient position as he tries to win back their esteem ... an explicit illustration of the New Jim Code.

When it comes to engineered inequity, there are many different types of "social credit" programs in various phases of prototype and implementation that are used for scoring and ranking populations in ways that reproduce and even amplify existing social hierarchies. Many of these come wrapped in the packaging of progress. And, while the idiom of the New Jim Code draws on the history of racial domination in the United States as a touchstone for technologically mediated injustice, our focus must necessarily reach beyond national borders and trouble the notion that racial discrimination is isolated and limited to one country, when a whole host of cross-cutting social ideologies make that impossible.

Already being implemented, China's social credit system is an exemplar of explicit ranking with far-reaching consequences. What's more, *Black Mirror* is referenced in many of the news reports of China's experiment, which started in 2014, with the State Council announcing its plans to develop a way to score the trustworthiness of citizens. The government system, which will require mandatory enrollment starting from 2020, builds on rating schemes currently used by private companies.

Using proprietary algorithms, these apps track not only financial history, for instance whether someone pays his bills on time or repays her loans, but also many other variables, such as one's educational, work, and criminal history. As they track all one's purchases, donations, and leisure activities, something like too much time spent playing video games marks the person as "idle" (for which points may be docked), whereas an activity like buying diapers suggests that one is "responsible." As one observer put it, "the system not only investigates behaviour – it shapes it. It 'nudges' citizens away from purchases and behaviours the government does not like."[55] Most alarmingly (as this relates directly to the New Jim Code), residents of China's Xinjiang, a predominantly Muslim province, are already being forced to download an app that aims to track "terrorist and illegal content."

Lest we be tempted to think that engineered inequity is a problem "over there," just recall Donald Trump's idea to register all Muslims in the United States on an electronic database – not to mention companies like Facebook, Google, and Instagram, which already collect the type of data employed in China's social credit system. Facebook has even patented a scoring system, though it hedges when asked whether it will ever develop it further. Even as distinct histories, politics, and social hierarchies shape the specific convergence of innovation and inequity in different contexts, it is common to observe, across this variation, a similar deployment of buzzwords, platitudes, and promises.

What sets China apart (for now) is that all those tracked behaviors are already being rated and folded into a "citizen score" that opens or shuts doors, depending on one's ranking.[56] People are given low marks for political misdeeds such as "spreading rumors" about government officials, for financial misdeeds such as failing to pay a court fine, or social misdeeds such as spending too much time playing video games. A low score brings on a number of penalties and restrictions, barring people from opportunities such as a job or a mortgage and prohibiting certain purchases, for example plane tickets or train passes.[57] The chief executive of one of the companies that pioneered the scoring system says that it "will ensure that the bad people in society don't have a place to go, while good people can move freely and without obstruction."[58]

Indeed, it is not only the desire to move freely, but all the additional privileges that come with a higher score that make it so alluring: faster service, VIP access, no deposits on rentals and hotels – not to mention the admiration of friends and colleagues. Like so many other technological lures, systems that seem to objectively rank people on the basis of merit and things we like, such as trustworthiness, invoke "efficiency" and "progress" as the lingua franca of innovation. China's policy states: "It will forge a public opinion environment where keeping trust is glorious. It will strengthen sincerity in government affairs, commercial sincerity, social sincerity and the construction of judicial credibility."[59] In fact, higher scores have become a new status symbol, even as low scorers are a digital underclass who may, we are told, have an opportunity to climb their way out of the algorithmic gutter.

72

Even the quality of people in one's network can affect your score – a bizarre scenario that has found its way onto TV shows like *Black Mirror* and *Community*, where even the most fleeting interpersonal interactions produce individual star ratings, thumbs up and down, giving rise to digital elites and subordinates. As Zeynep Tufekci explains, the ubiquitous incitement to "like" content on Facebook is designed to accommodate the desires of marketers and works against the interests of protesters, who want to express dissent by "disliking" particular content.[60] And, no matter how arbitrary or silly the credit (see "meow meow beenz" in the TV series *Community*), precisely because people and the state invest it with import, the system carries serious consequences for one's quality of life, until finally the pursuit of status spins out of control.

The phenomenon of measuring individuals not only by their behavior but by their networks takes the concept of social capital to a whole new level. In her work on marketplace lenders, sociologist Tamara K. Nopper considers how these companies help produce and rely on what she calls *digital character* – a "profile assessed to make inferences regarding character in terms of credibility, reliability, industriousness, responsibility, morality, and relationship choices."[61] Automated social credit systems make a broader principle of merit-based systems clear: scores assess a person's ability to conform to established definitions of good behavior and valued sociality rather than measuring any intrinsic quality. More importantly, the ideological commitments of dominant groups typically determine what gets awarded credit in the first place, automating social reproduction. This implicates not only race and ethnicity; depending on the fault lines of a given society, merit systems also codify class, caste, sex, gender, religion, and disability oppression (among other factors). The point is that multiple axes of domination typically converge in a single code.

Take the credit associated with the aforementioned categories of playing video games and buying diapers. There are many ways to parse the values embedded in the distinction between the "idle" and the "responsible" citizen so that it lowers the scores of gamers and increases the scores of diaper changers. There is the ableist logic, which labels people who spend a lot of time at home as "unproductive," whether they play video games or deal with a chronic illness; the conflation of economic productivity and upright citizenship is ubiquitous across many societies.

Consider, too, how gender norms are encoded in the value accorded to buying diapers, together with the presumption that parenthood varnishes (and, by extension, childlessness tarnishes) one's character. But one may wonder about the consequences of purchasing too many diapers. Does reproductive excess lower one's credit? Do assumptions about sex and morality, often fashioned by racist and classist views, shape the interpretation of having children and of purchasing diapers? In the United States, for instance, one could imagine the eugenic sensibility that stigmatizes Black women's fertility and celebrates White women's fecundity getting codified through a system that awards points for diapers purchased in suburban zip codes and deducts points for the same item when purchased in not yet gentrified parts of the city – the geography of social worth serving as a proxy for gendered racism and the New Jim Code. In these various scenarios, top-down reproductive policies could give way to a social credit system in which the consequences of low scores are so far-reaching that they could serve as a veritable digital birth control.

In a particularly poignant exchange toward the end of the "Nosedive" episode, Lacie is hitchhiking her way to win the approval of an elite group of acquaintances; and motorists repeatedly pass her by on account of her low status. Even though she knows the reason for being disregarded, when a truck driver of even lower rank kindly offers to give her a ride, Lacie looks down her nose at the woman ("nosedive" indeed). She soon learns that the driver has purposefully opted out of the coercive point system and, as they make small talk, the trucker says that people assume that, with such a low rank, she must be an "antisocial maniac." Lacie reassures the woman by saying you "seem normal." Finally, the trucker wonders about Lacie's fate: "I mean you're a 2.8 but you don't *look* 2.8." This moment is illuminating as to how abstract quantification gets embodied – that the difference between a 2.8 and a 4.0 kind of person should be self-evident and readable on the (sur)face. This is a key feature of racialization: we take arbitrary qualities (say, social score, or skin color), imbue them with cultural importance, and then act as if they reflected natural qualities in people (and differences between them) that should be obvious just by looking at someone.[62]

In this way speculative fiction offers us a canvas for thinking about the racial vision that we take for granted in our day-to-day lives. The White protagonist, in this case, is barred from housing, transportation, and relationships – a fictional experience that mirrors the forms of ethno-racial exclusions that many groups have actually experienced; and Lacie's low status, just like that of her real-life counterparts, is attributed to some intrinsic quality of her person rather than to the coded inequity that structures her social universe. The app, in this story, builds upon an already existing racial arithmetic, expanding the terms of exclusion to those whose Whiteness once sheltered them from harm. This is the subtext of so much science fiction: the anxiety that, if "we" keep going down this ruinous road, then *we might be next.*

Ultimately the danger of the New Jim Code positioning is that existing social biases are reinforced – yes. But new methods of social control are produced as well. Does this mean that every form of technological prediction or personalization has racist effects? Not necessarily. It means that, whenever we hear the promises of tech being extolled, our antennae should pop up to question what all that hype of "better, faster, fairer" might be hiding and making us ignore. And, when bias and inequity come to light, "lack of intention" to harm is not a viable alibi. One cannot reap the reward when things go right but downplay responsibility when they go wrong.

2

Default Discrimination

Is the Glitch Systemic?

GLITCH

- a minor problem
- a false or spurious electronic signal
- a brief or sudden interruption or irregularity
- may derive from Yiddish, glitsh – to slide, glide, "slippery place."[1]

When Princeton University media specialist Allison Bland was driving through Brooklyn, the Google Maps narrator directed her to "turn right on Malcolm Ten Boulevard," verbally interpreting the X in the street name as a Roman numeral rather than as referring to the Black liberation leader who was assassinated in New York City in 1965 (Figure 2.1).

Social and legal codes, like their byte-size counterparts, are not neutral; nor are all codes created equal. They reflect particular perspectives and forms of social organization that allow some people to assert themselves – their assumptions, interests, and desires – over others. From the seemingly mundane to the extraordinary, technical systems offer a mirror to the wider terrain of struggle over the forces that govern our lives.

ALBLA
@alliebland

Following ∨

Then Google Maps was like, "turn right on
Malcolm Ten Boulevard" and I knew there
were no black engineers working there

9:42 PM - 19 Nov 2013

3,656 Retweets **3,749** Likes

♡ 100   ⇄ 3.7K   ♡ 3.7K   ✉

Figure 2.1 Malcolm Ten
Source: Twitter @alliebland, November 19, 2013, 9:42 p.m.

Database design, in that way, is "an exercise in world-building," a normative process in which programmers are in a position to project their world views – a process that all too often reproduces the technology of race.[2] Computer systems are a part of the larger matrix of systemic racism. Just as legal codes are granted an allure of objectivity – "justice is (color)blind" goes the fiction – there is enormous mystique around computer codes, which hides the human biases involved in technical design.

The Google Maps glitch is better understood as a form of displacement or digital gentrification mirroring the widespread dislocation underway in urban areas across the United States. In this case, the cultural norms and practices of programmers – who are drawn from a narrow racial, gender, and classed demographic – are coded into technical systems that, literally, tell people where to go. These seemingly innocent directions, in turn, reflect and reproduce racialized commands that instruct people where they belong in the larger social order.[3]

78

Ironically, this problem of misrecognition actually reflects a solution to a difficult coding challenge. A computer's ability to parse Roman numerals, interpreting an "X" as "ten," was a hard-won design achievement.[4] That is, from a strictly technical standpoint, "Malcolm Ten Boulevard" would garner cheers. This illustrates how innovations reflect the priorities and concerns of those who frame the problems to be solved, and how such solutions may reinforce forms of social dismissal, regardless of the intentions of individual programmers.

While most observers are willing to concede that technology can be faulty, acknowledging the periodic breakdowns and "glitches" that arise, we must be willing to dig deeper.[5] A narrow investment in technical innovation necessarily displaces a broader set of social interests. This is more than a glitch. It is a form of exclusion and subordination built into the ways in which priorities are established and solutions defined in the tech industry. As Andrew Russell and Lee Vinsel contend, "[t]o take the place of progress, 'innovation,' a smaller, and morally neutral, concept arose. Innovation provided a way to celebrate the accomplishments of a high-tech age without expecting too much from them in the way of moral and social improvement."[6] For this reason, it is important to question "innovation" as a straightforward social good and to look again at what is hidden by an idealistic vision of technology. How is technology already raced?

This chapter probes the relationship between glitch and design, which we might be tempted to associate with competing conceptions of racism. If we think of racism as something of the past or requiring a particular visibility to exist, we can miss how the New Jim Code operates and what seeming glitches reveal about the structure of racism. Glitches are generally considered a fleeting interruption of an otherwise benign system, not an enduring and constitutive feature of social life. But what if we understand glitches instead to be a slippery place (with reference to the possible Yiddish origin of the word) between fleeting and durable, micro-interactions and macro-structures, individual hate and institutional indifference? Perhaps in that case glitches are not spurious, but rather a kind of signal of how the system operates. Not an aberration but a form of evidence, illuminating underlying flaws in a corrupted system.

Default Discrimination

At a recent workshop sponsored by a grassroots organization called Stop LAPD Spying, the facilitator explained that community members with whom she works might not know what algorithms are, but they know what it feels like to be watched. Feelings and stories of being surveilled are a form of "evidence," she insisted, and community testimony is data.[7] As part of producing those data, the organizers interviewed people about their experiences with surveillance and their views on predictive policing. They are asked, for example: "What do you think the predictions are based on?" One person, referring to the neighborhood I grew up in, responded:

> Because they over-patrol certain areas – if you're only looking on Crenshaw and you only pulling Black people

over then it's only gonna make it look like, you know, whoever you pulled over or whoever you searched or whoever you criminalized that's gonna be where you found something.[8]

Comments like this remind us that people who are most directly impacted by the New Jim Code have a keen sense of the default discrimination facilitated by these technologies. As a form of social technology, institutional racism, past and present, is the precondition for the carceral technologies that underpin the US penal system. At every stage of the process – from policing, sentencing, and imprisonment to parole – automated risk assessments are employed to determine people's likelihood of committing a crime.[9] They determine the risk profile of neighborhoods in order to concentrate police surveillance, or the risk profile of individuals in order to determine whether or for how long to release people on parole.

In a recent study of the recidivism risk scores assigned to thousands of people arrested in Broward County, Florida, ProPublica investigators found that the score was remarkably unreliable in forecasting violent crime. They also uncovered significant racial disparities:

> In forecasting who would re-offend, the algorithm made mistakes with black and white defendants at roughly the same rate but in very different ways. The formula was particularly likely to falsely flag black defendants as future criminals, wrongly labeling them this way at almost twice the rate as white defendants. White defendants were mislabeled as low risk more often than black defendants.[10]

The algorithm generating the risk score builds upon already existing forms of racial domination and reinforces them precisely because the apparatus ignores how race shapes the "weather." Literary scholar Christina Sharpe describes the weather as "the total climate; and the climate is antiblack."[11] For example, the survey given to prospective parolees to forecast the likelihood that they will recidivate includes questions about their criminal history, education and employment history, financial history, and neighborhood characteristics (among many other factors). As all these variables are structured by racial domination – from job market discrimination to ghettoization – the survey measures the extent to which an individual's life chances have been impacted by racism without ever asking an individual's race.[12]

Likewise, predictive policing software will always be more likely to direct police to neighborhoods like the one I grew up in, because the data that this software is drawing from reflect ongoing surveillance priorities that target predominantly Black neighborhoods.[13] Anti-Blackness is no glitch. The system is accurately rigged, we might say, because, unlike in natural weather forecasts, the weathermen are also the ones who make it rain.[14]

Even those who purportedly seek "fairness" in algorithmic decision-making are not usually willing to assert that the benchmark for whether an automated prediction is "unwarranted" is whether it strays from the proportion of a group in the larger population. That is, if a prediction matches the current crime rate, it is still unjust! Even so, many who are grappling with how to enact ethical practices in this arena still use the crime rate as the default measure of whether an algorithm is predicting fairly, when that very measure is a byproduct of ongoing regimes of selective policing and punishment.[15]

$$\frac{\delta A}{\delta t} = B + \frac{\eta D}{4} \nabla^2 A - \omega A + \theta \omega \delta$$

Figure 2.2   Patented PredPol Algorithm
Source: http://www.predpol.com/technology

Interestingly, the most commonly used algorithm in Los Angeles and elsewhere, called PredPol, is drawn directly from a model used to predict earthquake aftershocks (Figure 2.2). As author of *Carceral Capitalism*, Jackie Wang gives us this description: "In police departments that use PredPol, officers are given printouts of jurisdiction maps that are covered with red square boxes that indicate where crime is supposed to occur throughout the day . . . The box is a kind of *temporary crime zone*." She goes on to ask:

> What is the attitude or mentality of the officers who are patrolling one of the boxes? When they enter one of the boxes, do they expect to stumble upon a crime taking place? How might the expectation of finding crime influence what the officers actually find? Will people who pass through these temporary crime zones while they are being patrolled by officers automatically be perceived as suspicious? Could merely passing through one of the red boxes constitute probable cause?[16]

Let me predict: yes. If we consider that institutional racism in this country is an ongoing unnatural disaster, then crime prediction algorithms should more accurately be called crime *production* algorithms. The danger with New Jim Code predictions is the way in which self-fulfilling prophecies enact what they predict, giving the allure of accuracy. As the man behind PredPol's media strategy put it, "it sounds like fiction, but its more like science fact."[17]

Predicting Glitches

One of the most iconic scenes from *The Matrix* film trilogy deals with the power of predictions and self-fulfilling prophecies. The main protagonist, Neo, goes to visit the Oracle, a software program depicted as a Black woman in her late sixties. Neo is trying to figure out whether he is who others think he is – "the one" who is supposed to lead humanity in the war against the machines. As he tries to get a straight answer from the Oracle and to figure out whether she really has the gift of prophecy, she says, "I'd ask you to sit down, but you're not going to anyway. *And don't worry about the vase.*"

> NEO: What vase? [Neo knocks a vase to the floor]
> THE ORACLE: That vase.
> NEO: I'm sorry.
> THE ORACLE: I said don't worry about it. I'll get one of my kids to fix it.
> NEO: How did you know?
> THE ORACLE: What's really going to bake your noodle later on is, *would you still have broken it if I hadn't said anything.*[18]

This scene invites a question about real-life policing: Would cops still have warrants to knock down the doors in majority Black neighborhoods if predictive algorithms hadn't said anything?

The Matrix offers a potent allegory for thinking about

power, technology, and society. It is set in a dystopian future in which machines overrun the world, using the energy generated by human brains as a vital source of computing power. Most of humanity is held captive in battery-like pods, their minds experiencing an elaborate life-like simulation of the real world in order to pacify humans and maximize the amount of energy brains produce. The film follows a small band of freedom fighters who must convince Neo that the simulated life he was living is in fact a digital construction.

Early on in his initiation to this new reality, Neo experiences a fleeting moment of déjà vu when a black cat crosses his path – twice. Trinity, his protector and eventual love interest, grows alarmed and explains that this "glitch in the matrix" is not at all trivial but a sign that something about the program has been changed by the agents of the Matrix. The sensation of déjà vu is a warning sign that a confrontation is imminent and that they should prepare to fight.

The film's use of déjà vu is helpful for considering the relationship between seemingly trivial technical glitches and meaningful design decisions. The glitch in this context is a not an insignificant "mistake" to be patched over, but rather serves as a signal of something foundational about the structure of the world meant to pacify humans. It draws attention to the construction and reconstruction of the program and functions as an indication that those seeking freedom should be ready to spring into action.

A decade before the *Matrix* first hit the big screen, Black feminist theorist Patricia Hill Collins conceptualized systemic forms of inequality in terms of a "matrix of domination" in which race, class, gender, and other axes of power operated together, "as sites of domination and as potential sites of resistance."[19] This interlocking matrix operates at individual, group, and institutional levels, so that empowerment "involves rejecting the dimensions of knowledge, whether personal, cultural, or institutional, that perpetuate objectification and dehumanization."[20] Relating this dynamic to the question of how race "gets inside" technology, the Roman numeral glitch of Google Maps and others like it urge us to look again at the way our sociotechnical systems are constructed – by whom and to what ends.

Racist glitches – such as celebrity chef Paula Dean's admission that "yes, of course" she has used the N-word alongside her desire to host a "really southern plantation wedding" with all-Black servers;[21] or a tape-recorded phone call in which former Los Angeles Clippers owner and real estate mogul Donald Sterling told a friend "[i]t bothers me a lot that you want to broadcast that you're associating with black people"[22] – come and go, as provocative sound bites muffling a deeper social reckoning. In my second example, the scandal associated with Sterling's racist remarks stands in stark contrast with the hush and acceptance of a documented pattern of housing discrimination exercised over many years, wherein he refused to rent his properties to Black and Latinx tenants in Beverly Hills and to non-Korean tenants in LA's Koreatown.[23] In the midst of the suit brought by the Department of Justice, the Los Angeles chapter of the National Association for the Advancement of Colored People nevertheless honored Sterling with a lifetime achievement award in 2009. Only once his tape-recorded remarks went public in 2014 did the organization back out of plans to award him this highest honor for a second time, forcing the chapter president to resign amid criticism.

Dragging individuals as objects of the public condemnation of racist speech has become a media ritual and pastime. Some may consider it a distraction from the more insidious, institutionalized forms of racism typified by Sterling's real estate practices. The déjà vu regularity of all those low-hanging N-words would suggest that stigmatizing individuals is not much of a deterrent and rarely addresses all that gives them license and durability.

But, as with Trinity's response to Neo in the *Matrix* regarding his path being crossed twice by a black cat, perhaps if we situated racist "glitches" in the larger complex of social meanings and structures, we too could approach them as a signal rather than as a distraction. Sterling's infamous phone call, in this case, would alert us to a deeper pattern of housing discrimination, with far-reaching consequences.

Systemic Racism Reloaded

Scholars of race have long challenged the focus on individual "bad apples," often to be witnessed when someone's racist speech is exposed in the media – which is typically followed by business as usual.[24] These individuals are treated as glitches in an otherwise benign system. By contrast, sociologists have worked to delineate how seemingly neutral policies and norms can poison the entire "orchard" or structure of society, systematically benefiting some while subjugating others.[25]

Whereas racist glitches are often understood as transient, as signals they can draw our attention to discriminatory design as a durable feature of the social landscape since this nation's founding. As sociologists Joe Feagin and Sean Elias write, "[i]n the case of US society, systemic racism is foundational to and engineered into its major institutions and organizations."[26] This reorientation is also exemplified by Eduardo Bonilla-Silva's *Racism without Racists*, in which he defines "racialized social systems, or white supremacy for short ... as the totality of the social relations and practices that reinforce white privilege. Accordingly, the task of analysts interested in studying racial structures is to uncover the particular social, economic, political, social control, and ideological mechanisms responsible for the reproduction of racial privilege in a society."[27]

Taken together, this work builds upon the foundational insights of Charles V. Hamilton and Kwame Ture (née Stokely Carmichael), who developed the term "institutional racism" in 1967. While the authors discuss the linkage between institutional racism and what they describe as individual racism, they also state:

> This is not to say that every single white American consciously oppresses black people. He does not need to. Institutional racism has been maintained deliberately by the power structure and through indifference, inertia, and lack of courage on the part of the white masses as well as petty officials ... The line between purposeful suppression and indifference blurs.[28]

But taking issue with the overwhelming focus on top-down forces that characterize work on systemic racism, including Feagin and Elias' "theory of oppression,"

Michael Omi and Howard Winant highlight the agency and resistance of those subordinated by such systems. They say:

> To theorize racial politics and the racial state, then, is to enter the complex territory where structural racism encounters self-reflective action, the radical practice of people of color (and their white allies) in the United States. It is to confront the instability of the US system of racial hegemony, in which despotism and democracy coexist in seemingly permanent conflict.[29]

Strikingly, throughout this early work on institutional racism and structural inequality, there was very little focus on the role of technologies, beyond mass media, in advancing or undermining racial ideologies and structures. As Jessie Daniels notes in "Race and Racism in Internet Studies":

> The role of race in the development of Internet infrastructure and design has largely been obscured (Taborn, 2008). As Sinclair observes, "The history of race in America has been written as if technologies scarcely existed, and the history of technology as if it were utterly innocent of racial significance."[30]

Daniels' (2009) *Cyber Racism* illuminates how "white supremacy has entered the digital era" while acknowledging how those "excluded by the white-dominated mainstream media" also use the Internet for grassroots organizing and antiracist discourse.[31] In so doing, she challenges both those who say that technology is only a "source of danger" when it comes to the active presence of White supremacists online and those who assume that technology is "inherently democratizing."[32] Daniels echoes Nakamura's (2002, 2008) frustration with how

89

race remains undertheorized in Internet studies and urges more attention to the technology of structural racism. In line with the focus on glitches, researchers tend to concentrate on how the Internet perpetuates or mediates racial prejudice at the individual level rather than analyze how racism shapes infrastructure and design. And, while Daniels does not address this problem directly, an investigation of how algorithms perpetuate or disrupt racism should be considered in any study of discriminatory design.

Architecture and Algorithms

On a recent visit that I made to University of California at San Diego, my hosts explained that the design of the campus made it almost impossible to hold large outdoor gatherings. The "defensive" architecture designed to prevent skateboarding and cycling in the interest of pedestrians also deliberately prevented student protests at a number of campuses following the Berkeley free speech protests in the mid-1960s. This is not so much a trend in urban planning as an ongoing feature of stratified societies. For some years now, as I have been writing and thinking about discriminatory design of all sorts, I keep coming back to the topic of public benches: benches I tried to lie down on but was prevented because of intermittent arm rests, then benches with spikes that retreat after you feed the meter, and many more besides.

Like the discriminatory designs we are exploring in digital worlds, hostile architecture can range from the more obvious to the more insidious – like the oddly shaped and artistic-looking bench that makes it uncomfortable but not impossible to sit for very long. Whatever the form, hostile architecture reminds us that public space is a permanent battleground for those who wish to reinforce or challenge hierarchies. So, as we explore the New Jim Code, we can observe connections in the building of physical and digital worlds, even starting with the use of "architecture" as a common metaphor for describing what algorithms – those series of instructions written and maintained by programmers that adjust on the basis of human behavior – build. But, first, let's take a quick detour . . .

The era commonly called "Jim Crow" is best known for the system of laws that mandated racial segregation and upheld White supremacy in the United States between 1876 and 1965. Legal codes, social codes, and building codes intersected to keep people separate and unequal. The academic truism that race is "constructed" rarely brings to mind these concrete brick and mortar structures, much less the digital structures operating today. Yet if we consider race as itself a technology, as a means to sort, organize, and design a social structure as well as to understand the durability of race, its consistency and adaptability, we can understand more clearly the literal architecture of power.

Take the work of famed "master builder" Robert Moses, who in the mid-twentieth century built hundreds of structures, highways, bridges, stadiums, and more, prioritizing suburbanization and upper-middle-class mobility over public transit and accessibility to poor and working-class New Yorkers. In a now iconic (yet still disputed) account of Moses' approach to public works, science and technology studies scholar Langdon

Winner describes the low-hanging overpasses that line the Long Island parkway system. In Winner's telling, the design prevented buses from using the roads, which enabled predominantly White, affluent car owners to move freely, while working-class and non-White people who relied on buses were prevented from accessing the suburbs and the beaches. And while the veracity of Winner's account continues to be debated, the parable has taken on a life of its own, becoming a narrative tool for illustrating how artifacts "have politics."[33]

For our purpose, Moses' bridges symbolize the broader architecture of Jim Crow. But, whereas Jim Crow laws explicitly restricted Black people from numerous "White only" spaces and services, the physical construction of cities and suburbs is central to the exercise of racial power, including in our postcivil rights era. And, while some scholars dispute whether Moses intended to exclude Black people from New York suburbs and beaches, one point remains clear: the way we engineer the material world reflects and reinforces (but could also be used to subvert) social hierarchies.

Yet plans to engineer inequity are not foolproof. In April 2018 a group of high school students and their chaperones returning from a spring break trip to Europe arrived at Kennedy Airport and boarded a charter bus that was headed to a Long Island shopping center where parents waited to pick up their kids. As they drove to the mall, the bus driver's navigation system failed to warn him about the low-hanging bridges that line the Long Island parkway and the bus slammed violently into the overpass, crushing the roof, seriously wounding six, and leaving dozens more injured. As news reports pointed out, this was only the latest of hundreds of similar accidents that happened over the years, despite numerous warning signs and sensor devices intended to alert oncoming traffic of the unusually low height of overpasses. Collateral damage, we might say, is part and parcel of discriminatory design.

From what we know about the people whom city planners have tended to prioritize in their designs, families such as the ones who could send their children to Europe for the spring break loom large among them. But a charter bus with the roof shaved off reminds us that tools of social exclusion are not guaranteed to impact only those who are explicitly targeted to be disadvantaged through discriminatory design. The best-laid plans don't necessarily "stay in their lane," as the saying goes. Knowing this, might it be possible to rally more people against social and material structures that immobilize some to the benefit of others? If race and other axes of inequity are constructed, then perhaps we can construct them differently?

When it comes to search engines such as Google, it turns out that online tools, like racist robots, reproduce the biases that persist in the social world. They are, after all, programmed using algorithms that are constantly updated on the basis of human behavior and are learning and replicating the technology of race, expressed in the many different associations that the users make. This issue came to light in 2016, when some users searched the phrase "three Black teenagers" and were presented with criminal mug shots. Then when they changed the phrase to "three White teenagers," users were presented with photos of smiling, go-lucky youths; and a search for "three Asian teenagers" presented images of scantily clad girls and women. Taken together, these images reflect and reinforce popular stereotypes of Black criminality, White innocence, or Asian women's sexualization that underpin much more lethal and systemic forms of punishment, privilege, and fetishism respectively.[34] The original viral video that sparked the controversy raised the question "Is Google being racist?," followed by a number of analysts who sought to explain how these results were produced:

> The idea here is that computers, unlike people, can't be racist but we're increasingly learning that they do in fact take after their makers . . . Some experts believe that this problem might stem from the hidden biases in the massive piles of data that algorithms process as they learn to recognize patterns . . . reproducing our worst values.[35]

According to the company, Google itself uses "over 200 unique signals or 'clues' that make it possible to guess what you might be looking for."[36] Or, as one observer put it, "[t]he short answer to why Google's algorithm returns racist results is that society is racist."[37] However, this does not mean that we have to wait for a social utopia to float down from the clouds before expecting companies to take action. They are already able to optimize online content in ways that mitigate bias. Today, if you look up the keywords in Noble's iconic example, the phrase "Black girls" yields images of Black Girls Code founder Kimberly Bryant and #MeToo founder Tarana Burke, along with images of organizations like Black Girls Rock! (an awards show) and Black Girls Run (a wellness movement). The technical capacity was always there, but social awareness and incentives to ensure fair representation online were lacking. As Noble reports, the pornography industry has billions of dollars to throw at companies in order to optimize content, so advertising cannnot continue to be the primary driver of online content. Perhaps Donald Knuth's proverbial warning is true: "premature optimization is the root of all evil."[38] And so the struggle to democratize information gateways continues.[39]

A number of other examples illustrate algorithmic discrimination as an ongoing problem. When a graduate student searched for "unprofessional hairstyles for work," she was shown photos of Black women; when she changed the search to "professional hairstyles for work," she was presented with photos of White women.[40] Men are shown ads for high-income jobs much more frequently than are women, and tutoring for what is known in the United States as the Scholastic Aptitude Test (SAT) is priced more highly for customers in neighborhoods with a higher density of Asian residents: "From retail to real estate, from employment to criminal justice, the use of data mining, scoring and predictive software . . . is proliferating . . . [And] when software makes decisions based on data, like a person's zip code, it can reflect, or even amplify, the results of historical or institutional discrimination."[41]

A team of Princeton researchers studying associations made with Black-sounding names and White-sounding names confirmed findings from employment audit studies[42] to the effect that respondents make negative associations with Black names and positive associations with White ones. Caliskan and colleagues show that widely used language-processing algorithms trained on human writing from the Internet reproduce human biases along racist and sexist lines.[43] They call into question the assumption that computation is pure and unbiased, warning that, "if we build an intelligent system that learns enough about the properties of language to be able to understand and produce it, in the process it will also acquire historic cultural associations, some of which can be objectionable. Already, popular online translation systems incorporate some of the biases we study ... Further concerns may arise as AI is given agency in our society."[44] And, as we shall see in the following chapters, the practice of codifying existing social prejudices into a technical system is even harder to detect when the stated purpose of a particular technology is to override human prejudice.

3

Coded Exposure

Is Visibility a Trap?

I think my Blackness is interfering with the computer's ability to follow me.

Webcam user[1]

EXPOSURE

- the amount of light per unit area
- the disclosure of something secret
- the condition of being unprotected
- the condition of being at risk of financial loss
- the condition of being presented to view or made known.[2]

In the short-lived TV sitcom *Better off Ted*, the writers parody the phenomena of biased technology in an episode titled "Racial Sensitivity." This episode presents the corporation where the show takes place installing a "new state of the art system that's gonna save money," but employees soon find there is a "glitch in the system that keeps it from recognizing people with dark skin."[3] When the show's protagonist confronts his boss, suggesting the sensors are racist, she insists otherwise:

> The company's position is that it's actually the opposite of racist because it's not targeting black people, it's just ignoring them. They insist that the worst people can call it is indifferent . . . In the meantime, they'd like to remind everyone to celebrate the fact that it does see Hispanics, Asians, Pacific Islanders, and Jews.[4]

The show brilliantly depicts how the default Whiteness of tech development, a superficial corporate diversity ethos, and the prioritization of efficiency over equity work together to ensure that innovation produces social containment.[5] The fact that Black employees are unable to use the elevators, doors, and water fountains or turn the lights on is treated as a minor inconvenience in service to a greater good. The absurdity goes further when, rather than removing the sensors, the company "blithely installs separate, manually operated drinking fountains for the convenience of the black employees,"[6] an incisive illustration of the New Jim Code wherein tech advancement, posed as a solution, conjures a prior racial regime in the form of separate water fountains.

Eventually the company sees the error of its ways and decides to hire minimum-wage-earning White employees to follow Black employees around the building, so that the sensors will activate. But then the legal team determines that, for each new White worker, they must hire an equal number of Black workers, and on and on, in a spiraling quota that ends when the firm finally decides to reinstall the old sensors.

Playing off of the political anxieties around reverse discrimination and affirmative action, the episode title

"Racial Sensitivity" – a formula that usually designates a charge brought against Black people who call attention to racism – is a commentary on the company's insensitivity and on the absurdity of its fixes. The writers seem to be telling us that more, not less, sensitivity is the solution to the technological and institutional dilemma of coded inequity. The episode also manages to illustrate how indifference to Blackness can be profitable within the logic of racial capitalism until the social costs become too high to maintain. [7]

Multiply Exposed

Some technologies fail to see Blackness, while others render Black people hypervisible and expose them to systems of racial surveillance.[8] Exposure, in this sense, takes on multiple meanings.[9] Exposing film is a delicate process – artful, scientific, and entangled in forms of social and political vulnerability and risk. Who is seen and under what terms holds a mirror onto more far-reaching forms of power and inequality. Far from being neutral or simply aesthetic, images have been one of the primary weapons in reinforcing and opposing social oppression. From the development of photography in the Victorian era to the image-filtering techniques in social media apps today, visual technologies and racial taxonomies fashion each other.[10]

Photography was developed as a tool to capture visually and classify human difference; it also helped to construct and solidify existing technologies, namely the ideas of race and assertions of empire, which required visual evidence of stratified difference.[11] Unlike older

99

school images, such as the paintings and engravings of exotic "others" that circulated widely before the Victorian period, photographs held an allure of objectivity, a sense that such images "were free from the bias of human imagination . . . a neutral reflection of the world."[12] Yet such reflections were fabricated according to the demands and desires of those who exercised power and control over others. Some photographs were staged, of course, to reflect White supremacist desires and anxieties. But race as a means of sorting people into groups on the basis of their presumed inferiority and superiority was staged in and of itself, long before becoming the object of photography.

What of the modern photographic industry? Is it more democratic and value-neutral than image was in previous eras? With the invention of color photography, the positive bias toward lighter skin tones was built into visual technologies and "presented to the public as neutral." Neutrality comes in the idea that "physics is physics," even though the very techniques of color-balancing an image reinforce a dominant White ideal.[13] And when it comes to the latest digital techniques, social and political factors continue to fashion computer-generated images. In this visual economy, race is not only digitized but heightened and accorded greater value.

This chapter traces the complex processes involved in "exposing" race in and through technology and the implications of presenting partial and distorted visions as neutral and universal. Linking historical precedents with contemporary techniques, the different forms of "exposure" noted in the epigraph serve as a touchstone for considering how the act of viewing something or someone may put the object of vision at risk. This kind of scopic vulnerability is central to the experience of being racialized.

In many ways, philosopher and psychiatrist Frantz Fanon's classic text *Black Skin, White Masks* is a meditation on scopic vulnerability. He describes the experience of being looked at, but not truly seen, by a White child on the streets of Paris:

> "Look, a Negro!"
> It was an external stimulus that flicked over me as I
>   passed by.
> I made a tight smile.
> "Look, a Negro!" It was true. It amused me.
> "Look, a Negro!" The circle was drawing a bit tighter. I
>   made no secret of my amusement.
> "Mama, see the Negro! I'm frightened!" Frightened!
>   Frightened! Now they were beginning to be afraid of
>   me. I made up my mind to laugh myself to tears, but
>   laughter had become impossible.

This story reveals to us that a key feature of Black life in racist societies is the constant threat of exposure and of being misread; and that being exposed is also a process of enclosure, a form of suffocating social constriction.

In a beautiful essay titled "Skin Feeling," literary scholar Sofia Samatar reminds us: "The invisibility of a person is also the visibility of a race . . . to be constantly exposed as something you are not."[14] Yet, in the distorted funhouse reflection of racist conditioning, the White children are the ones who fancy themselves as being at risk. Fanon's experience on the streets of Paris foreshadows the technologically mediated forms of exposure that proliferate Black life today. Whether we are talking about the widespread surveillance systems built into urban landscapes or the green light sitting above your laptop screen, detection and recognition are easily conflated when the default settings are distorted by racist logics.[15]

Finally, as it circulates in the domain of finance, the term "exposure" quantifies how much one stands to lose in an investment. If, as legal scholar Cheryl I. Harris argues, Whiteness is a form of property and if there is a "possessive investment in whiteness" (as sociologist George Lipsitz describes it), then visual technologies offer a site where we can examine how the value of Whiteness is underwritten through multiple forms of exposure by which racialized others are forcibly and fictitiously observed but not seen. That said, photography has also been a powerful tool to invest in Blackness. Take cultural studies scholar and media activist Yaba Blay's work on the social, psychic, and public health harms associated with skin bleaching. In addition to scholarly analysis, she created a media campaign called Pretty.Period, which counters the faux compliment that dark-skinned women must routinely endure: "you're pretty *for a dark-skinned girl*." By exposing the gendered racism coded in the qualifier, Blay responds "*No*, we're pretty PERIOD."[16] The campaign has produced an expansive archive with thousands of striking images of dark-skinned women of all ages across the African diaspora whose beauty is not up for debate. Period.

But divesting away from Whiteness in this way too often requires investing in ableist notions of gender, beauty, sexuality, and desire. In her talk "Moving toward the Ugly: A Politic beyond Desirability," Mia Mingus recognizes "the brilliance in our instinct to move toward beauty and desirability," but she also wrestles with the way in which "the generational effects of global capitalism, genocide, violence, oppression, and trauma settle into our bodies." She calls for a

> shift from a politic of desirability and beauty to a politic of ugly and magnificence . . . The magnificence of a body that shakes, spills out, takes up space, needs help, moseys, slinks, limps, drools, rocks, curls over on itself . . . The magnificence of bodies that have been coded, not just undesirable and ugly, but un-human . . . Moving beyond a politic of desirability to loving the ugly. Respecting Ugly for how it has shaped us and been exiled. Seeing its power and magic, seeing the reasons it has been feared. Seeing it for what it is: some of our greatest strength. Because we all do it. We all run from ugly.[17]

Mingus' intervention exposes the interlocking effects of racism, ableism, capitalism, heterosexism, and more. A multiple exposure that, like the ghost images that appear on photographs, haunts our discussion of race and technology. Like Blay, Mingus is not only an observer. She reminds us that those who are multiply exposed also engage in liberatory forms of scopic resistance and recoding: dark-skinned :: beautiful *and* ugly :: magnificent.

Exposing Whiteness

The most concrete technique through which Whiteness has fashioned photography is the Shirley Cards produced by Kodak from the 1950 to 1990s (see Figure 3.1). The cards were an integral part of film exposure methods and used the image of a White woman to standardize the exposure process. Since the model's skin was set as

Figure 3.1   Shirley Card
Source: Kodak Color Dataguide, 1976

the norm, darker skinned people in photographs would be routinely underexposed. In short, skin tone biases were embedded in the "actual apparatuses of visual reproduction."[18] As one photographer recently put it, "It turns out, film stock's failures to capture dark skin aren't a technical issue, they're a choice."[19] This also implies we can choose otherwise.

Photographers developed a range of "fixes" for under-exposure in order to calibrate the color; for instance they could add more lighting to darker subjects. But these only worked for images containing a single varia-tion. If more than one skin tone were represented in an image, such fixes were harder to employ.

At least three social shifts propelled more fun-damental changes to this form of discriminatory design. As public schools in the United States began desegregating and students of different skin tones were photographed for yearbooks in the same frame, the technical fixes that could be employed when a Black child was photographed alone were not useful. In particular, Black parents, objecting to the fact that their children's facial features were rendered blurry, demanded higher-quality images.[20] But the photographic industry did not fully take notice until companies that manufactured brown products like chocolate and wooden furniture began complaining that photographs did not depict their goods with enough subtlety, showcasing the varieties of chocolate and of grains in wood.

Finally, as US-based visual technologies circulated in non-European countries, the bias toward lighter skin tones grew ever more apparent. Competition in Asian markets propelled Kodak to follow Fuji in "ethnicizing" Shirley Cards (Figure 3.2). Kodak continued research

Figure 3.2   Diverse Shirley
Source: Kodak multiracial Shirley card, 1996

on skin tone preferences in different countries. Roth describes a resultant "geography of emulsions," in which "film inventory is batched by region and distributed" according to the skin color biases of the various parts of the world.[21] The market and profitability imperative of tailoring technologies to different populations is an ongoing driver of innovation.

But the hegemony of Whiteness is exposed not only in the context of the global competition to capture different regional markets. It is also exposed through practices that are more explicitly political. In South Africa, for example, Polaroid's ID2 camera, with its added flash "boost button," was used to better capture Black citizens' images for the infamous passbooks that violently restricted the movement of Black people throughout the country.

Polaroid's profit from South African apartheid spurred widespread protest against the company. The protest was led by the Polaroid Revolutionary Workers' Movement, which was founded by several African American employees in the United States, most notably photographer Ken Williams and chemist Caroline Hunter. The Workers' Movement "pointed out that part of Polaroid's profit in South Africa was earned from the sale of photo-identification units" that were used

to photograph Black South Africans for the much hated "reference" books or "passbooks," which control the movements of Blacks into urban areas in the Republic of South Africa. If a Black is without one of these documents he is subject to imprisonment, a fine, or deportation from the urban area in which he was found.[22]

One of the flyers that the Workers' Movement posted around the office summed up the problem: "Polaroid Imprisons Black People in 60 Seconds."[23]

After initial protests, Polaroid experimented with ways to improve the conditions of its Black South-African workers, but activists deemed the reforms inadequate and continued pressuring the company over a seven-year period, until finally Polaroid pulled out of South Africa completely. This move, in turn, propelled the broader movement for boycott, divestment, and sanctions throughout the 1980s, which prompted other companies to withdraw from South Africa too.[24] In short, the use of visual technologies "in systems set up to classify people is an important aspect of the history of photography,"[25] one that connects the design of technology and social policy.

Aiming to expose the Whiteness of photo technologies, London-based artists Adam Broomberg and Oliver Chanarin used decades-old film and Polaroid's ID-2 camera, which were the ones used for passbooks, to take pictures across South Africa for a month (see Figure 3.3).

Their exhibit, "To Photograph the Details of a Dark Horse in Low Light" (a line taken from a Kodak statement touting the ability of Kodak film to depict dark skin accurately), aims to explore "the radical notion that prejudice might be inherent in the medium of photography." Here the artists echo an assertion made by photographer Jean-Luc Godard who, in 1977, was invited on an assignment to Mozambique but refused to use Kodak film, saying that it was inherently "racist." According to Broomberg, the light range was so narrow that, "if you exposed film for a white kid, the black kid sitting next to him would be rendered invisible except

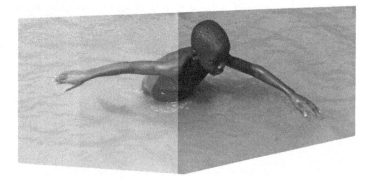

Figure 3.3 Strip Test 7
Source: "To Photograph the Details of a Dark Horse in Low Light," Broomberg and Chanarin, 2012

for the whites of his eyes and teeth."[26] You might be thinking, *surely* this is no longer an issue.

In 2009, Hewlett Packard's MediaSmart webcam demonstrated how the camera would pan to follow a White face but would stop when individuals with dark skin entered the frame.[27] The issue, according to HP, was that "the software has difficulty recognizing facial features in lower light levels."[28] *What are we to make of such enduring invisibility?* That new tools are coded in old biases is surprising only if we equate technological innovation with social progress. The popular trope that technology is always one step ahead of society is not only misleading but incorrect, when viewed through the lens of enduring invisibility.

Just as Polaroid, Kodak, and others attempted to design differently so that their cameras could vividly represent a broader spectrum of skin tones, so too companies that manufacture digital cameras today are working to address bias in the design and marketing of their products. In developing smartphones for sub-Saharan Africa, China's Tecno Mobile made it a point to emphasize the quality of images for Black customers:

> In one such ad, a wide screen smartphone is shown on a black page with the image of a black woman showing on the screen. The words "capture the beauty of darkness" are written in bold beneath the image, followed by the line "The phone is powered for low-light shooting." The ad labels the phone, "Camon C8," as a solution for a commonly held frustration with mobile phone cameras that render poor quality photos of dark-skinned subjects in low-light settings.[29]

In the United States, the default settings of photo technologies, both past and present, tend to cater to lighter-skinned subjects. This is not simply a benign reflection of designers' or technicians' unexamined biases, nor is it an inevitable result of technological development, as China's Tecno Mobile demonstrates. In the next section we observe how visual technologies expose Whiteness and regularly reinforce racist visions, although the way such images circulate and gain meaning is not always a direct reflection of their initial settings.

Exposing Difference

In her study of colonial-era photography, visual anthropologist Deborah Poole argues that we must not assume a singular interpretation of the relationship between images and society, one that looks for an all-encompassing "gaze" to exercise domination and control. Rather it is important to investigate the social nature of vision, because, once "unleashed in society, an image can acquire myriad interpretations or meanings according to the different codes and referents brought to it by its diverse viewers."[30] In examining the complex coding of racial desire and derision, Poole's insights remind us that domination and surveillance typically go hand in hand with "the pleasure of looking." The seeming adoration poured on racialized others via visual technologies, however, does not in itself signal a decline in racism and domination.

The desire to see others in a derogatory or in an exotic light, just as much as the practice of invisibilizing them, reproduces long-standing forms of authority and hierarchy. When it comes to representing racialized others, the interplay between desire and derision, longing and loathing can get lost in the strict focus on how visual technologies fail to see darker-skinned people.[31] We can overlook the technology – racism – that precedes technological innovations.

In 2015 Google Photo came under fire because its auto-labeling software tagged two Black friends as "gorillas"[32] – a racist depiction that goes back for centuries, being formalized through scientific racism and through the association of Black people with simians in the Great Chain of Being. It found its modern incarnation in cartoons of former First Lady Michelle Obama and in Roseanne Barr's aforementioned racist tweets against Valerie Jarrett and was resuscitated in algorithms that codify representations used for generations to denigrate people of African descent. This form of machine bias extends beyond racialized labels, to the very exercise of racist judgments, as the beauty contest described in Chapter 1 made clear.

Similarly, in his examination of video game avatars,

computer scientist and artist D. Fox Harrell found that, when he attempted to make an African-inspired avatar that looked like him, it "was automatically made less intelligent." He explains:

> Prejudice, bias, stereotyping, and stigma are built not only into many games, but other forms of identity representations in social networks, virtual worlds, and more. These have real world effects on how we see ourselves and each other. Even in systems that have very open identity creation options, like Second Life, there are still different valuations for skins, social groups and categories being formed.[33]

The impact of having seemingly "racist robots" as judges in beauty contests and as players in video games may seem trivial, but similar biases are built into the technological systems used by police, where they have more lethal consequences.

In social theorist Michel Foucault's classic formulation, "visibility is a trap." Foucault explained how power is exercised through techniques of surveillance in which people are constantly watched and disciplined, "the object of information, never a subject of communication." The *less obvious* the mechanism, the *more powerful* the disciplinary function of surveillance. It is tempting to point to the smart recording devices we carry around in our pockets and exclaim that "we are all caught inside the digital dragnet!" But, the fact is, we do not all experience the dangers of exposure in equal measure. Consider the "If you *see* something, *say* something" signs that litter public spaces, the brigade of White women reporting Black people to the police, the broken windows policies that license law enforcement to discipline small infractions like vandalism and toll-jumping, allegedly in order to deter and prevent larger crimes, and police body cameras that supposedly capture what "really" happened when an officer harasses or kills someone: clearly people are exposed differently to the dangers of surveillance.

In the most comprehensive study of its kind, a group of researchers at Georgetown Law School obtained over 10,000 pages of information from more than 100 police departments across the country, to examine how the use of facial recognition software impacts different communities. They found that "[t]he databases they use are disproportionately African American, and the software is especially bad at recognizing Black faces, according to several studies."[34] What's more, the different global settings in which AI is taught to "see" impacts the technical settings designed to identify individuals from various groups. It turns out that algorithms "developed in China, Japan, and South Korea recognized East Asian faces far more readily than Caucasians. The reverse was true for algorithms developed in France, Germany, and the United States, which were significantly better at recognizing Caucasian facial characteristics."[35] This suggests that the political–geographic setting augments the default setting of Whiteness. The ethnoracial makeup of the software design team, the test photo databases, and the larger population of users influence the algorithms' capacity for recognition, though not in any straightforward sense.

For instance, when it comes to datasets, a 2012 study found that an algorithm trained "exclusively on either African American or Caucasian faces recognized members of the race in its training set more readily than members of any other race."[36] Scholars at Georgetown University's Center on Privacy and Technology point out that the disparities in facial recognition across racial groups may be introduced "at a number of points in the process of designing and deploying a facial recognition system":

> The engineer that develops an algorithm may program it to focus on facial features that are more easily distinguishable in some race than in others – the shape of a person's eyes, the width of the nose, the size of the mouth or chin. This decision, in turn, might be based on preexisting biological research about face identification and past practices which themselves may contain bias. Or the engineer may rely on his or her own experience in distinguishing between faces – a process that is influenced by the engineer's own race.[37]

Now consider that these software programs are used by police departments all over the country; in those departments "digital eyes watch the public," comparing individual faces in real time to "hot lists" that are filled disproportionately with Black people – and these also happen to be the least recognizable figures in the world of facial recognition software.

The humor in the much circulated HP MediaSmart video of the Black user quoted in this chapter's epigraph saying "I think my blackness is interfering with the computer's ability to follow me" turns deadly in the context of digitally mediated police profiling, where suspects are caught in the crosshairs of being seen too much via surveillance practices and not enough via software; one's own body is called upon to testify against itself. Guilty, guilty, guilty. The life sciences, in turn, are routinely used to arbitrate guilt.[38]

Exposing Science

In the documentary film *DNA Dreams*, viewers are taken inside of "the world's largest genomics organization," which is based in Shenzen, China. Thousands of scientists are working there to uncover the genetics of intelligence (among other traits). In a scene haunted by the famous words of Martin Luther King, Jr., the chair of the institute is shown speaking to a packed and spellbound audience: "I have a dream. We have a dream. That we are going to sequence every living thing on Earth, that we are going to sequence everyone in the world." Until then, the institute was studying the DNA of 2,000 people considered highly intelligent in order to isolate the alleles that supposedly made them smart. If this sounds like something human beings have tried before, it is because the desire to propagate "good genes" was the basis of a popular, "progressive," but ultimately deadly movement called eugenics.

Negative eugenics, discouraging the reproduction of those whom society deems "unfit," is what most people associate with the practice, because it led to widespread sterilization programs in which US scientists inspired Nazi doctors to scale up this practice to the point of genocide. The popularity of eugenics gained steam following the 1927 Supreme Court decision in *Buck v. Bell* – a decision to uphold the involuntary sterilization of those deemed intellectually disabled: "It is better for all the world, if instead of waiting to execute degenerate offspring for crime, or to let them starve for their imbecility, society can prevent those who are manifestly unfit from continuing their kind." We see how the law becomes an instrument for perpetuating deeply discriminatory practices under the guise of reason, neutrality, and social betterment for "all the world." Negative eugenic practices such as prison sterilization are still with us; as recently as in 2013, doctors in California prisons were coercing women to undergo sterilization, and in 2017 a Tennessee judge offered shorter sentences if prisoners agreed to sterilization.[39] "Positive" eugenics, on the other hand, encourages the reproduction of populations that society already values. State fairs would host "fitter family contests" and people would submit their kids to measurements and tests, in the hope of receiving a eugenics certificate as part of the festivities.

Despite obvious links to a previous era of eugenics justified on scientific grounds, the scientists in *DNA Dreams* disavow the connection. In a scene that depicts some of the key players eating dinner and discussing how their research could allow parents to screen embryos and choose the one that will become the smartest, one of them argues: "This isn't even positive eugenics that we're taking about, we're not encouraging smart people to have kids, we're encouraging everyone who has kids to have the best kids they possibly could have."[40] The dream they are selling is what we might call Equal Opportunity Eugenics.

The fact that we may all, ultimately, be able to access the tools of eugenic selection does not make such processes less eugenic. It just means that the intertwining projects of racism and ableism are all-encompassing.[41] This is yet another example of how those who design the world according to their own values and biases are employing the rhetoric of "inclusion" as progressive veneer for deeply discriminatory practices. This goes much deeper than a marketing scheme and takes us well beyond one institute in China. The fact is, despite its bad Nazi press, under one description or another eugenics has typically been espoused by those in the United States and Europe who consider themselves social progressives.

A story by Kathryn Paige Harden titled "Why Progressives Should Embrace the Genetics of Education," recently published in the *New York Times* (July 24, 2018), reported on a massive US-based study and implored those who "value social justice" to harness the genomic revolution. In a savvy slippage between genetic and environmental factors that would make the founders of eugenics proud, the author asserts that "knowing which genes are associated with educational success will help scientists understand how different environments also affect that success." But, as many critics have pointed out since, the problem is not a lack of knowledge![42] One observer put it best: "I cannot imagine a subject on which we know more about than the environments under which children learn best. It has been the subject of study and discussion for well more than a century. Are we suddenly unsure that poverty has a negative effect on educational attainment?"[43]

It is not the facts that elude us, but a fierce commitment to justice that would make us distribute resources so that all students have access to a good educational environment. Demanding more data on subjects that we already know much about is, in my estimation, a perversion of knowledge. The *datafication of injustice* . . . in which the hunt for more and more data is a barrier to acting on what we already know. We need something like an academic equivalent of "I said what I said!"

– the catchphrase of reality TV star NeNe Leakes – for those who insist on digging deeper and deeper into the genome for scientific solutions to social problems.

The desire to sort good and bad human traits, encouraging the former and discouraging the latter, is also animated by a belief that humans can be designed better than they currently are. Correction: a belief that more humans can be like those already deemed superior. But in all this one forgets to question who was granted authority to make these value judgments in the first place. Genetic discrimination, in turn, does not just describe what prospective parents have to do if they decide to select supposedly smart fetuses over their average siblings. Discriminatory design happens much earlier in the process, in the decisions that researchers make as to what behaviors to categorize as intelligent in the first place. As philosopher Ian Hacking (2006) put it in "Making Up People," when we identify which people to control, help, change, or emulate as "geniuses," methods of classification change those who [sic] scientists set out to study.[44] And not just change them, but actually create and re-create kinds of people in the process of naming and studying, which becomes a materialization of the scientific imagination.

Another contributor to this process is the decision to ignore the great impact of environmental factors on complex human traits such as intelligence, and the fact that a full "98% of all variation in educational attainment is accounted for by factors other than a person's simple genetic makeup."[45] Like those Beauty AI app designers who seemed to think that there was some universal standard of beauty against which all of humanity could be judged and who expressed surprise when the algorithms they trained showed an overwhelming preference for White contestants, those who hunt for the genetic basis of IQ have already accepted dominant standards of intelligence, starting with their selection of the 2,000 individuals deemed smart enough to be studied. And, given the powerful bioinformatic tools at their disposal, they may very well identify shared alleles in their sample, finding evidence for what they seek without questioning the basic premise to begin with.

In this way *DNA Dreams* brings to life the dystopian nightmare we encounter in the 1997 film *Gattaca*, in which the main character Vincent, played by Ethan Hawke, narrates: "I belonged to a new underclass, no longer determined by social status or the color of your skin. No, we have discrimination down to a science."[46] As in so much science fiction, the Whiteness of the main protagonist is telling. Not only does it deflect attention away from the fact that, in the present, many people already live a version of the dystopia represented in the film in future tense. The "unbearable Whiteness" of sci-fi expresses itself in the anxiety underlying so many dystopian visions that, if we keep going down this road, "We're next."[47] Whether it's Keanu Reeves in *The Matrix*, Matt Damon in *Elysium*, Chris Evans in *Snowpiercer* – all characters whose Whiteness, maleness, straightness, and (let's just admit) cuteness would land them at the top of the present social order – they all find themselves in a fictional future among the downtrodden. Viewers, in turn, are compelled to identify with the future oppression of subordinated White people without necessarily feeling concern for the "old" underclasses in our midst. So, while *DNA Dreams* sits in the shadow of *Gattaca*, *Gattaca*-like representations can overshadow the everyday theft of opportunity, stratified as it is by race and justified by eugenic-like judgments about the value of different human lives.

So, lest we assume that eugenics simply faded away with the passing of laws and the rise of bioethics, its ideology persists in many areas of life well beyond the field of genomics; it endures, namely, in how lives of White and wealthy people continue to be valued over others. Reproduction, in turn, is not simply about the act of procreation but about access to the full range of symbolic and material goods (things like respect and dignity, quality healthcare, and education) that affirm life.[48] In that way, the Movement for Black Lives is implicitly an *anti-eugenics* movement. The aim is not just to stop premature deaths that result from police violence but to foster economic, social, and political power and resources that will sustain Black life more broadly.[49] Fostering life, in turn, requires reckoning with the multiple ways science and technology can expose people to death – from Dr. J. Marion Sims' experiments carried out on unanaesthetized enslaved women and designed to hone gynecological techniques, to then President Barack Obama's 563 drone strikes that killed hundreds. We have good reason to be skeptical of the way tech cheerleaders feign innocence when it comes to the racial dimensions of these harms.

In 2016, the *20/20* television show on ABC released an image of a suspect in the murder of a woman in Chapel Hill, North Carolina. The image was created by the company Parabon NanoLabs, which charges $3,600 to analyze a sample and to produce a composite sketch using technology funded by the Department of Defense. The director of bioinformatics at Parabon NanoLabs explained: "It's not meant to be a driver's license photograph. It's really intended for lead generation, for prioritizing the suspect list. The people who match go to the top."[50]

In this case, the image depicted a "Latino man, with likely olive skin, brown or hazel eyes and black hair . . . He is shown at age 25 years old and a typical body mass index of 22, which are default settings when the company does not have that information."[51] But, as Pamela Sankar insists, ancestry-informative markers (AIMS) are "associated probabilistically with a population, not predictably with an individual."[52] Yet, Parabon said it was 85.7 percent confident about the suspect's skin shade and 93.8 percent confident about his eye color; so essentially this is a high-tech form of racial profiling that exemplifies the New Jim Code.

The gradual incorporation of forensic DNA phenotyping or "genetic fingerprinting" in police work draws together concerns about biased databases and racialized predictions.[53] Unlike the more common form of genetic testing, in which DNA is used to confirm or rule out the identity of an individual suspect, phenotyping is a predictive technology. And unlike an artist's sketch that relies on the memory of an eye witness, trace evidence at a crime scene is used by officers to produce a computer-generated image. The image is created by comparing the crime scene sample and particular points in the genome (i.e. AIMS) to samples in an existing database, in order to predict the appearance of a suspect.[54]

But the relationship between genes and facial variation is not at all clear. Nevertheless a number of companies sell this service to law enforcement, even as experts question the accuracy of the technology. In a *New York Times* article titled "Building a Face, and a Case, on DNA," Benedikt Hallgrimsson, head of the Department of Cell Biology and Anatomy, who studies the development of faces at University of Calgary, cautions: "A bit of science fiction at this point." His article conjures a dystopian reality, if such techniques are used to insulate existing forms of racial profiling from charges of bias. And, as Foucault reminds us, "the guilty person is only one of the targets of punishment. For punishment is directed above all at others, at all the *potentially* guilty."[55]

Even before the algorithmic predictions we have today, predictive guilt has been a cornerstone of police work. In the Supreme Court's decision in the case of *Terry v. Ohio* (1968), the court ruled that "a police officer may stop a suspect on the street and frisk him or her *without* probable cause to arrest, if the police officer has a *reasonable suspicion* that the person has committed, is committing, *or is about to* commit a crime and has a reasonable belief that the person 'may be armed and presently dangerous.'"[56] A 2010 report titled Platform for Prejudice explains that the Nationwide Suspicious Activity Reporting Initiative "reflects the new philosophy called Intelligence-Led Policing. The term itself is misleading. Pre-Emptive Policing, the more accurate term, emphasizes surveillance and seizures of individuals *before* a criminal 'predicate' exists." While some, including the authors of this report, may note that pre-emptive policing is hardly "compatible with American Constitutional principles such as the presumption of innocence and the warrant requirement," we can also consider how, as Simone Browne has shown, the practice *is* consistent with the long history of racial surveillance endured by Black people.[57]

Forensic DNA phenotyping, in turn, gives officers license to suspect anyone who fits the generic description of the image. As Stanford bioethicist Pamela Sankar cautions, "[i]t seems possible that instead of making suspect searches more exact, the vagueness of FDP descriptions might make them more vulnerable to stereotyping. Of course, the same might be said of most descriptions the police are handed when it comes to certain suspects. Other descriptions, however, are not based on genetics."[58] That is, when the bias is routed through technoscience and coded "scientific" and "objective," a key feature of the New Jim Code, it becomes even more difficult to challenge it and to hold individuals and institutions accountable.

And yet, as Britt Rusert so poignantly chronicles in *Fugitive Science: Empiricism and Freedom in Early African American Culture*, Black scientists, scholars, and artists have resisted and subverted racist science at every turn. Their radical empiricism takes special issue with the visual dimensions of scientific racism, producing a counterarchive that offers "competing visual evidence" of Black humanity and sociality and refuting the derogatory images of scientific writings and the popular press alike. Drawing upon Shawn Michelle Smith's discussion of the "scopic regime" that supported scientific racism, Rusert demonstrates that "[t]he ground of the visual became a key site upon which African Americans waged their battle against racist science, print, and popular culture in the 1830s and 1840s."[59] And the battle still rages!

Racial representations engineered through algorithmic codes should be understood as part of a much longer visual archive. The proliferation of digitized racial visions, from HP's blurry blackness to Google's gorilla tags, is also an occasion for the creation of subversive countercodings. After it was revealed that the Miami Police Department used images of Black men for target practice, a movement of clergy and other activists initiated the hashtag #UseMeInstead circulating their own, predominantly White photos. In another form of subversive visualization, activists called out the way media outlets circulate unflattering photos of Black youths murdered by police or White vigilantes. They used the hashtag #IfTheyGunnedMeDown and asked the question "Which one would they use?" with dueling photos of themselves looking stereotypically "thuggish" (e.g. not smiling, wearing a hoodie, throwing up hand signs, smoking, or holding alcohol) and "respectable" (e.g. smiling, wearing a graduation gown or suit, playing with a baby, or wearing a military uniform).

Whether owing to the overrepresentation of Black people in TV news reports of criminal suspects or to the decision of media outlets to use more "thuggish" photos when reporting on Black victims, racism runs all the way through the visual representation of crime and victimization.[60] Style, comportment, and context become the codes through which mass audiences are hailed in the Fanonian sense of "Look, a Negro!" But, through social media technologies, the hashtag phenomenon allows people to decode and recode these mediated hails astutely and collectively,[61] demonstrating how popular representations criminalize Black victims of state-sanctioned violence and revealing, through visual performance, how racialized distortions continue apace, even when they have no explicit mentions of race to rely on.

Exposing Privacy

Fanon's (2008) *Black Skin, White Masks* reverberates through the work of MIT Media Lab researcher Joy Buolamwini, who discovered that the facial recognition technology with which she was working could detect the contours of her face only when she put on a White mask. This is what she calls the "coded gaze." Buolamwini established the Algorithmic Justice League as part of her quest for "full spectrum inclusion," to counter the bias she experienced.[62] She asks: "If we do not improve the systems and they continue to be used, what are the implications of having innocent people identified as criminal suspects?"

While inclusion and accuracy are worthy goals in the abstract, given the encoding of long-standing racism in discriminatory design, what does it mean to be included, and hence more accurately identifiable, in an unjust set of social relations? Innocence and criminality are not objective states of being that can be detected by an algorithm but are *created* through the interaction of institutions and individuals against the backdrop of a deeply racialized history, in which Blackness is coded as a criminal. Inclusion in this context is more akin to possession, as in Fanon's plea that the "tool never possess the man," where possession alerts us to the way freedom is constrained.

Consider a population-wide facial recognition program in which the Zimbabwean government has contracted a China-based company to track millions of Zimbabwean citizens in order to make the Chinese database more comprehensive by "more clearly identify[ing] different

124

ethnicities." The benefit for Zimbabwe is access to a suite of technologies that can be used by law enforcement and other public agencies, while positioning China to become "the world leader in artificial intelligence."[63] *Transnational algorithmic diversity training par excellence!* Perhaps. Or, better, neocolonial extraction for the digital age in which the people whose faces populate the database have no rights vis-à-vis the data or systems that are built with their biometric input. Not only that. Since the biggest application of facial recognition is in the context of law enforcement and immigration control, Zimbabwe is helping Chinese officials to become more adept at criminalizing Black people within China and across the African diaspora.

Racist structures do not only marginalize but also forcibly center and surveil racialized groups that are "trapped between regimes of invisibility and spectacular hypervisibility,"[64] threatened by inclusion in science and technology as objects of inquiry. Inclusion is no straightforward good but is often a form of unwanted exposure. Jasmine Nichole Cobb's insight that "invisibility is ... part of the social condition of blackness in modernity as well as an important representational tactic for people of African descent" – what Rusert describes as that "dialectic of calculated visibility and strategic invisibility" – is relevant to countering the New Jim Code.[65]

The figure of Saartjie ("Sara") Baartman illustrates the violent underside of being forcibly seen. Baartman, who was taken from South Africa to Europe in 1810, was publicly displayed for large audiences in London and Paris, photographed, studied, and eventually dissected in death by the leading scientist of the time, Georges

Cuvier, and her skeleton, brain, and genitals were sub-
sequently put on display until 1974. Baartman's horrific
exposure in life and death illustrates the connection
between visual and scientific technologies. While many
people have heard some version of her story in scholarly
texts and popular works, few know of Baartman's eventual repatriation to and burial in South Africa in 2002,
through which the evidentiary politics surrounding her
identity came to a climax. The protracted negotiations
between South Africa and France for the return of
Baartman's remains – her skeleton, brain, and genitals –
were stalled by French claims that the remains had been
lost and could not be identified among the museum's
holdings. Consider that "Baartman was one of thousands from Europe's former colonial territories whose
remains had been gathered in metropolitan museums."
In 2002, "once the French government [finally] agreed
to return them, a dispute arose about the veracity of the
physical remains offered by the French."[66]

Despite this, the South African committee that nego-
tiated her return declined to have the remains tested
to verify whether they belonged to Baartman, or even
whether the three sets of remains belonged to the same
person. For the committee, to do so would amount
to a replication of the violation, repeating once again
the "great long insult" to which Baartman had been
subjected during her life. Instead, on August 9, 2002,
Baartman was given a ceremonial burial in Hankey,
South Africa, near the place where she was born. This
decision of not exposing Baartman's remains to scrutiny
yet again was the South African committee's assertion
and attempt to define a way of knowing differently,
whereby it decided to accept without further DNA

testing that the remains offered by France belonged to Baartman. This signaled an end to the invasive visibility to which Baartman was subjected during her lifetime and for 159 years after her death.

In "Baartman and the Private: How Can We Look at a Figure That Has Been Looked at Too Much," South African gender studies scholar Gabeba Baderoon explains how "dominated peoples have long crafted a way to exist and keep their histories outside of conventional archives." The politics of knowledge, in other words, is deeply entangled in a politics of the private and in who gets to lay claim to privacy and subjectivity. The assertion of "privacy" in this context is not the same as *privatizing* – an economic calculation "outside history," made for the purpose of maximizing profits; rather, in Baderoon's theory of the private, it draws attention to the "intimate, personal, closed, hidden, *coded*, secret, veiled, unknown, the apparently meaningless, the invisible, the ordinary, the in-between, the silent . . . the underside . . . unofficial . . . unpredictable, and unreliable in dominant views of history."[67]

What is privacy for already exposed people in the age of big data? For oppressed people, I think privacy is not only about protecting some things from view, but also about what is strategically exposed. This might look like Mamie Till-Mobley, mother of slain teenager Emmett Till, choosing to expose the mutilated body of her son because "I think everybody needs to know what happened." It could also look like the organization Stop LAPD Spying Coalition, exposing the lies of law enforcement officials who claim not to know about the very surveillance techniques that the organization records them using. Organizers participate in

community events, public rallies, and protests and pro-
ceed to "watch the watchers." In one video, activists are
shown interviewing police officers who act as if they had
never heard of "Freedom on the Move" vans – a mobile
video surveillance system "intended for use by military,
border patrol, and law enforcement agencies"; and,
just as they make these denials, the video cuts to the
vans driving by the May Day rally.[68] Countering these
forms of technological exposure, Stop LAPD Spying
Coalition created "A People's Audit," which includes
survey results of community members' experiences of
preemptive policing and harassment.[69] If surveillance
treats people like a "surface," then countering this form
of violent exposure can entail listening deeply to the
everyday encounters of those who are forcibly watched.
This points to a different way of making sense and
knowledge of the world, a theory of privacy predicated
on mutual respect and dignity.

Exposing Citizenship

Coded exposure is not simply an American phenomenon,
nor is it an issue that exists only when societies explicitly
use the language of "race" in social and political life.
Caste, religion, nationality, and disability are routinely
racialized, to the extent that they signify immutable
and stratified human differences. Moving beyond the
US context, digitizing identity in governmental practices
can lead to new forms of surveillance, coercion, and
subordination.[70] UK's Human Provenance Pilot Project,
India's Unique Identity Project (UID), and Kuwait's
National DNA Initiative show how the racialization of

inequality produces an allure of objectivity and inevitability that makes it even harder to question and change the techno status quo.

In 2009, the UK Border Agency (UKBA) initiated the Human Provenance Pilot Project (HPPP), with the aim of using genetic ancestry testing and isotope analysis to vet asylum claims.[71] If, over the course of a standard interview, caseworkers grew suspicious of an applicant's story, they would request samples of saliva, nails, and hair. The primary targets of the project were East Africans. Somali applicants escaping persecution were eligible for asylum, so if the tests indicated that someone was from Kenya – a phenomenon dubbed "nationality swapping" – that person was scheduled for deportation. A letter from the deputy director of the project stated that "all samples will be provided voluntarily,"[72] but caseworkers were encouraged to regard refusal to submit samples with suspicion. The official protocol instructed:

> If an asylum applicant refused to provide samples for the isotope analysis and DNA testing the case owner could draw a negative inference as to the applicant's credibility ... There must be other compelling evidence which also clearly demonstrates that the applicant has attempted to conceal information or mislead the UKBA. It must not be stated within the RFRL [Reasons for Refusal Letter] in isolation and must certainly not be stated as a primary reason for refusing the applicant's asylum claim.[73]

Following the protests of refugee advocates and journalists – and not through any regulatory or oversight governing body – the project came under widespread scrutiny. In the process, academic scientists expressed shock and disgust, insisting that the techniques used could not diagnose nationality in the way the project assumed.[74] David Balding, a population geneticist at Imperial College London, noted that "genes don't respect national borders, as many legitimate citizens are migrants or direct descendants of migrants, and many national borders split ethnic groups."[75] Mark Thomas, a geneticist of University College London who called the HPPP "horrifying," contended that determining a person's ancestry – as distinct from nationality – is more complicated than many believe: "[mitochondrial] DNA will never have the resolution to specify a country of origin. Many DNA ancestry testing companies have sprung up over the last 10 years, often based on mtDNA, but what they are selling is little better than genetic astrology," he said. "Dense genomic SNP data does [sic] have some resolution . . . but not at a very local scale, and with considerable errors."[76] Likewise, Alec Jeffries, one of the pioneers of human DNA fingerprinting, wrote:

> The Borders Agency is clearly making huge and unwarranted assumptions about population structure in Africa; the extensive research needed to determine population structure and the ability or otherwise of DNA to pinpoint ethnic origin in this region simply has not been done. Even if it did work (which I doubt), assigning a person to a population does not establish nationality – people move! The whole proposal is naive and scientifically flawed.[77]

Janet Montgomery, an isotope specialist at Durham University, explained that, "unless the border between Somalia and Kenya represented some major geological or hydrological division, I cannot see how isotopes will discriminate between people living there let alone living at/on the border." Montgomery insisted: "Isotopes do not respect national borders or convey some inherent national attribute. They are not passports."[78]

Despite such severe criticism from the scientific community, the HPPP did not initially shut down; nor did it rule out the possibility of reintroducing a similar initiative in the future. In their defense, representatives of the UKBA insisted that only asylum-seekers who had already failed linguistic tests (another contested method of determining nationality) would be asked to provide mouth swabs, hair, and nail samples.[79] The UKBA also released the following written response to scientific criticisms:

> Ancestral DNA testing will not be used alone but will combine with language analysis, investigative interviewing techniques and other recognized forensic disciplines. The results of the combination of these procedures may indicate a person's possible origin and enable the UK Border Agency to make further enquiries leading to the return of those intending on abusing the UK's asylum system. This project is working with a number of leading scientists in this field who have studied differences in the genetic backgrounds of various population groups.[80]

Several prominent scientists said they suspected that private labs, which were under much less regulatory oversight, had been involved in the project. And, while the UKBA has since tried to downplay the significance of the project, in the words of archaeologist Jessica Pearson, "[i]t's peoples' lives we're dealing with."[81]

The idea that the HPPP was "voluntary" conceals the threat of deportation, which was made if applicants did not consent to testing. It is false to say that one has a choice when one of the two available choices automatically implies penalization. As Richard Tutton, Christine Hauskeller, and Steve Sturdy (2014) explain, "In the UK, official and popular attitudes to those who request sanctuary have become dominated by a hermeneutic of suspicion. Public and policy discourses portray asylum seekers as mostly 'bogus' refugees seeking admission to the country for economic, not humanitarian, reasons";[82] this also ignores that economic dispossession is itself a global humanitarian crisis.

The quest for scientific tools to determine ancestry and arbitrate group membership continues apace toward a variety of political and biomedical ends. The scientists' near uniform criticism of the UK project serves to highlight a key feature of the underlying science – its refusal to adhere to "terms of use" insofar as the UKBA was unwilling to shut down the project completely. Also essential to this discussion is the fact that such technologies of identity do not simply offer more objective means of confirming or disconfirming conventional identity claims; they actually redefine the social categories of identity on which immigration and asylum decisions are based. The HPPP stands as a salutary warning about the ways in which supposedly objective technologies of identification are increasingly being used at international borders to disempower the already vulnerable still further.[83]

Turning now to India: there the government aims to create a unique 12-digit ID for every resident called an Aadhaar (which means "foundation" in Hindi). An Aadhaar number is tied to individual demographic and biometric markers and is needed when applying for hundreds of welfare programs, as well as for things such as a driver's license and college degree. The explicit purpose of the ID program is to avoid duplicates in the system and to provide insight into the economy, including the efficacy of aid programs, so as to allow the government and expert organizations to make more informed decisions. But what about those who wish to opt out?

According to WikiLeaks spokesperson Jacob Appelbaum, the Aadhaar program is likely to "create a digital caste system because going by the way it is now being implemented, if you choose not to be part of the system, you will be the modern-day equivalent of an outcast. In theory, you are supposed to have the freedom to choose but in reality, the choice will only be whether to be left out or left behind."[84] There are already reports of citizens being denied welfare services, including children unable to receive school lunches when their Aadhaar could not be authenticated.[85] In this way the New Jim Code gives rise to digital untouchables.

Although the Aadhaar Act of 2016 says that the UID is voluntary, it makes digital identity such "an integral part of every aspect of being a resident/citizen of the country"[86] that it can be said to *produce* illegality rather than screen for it. As Appelbaum notes, "not having Aadhaar would effectively be a criminal offence because it would turn perfectly law-abiding, tax-paying citizens into non-compliant ones on account of not having been able to pay one's taxes."[87] Aadhaar critics warn that the initiative will further harm the most vulnerable: "Naturally, women, Dalits, transgenders, religious and sexual minorities, who are anyway part of vulnerable and marginalised groups, would be far more susceptible to state policing of bodies and possible discrimination via Aadhaar than upper caste Hindu men, simply because the latter's entrenched privileges will ensure the least surveillance for themselves."[88] Famed Indian writer Arundhati Roy has criticized the program as a "containment technique . . . perhaps one of the most ambitious and expensive information gathering projects in the world" and as an ill-conceived investment, given more pressing priorities:

> People don't have clean drinking water, or toilets, or food, or money, but they will have election cards *and* UID numbers. Is it a coincidence that the UID project . . . will inject massive amounts of money into a slightly beleaguered IT industry? To digitize a country with such a large population of the illegitimate and "illegible" – people who are for the most part slum dwellers, hawkers, Adivasis without land records – will criminalize them, turning them from illegitimate to illegal.[89]

Even as cases of Aadhaar data being hacked or sold make their way through Indian courts, an Indian finance minister suggested that adding DNA data into the biometric mix may actually be next.[90]

While India has yet to take that step, in 2015 Kuwait passed a law requiring citizens, residents, and visitors to submit DNA samples to a massive genetic database. According to one report, "[i]t sounds like an idea from a bad science-fiction novel . . . Such a database would be the first of its kind in the world."[91] It would include 1.3 million citizens and 2.9 million expatriates, costing approximately $400 million. A station would be set up at the airport, where all new arrivals would be required to submit cheek swabs or blood samples. Newborn babies would be tested and, in order for citizens to receive their new passports, they would have first to submit their DNA.

Although a court struck down Kuwait's DNA Law in 2017, the government expected about 200,000 people to refuse testing, and serious punishments awaited them, including a year in jail or a $33,000 fine for "refusers," and seven years in prison for those who forged samples. Officials originally passed the law after an ISIS-linked man set off a bomb in a mosque killing 27 people. Proponents say that the database could help fight terrorism and crime as well as identify victims of large-scale attacks. Critics warned that there is more to the story, and that the already fraught status of the Bidoon minority is further threatened by this new law, because DNA tests will likely be used to arbitrate citizenship. The Bidoon are stateless descendants of nomadic Arab tribes that the Kuwaiti government considers "illegal residents," though some have acquired citizenship over the years through marriage and adoption. As one report explained,

> Kuwaiti citizenship is restricted to families that have been there since 1920, and is passed down through fathers' bloodlines, with few exceptions ... Being an oil-rich country, Kuwaiti citizenship [sic] comes with a long list of benefits, including free education through college, free healthcare, grocery subsidies, unemployment benefits, and monthly government checks per child. Essentially, the law will allow the government to restrict access to citizenship based on verifiable bloodlines.[92]

A researcher at the Human Rights Watch explained:

> As the law was being passed, people who knew the intricacies of the Bidoon issue were saying, "This law has

nothing to do with terrorism and criminal activity, but it has more to do with the state at a moment when oil prices are down and the state has to suddenly talk about taxing its own citizens and cutting all sorts of benefits. This might actually be an attempt to significantly cut the benefits to this community."[93]

The likelihood that the law would have been applied in this manner is supported by a number of government statements. As one official explained, the DNA database would "aid in the verification of Kuwaiti citizens";[94] another said that the data would help "arrest forgers and others who falsely claim their lineage."[95] The United Nations Human Rights Commission, among other organizations, is concerned that copycat laws in other countries will soon follow, especially as xenophobia is on the rise throughout the world.

Nothing short of a collective and sustained effort that, like the aforementioned Polaroid Revolutionary Workers' Movement, draws together those who work inside and outside powerful institutions can begin to counter the many violent exposures underway.

4

Technological Benevolence

Do Fixes Fix Us?

- to repair
- to get even with
- to make firm, stable, or stationary
- to influence the actions, outcome, or effect of by improper or illegal methods.

Like more and more people released from immigrant detention centers, Grace, a single mother from El Salvador, was imprisoned for over a year before being released with an ankle monitor – what families call "grilletes," Spanish for shackles. "It's like they make us free, but not totally free. It's the same psychological game as detention. They aren't freeing us totally. It's, 'If you break a rule, if you don't tell us you're leaving, we'll put you in detention again.'"[1] Pseudo-freedom offers more opportunity to control and capitalize on the electronic afterlives of imprisonment. Quite literally, those wearing the shackle must pay for their containment. The same companies that have federal contracts with Immigration and Customs Enforcement

(ICE) and profit from immigrant prisons have moved into the ankle monitor business now that holding families seeking asylum has come under intense public criticism.[2] In fact, as I write this, Microsoft employees are demanding that the company drop a $19.4 million contract with ICE for facial recognition and identification software – what Microsoft originally dubbed "transformative technologies for homeland security and public safety."[3] Technical fixes operate in a world of euphemisms, where nothing is as it seems. One of the companies with longstanding ties to ICE, GEO Group, calls their facilities "family residential centers," while lawyers and human rights advocates rightly call them "family prisons."[4] Likewise, the purportedly more humane alternatives to prison, part of a growing suite of "technocorrections," should just be called what they are – *grilletes*.

As the devastation wrought by racist policing and mass incarceration in the United States gains widespread attention – from President Obama's Fair Sentencing Act (2010) to the Supreme Court's decision in *Brown v. Plata* (2011), which addresses prison overcrowding, and to the publication of books such as Michelle Alexander's (2012) *The New Jim Crow* – many proposed reforms incorporate technology designed to address the crisis. Foremost in this trend is the popularity of using electronic monitoring (EM) technologies to resolve the unsustainable and unconstitutional overcrowding of jails and prisons by having "mass monitorization" rather than mass incarceration.[5] Whereas ankle bracelets are typically associated with white-collar crimes and relatively privileged felons (think Martha Stewart), they are now being rolled out on a much larger scale, such as Philadelphia's pilot program, where 60 percent of inmates are waiting for trial and 72 percent are people of color.[6] Proponents argue that EM costs less, increases public safety, and allows those monitored to integrate into work and family life, as they either await trial or serve parole.

But, as those who have been subjected to EM and those who have researched the implications of mass monitorization argue, its depiction as an "alternative" to incarceration is based on a number of faulty assumptions; EM should more aptly be called "E-carceration."[7] Researcher, author, and activist James Kilgore recalls serving parole with an ankle bracelet and having to choose between taking his ill mother to the hospital or adhering to the mobility restrictions of his monitor.[8] He argues:

> An alternative to incarceration must embody an alternative mindset. This means rejection of the punitive, racist mentality that has dominated US criminal justice and social policy for more than three decades. An alternative to incarceration must recognize the full humanity and rights of people with felony convictions and their loved ones.[9]

Most EM is being used in pre-trial release programs for those who cannot afford bail, employing GPS to track individuals at all times – a newfangled form of incarceration before conviction. As founder and executive director of the Center for Media Justice, Malkia Cyril stresses: "There is increasing evidence that the algorithmic formulas used to make these decisions [about who should be assigned e-monitoring] contain deep-seated racial bias, so we must explore the extent to which EM both infringes upon core civil rights and represents a new frontier to compile surveillance data."[10] The very solutions to mass incarceration and prison overcrowding, in other words, give rise to innovative forms of injustice. They are, in short, racial fixes that harm even as they purport to help.[11]

Technological Benevolence

Numerous efforts are also underway to develop technologies that ameliorate social cleavages. These interventions explicitly aim at addressing bias of different kinds, but some of them can still end up reinforcing the New Jim Code. Take, for example, new artificial intelligence techniques for vetting job applicants. A company called HireVue aims to "reduce unconscious bias and promote diversity" in the workplace by using an AI-powered program that analyzes recorded interviews of prospective employees. It uses thousands of data points, including verbal and nonverbal cues such as facial expression, posture, and vocal tone, and compares jobseekers' scores to those of existing top-performing employees in order to decide whom to flag as a desirable hire and whom to reject.

The sheer size of many applicant pools and the amount of time and money that companies pour into recruitment is astronomical. Companies like HireVue can narrow the eligible pool at a fraction of the time and cost, and hundreds of companies and organizations – including Hilton, HBO, Boston Red Sox, and Atlanta Public Schools – have signed on. Another added value, according to HireVue, is that there is a lot that a human interviewer misses but

140

that AI can keep track of so as to make "data-driven talent decisions." The CEO of MYA Systems, another company in the AI-powered recruitment business, described some of the benefits thus: "a 79% reduction in the time it took to fill each position, and a 144% increase in productivity per recruiter who used the technology."[12] But efficiency and effectiveness are not the only drivers. AI programs are called upon to bypass human bias when it comes to evaluating job candidates.

Recall that the problem of employment discrimination is widespread and well documented. Wouldn't that be a good reason to outsource decisions to AI? And, if so, is the solution to ensure that the algorithm is not exposed to prejudicial associations, so that it avoids replicating our worst tendencies? Not quite, says the Princeton team working on natural language processing mentioned earlier, because exposure to negative biases can be instructive on how *not* to act – at least for humans. Some warn that completely shielding AI from the "bad" and saturating it in the "good" is not necessarily the way to go. Instead the question is how to code a machine that can vacuum up all the beauty and ugliness from humanity, yet remain without prejudice – an idea we will come back to.

But for now it should be clear why technical fixes that claim to bypass and even overcome human biases are so desirable, even *magical*. Ed Finn, director for the Center for Science and the Imagination at the University of Arizona, connects the cultural power we grant to algorithms with a longer genealogy of symbols and sorcery, arguing that "computation casts a cultural shadow that is informed by this long tradition of magical thinking."[13] Magical for employers, perhaps, looking to streamline the grueling work of recruitment, but a *curse* for many job seekers.

Whereas the CEO of MYA Systems describes "a very human-like interaction" in the algorithmic vetting process, those who are on the hunt for jobs recount a much different experience. According to one report, applicants are frustrated not only by the lack of human contact, but also because they have no idea how they are evaluated and why they are repeatedly rejected. One job seeker described questioning every small movement and micro-expression and feeling a heightened sense of worthlessness because "the company couldn't even assign a person for a few minutes. The whole thing is becoming less human."[14]

Less human in terms of interaction, yes, and still discriminatory. One headline put it bluntly: "Your Next Interview Could Be with a Racist Robot." As Stanford University computer scientist Timnit Gebru warns, "[i]t's really dangerous to replace thousands of human [perspectives] with one or two algorithms." This sentiment is echoed by Princeton University computer science professor Arvind Narayanan, who tweeted this in response to AI-power employment decisions:

> Human decision makers might be biased, but at least there's a *diversity* of biases. Imagine a future where every employer uses automated resume screening algorithms that all use the same heuristics, and job seekers who do not pass those checks get rejected everywhere.

In October 2018, Amazon scrapped an AI recruitment tool when it realized that the algorithm was discriminating against women. The system ranked applicants on a score of 1 to 5; it was built using primarily the resumes of men over a ten-year period and downgraded applications that listed women's colleges or terms such as "women's chess club." But even after programmers edited the algorithm to make it remain "gender neutral" to these obvious words, Amazon worried that "the machines would devise other ways of sorting candidates that proved discriminatory."[15] They rightly understood that neutrality is no safeguard against discriminatory design. In fact, given tech industry demographics, the training data were likely much more imbalanced by race than by gender, so it is probable that the AI's racial bias was even stronger than the reported gender bias.

Some job seekers are already developing ways to subvert the system by trading answers to employers' tests and by creating fake applications as informal audits of their own. In fact one HR employee for a major company recommends "slipping the words 'Oxford' or 'Cambridge' into a CV in invisible white text, to pass the automated screening."[16] In terms of a more collective response, a federation of trade unions called UNI Global Union has developed "a charter of digital rights for workers touching on automated and AI-based decisions, to be included in bargaining agreements."

The danger of New Jim Code impartiality is the neglect of ongoing inequity perpetuated by colorblind designs. In this context, algorithms may not be just a veneer that covers historical fault lines. They also seem to be streamlining discrimination – making it easier to sift, sort, and *justify* why tomorrow's workforce continues to be racially stratified. Algorithmic neutrality reproduces algorithmically sustained discrimination.

Fixing Diversity

Diversity Inc., a company I introduced to you earlier, does not employ fancy machine learning algorithms but statistics that use people's first and last names to predict their ethnicity. Ethno-racially coded names are a resource for computer coding and thus a valuable commodity in many other industries that are looking to tailor their products to different groups. One of the things I find fascinating in this context is how ethnicity operates as a proxy for individuality. So, when people who work in direct marketing talk about ethnic targeting, they see this as acknowledging individuals, not groups. To them, it is the opposite of making vague generalizations, even when ethnic stereotypes are employed. For example, one industry insider who uses names to predict ethnicity explains: "There is no such thing as an average Joe or Jane, Asian Americans have different values than Jewish Americans, if you know someone's ethnicity or religion, you can predict quite a few things."[17]

Even more interesting is that Diversity Inc. in particular has delineated over 150 distinct ethnicities and "builds" new ones for companies that need to reach a subgroup that is not already represented in their database. The language of "building" an ethnicity resonates with our earlier discussion about algorithms and architecture. Now, let's take a slightly closer look at how computer coding in this context relates to other sorts of ethno-racial coding.

During an interview with Diversity Inc.'s director of research and product development, she walked me through a typical presentation used to pitch the value of the company's software to prospective clients. I learned that their products are especially valuable to those industries not allowed to collect ethno-racial data directly from individuals because of civil rights legislation that attempts to curb how these data are used to discriminate. But now those who work in finance, housing, and healthcare can use predictive software programs to ascertain information that they cannot request directly. The US Health Insurance Portability and Accountability Act (HIPAA) privacy rule, for example, strictly monitors the collection, storage, and communication of individuals' "protected health information," among other features of the law. This means that pharmaceutical companies, which market to different groups, need indirect methods to create customer profiles, because they cannot collect racial-ethnic data directly.

This is where Diversity Inc. comes in. Its software programs target customers not only on the basis of race and ethnicity, but also on the basis of socioeconomic status, gender, and a growing list of other attributes. However, the company does not refer to "race" anywhere in their product descriptions. Everything is based on individuals' names, we are told. "A person's name is data," according to the director of research and product development. She explains that her clients typically supply Diversity Inc. with a database of client names and her team builds knowledge around it. The process, she says, has a 96 percent accuracy rate, because so many last names are not shared across racial–ethnic groups – a phenomenon sociologists call "cultural segregation."[18] In the context of tailored advertising, segregation has the added value of facilitating valuable prediction, innovation, and wealth generation.

Interestingly, African Americans and Filipino Americans are two groups whose common surnames are not as highly predictive as those of other groups, because more often than not they have inherited the last names of White people who once enslaved and colonized their ancestors. For this reason, Diversity Inc. triangulates African American and Filipino American surnames with other data points, namely zip codes. For example, in order to assign a racial–ethnic identity to "Sarah Johnson," her name would be coded in this manner:

SARAH: Generic first name
JOHNSON: English surname does not predict ethnicity
ZIP CODE: Majority Black neighborhood
ETHNICITY: African American

We can see how racially segregated neighborhoods, which are the ongoing legacy of Jim Crow policies of a previous era, may yield profitable insights about identity and consumer habits.

The financial value of segregation was one of the justifications for redlining policies in the early to mid-twentieth century in which banks, with the support of the federal government, mapped cities into color-coded zones, investing in White neighborhoods and depriving Black ones. In my grandmother's neighborhood, Leimert Park Los Angeles, marketing campaigns from the 1940s lured White home buyers by touting "beneficial restrictions that absolutely SECURES the security of your investment."[19] These racially restrictive covenants were the main tool that individual homeowners, neighborhood associations, and developers

146

used in order to prevent Black people from purchasing property.

Whereas laws and practices of a previous era blatantly encouraged segregation to reinforce racial hierarchy, today companies are more interested in curating a range of markets to bolster their profit margin. And, whereas the purpose of identifying an individual's race during the Jim Crow era was to discriminate effectively, now the stated aim is to "better serve" or "include" different groups.[20] By fixing group identities as stable features of the social landscape, these technical fixes offer a kind of remedy for the shortcomings of a mass-marketing approach to consumer life. Difference is monetized and, through software techniques, now codified beyond the law, in the digital structures of everyday life, through what Safiya Noble incisively calls "technological redlining."[21]

This is not simply a story of "then" versus "now." It is about how historical processes make the present possible; it is about the continuity between Jim Crow and the New Jim Code. Those who wanted to maintain White supremacy by controlling wealth and property used redlining and restrictive covenants to create neighborhoods separated by race. These same geographic divisions are now a source of profit for those who want to gear their products and services to different racial–ethnic groups. But whether or not we consider this latter process "racist" depends in part on how well we think a group is being targeted – accurately seen, unfairly ignored, or falsely distorted.

The broader point is that racialized zip codes are the output of Jim Crow policies and the input of New Jim Code practices. Without them, entities would be unable to navigate the antidiscriminatory ethos of civil rights legislation, and companies like Diversity Inc. would have a much harder time predicting Blackness as part of what they sell to firms and organizations.

The emergence of companies like Diversity Inc., which create racial–ethnic data to be sold to others, also invites questions about possible negative consequences in terms of privacy, surveillance, and discrimination. The fact that there is no democratic oversight of this process is worrisome. The public is just supposed to trust that these tools will not be used to create a Muslim database that uses Arab names as a proxy for direct profiling. Racial fixes, in this way, are duplicitous and multiplicitous, two-faced and wide-ranging. We find them well beyond the realm of policing and prisons, in the seemingly more benign arenas of work and school. Here racial fixes often come wrapped in the language of diversity – celebrated as a self-evident good, a recognition of one's individuality or identity, touted on university websites and employee trainings, a cheery antidote for those suffering from racial queasiness. For this reason, in social justice circles "diversity" is often mocked as a feel-good panacea, a poor proxy for more substantive transformations of the racial status quo, cosmetic and episodic gestures . . . without lasting movement.

Diversity mission statements are part of a larger repertoire of "happy talk," which involves a willingness to acknowledge and even revel in cultural difference without seriously challenging the ongoing structural inequality.[22] It is the difference between international food fairs held by many schools and the racialized tracking systems that shape the day-to-day experiences and opportunities of students at those same institutions.

"Eating the other," to borrow bell hooks' classic formulation, is not a sign of cultural recognition, nor does it challenge oppressive systems. On Columbus Day, as I sat in a local café working on this book, I overheard a group of White men clad in power suits, bankers in town for a meeting if I had to guess, as their conversation moved seamlessly from stock market trends to mocking Indigenous People's Day and to their favorite places for getting ethnic food. The pleasure of devouring difference – literally, through food, and figuratively, through music, travel, sex, and more – masks power differentials and dampens the prospects for concrete political action that might lead to a more lasting social transformation.[23] It exemplifies a kind of racial fix(ation) in which those feasting at the table of cultural diversity assume that their own pleasure is shared with those who are being consumed.

In *The Enigma of Diversity*, sociologist Ellen Berry explains how those who champion a flat conception of diversity have "redefined racial progress for the post-civil rights era, from a legal fight for equal rights to a celebration of cultural difference as a competitive advantage" in which everyone (theoretically) wins.[24] More pointedly, the late political scientist Lee Ann Fujii reminds us that the lack of genuine diversity "maintains a racialized way of seeing the world. This lens of default Whiteness is assumed to be neutral, unraced, and ungendered, and therefore 'scientifically' sound. But Whiteness is anything but."[25] Finally, legal scholar Nancy Leong details how institutions commodify racial diversity for their own benefit, defining, in her analysis, racial capitalism as "the process of deriving social and economic value from the racial identity of another person."[26]

Building on these critiques, we can consider how technologies mediate racial capitalism by encoding racialized distinctions "in service" to diverse populations. And sociotechnical interventions rely on fixed notions of ethno-racial difference to solve different kinds of problems. Most importantly, a racial fix is itself a social technology that creates vertical realities – freedom, security, and happiness above and bondage, precarity, and misery below – all the while masking and distorting the lives of the latter from those who experience the former.

Racial Fixes

A racial fix must continually burnish its benevolence, which is made easier by conjuring the noble-sounding ambitions of technoscience. The HBO series *Silicon Valley* parodies this techno-benevolence to great effect. In a scene that showcases hopeful software developers presenting at TechCrunch, a conference where only the most promising ideas attract top investors, the writers spoof these rapid-fire and painfully earnest pitches (each line designating a different speaker):

> We're here to revolutionize the way you report bugs on your mobile platform!
> We will revolutionize location-based news aggregation as you know it!
> We're making the world a better place through Paxo's algorithms for consensus protocols!
> And we're making the world a better place through software defying data centers for cloud computing!
> . . . a better place for canonical data models to communicate between end points.

... a better place through scalable, fault tolerant, distributed, ACID transactions.
And we are truly, local, mobile, social.
And we're completely SoMoLo ...
And we're MoLoSo.
We are MoSoLo, bro.[27]

The scene plays with the connection between buzzwords and benevolence, making fun of the do-good sound bites that characterize the *revolutionary* culture of innovation: "health," "safety," "efficiency," and even "diversity" mask newfangled forms of classification and control, which often take shape under the rubric of customization and individualization. The scene eventually whittles down the sound bites into virtuous acronyms, where each start-up offers a different configuration of the same three buzzwords – local, mobile, social – exposing how the same features are simply reordered to give the illusion of choice. Indeed, as I explore below, if people do not truly have the choice to wiggle free from the suffocating embrace of techno-benevolence without repercussions, that is a sign of fixity – an innovation that constrains.

Racial fixes are appealing, in part because they come wrapped in an aura of personalization: they are products and experiences specially tailored just for you, goes the marketing mantra. Novel software programs permit businesses to personalize in appealing and creative ways, building on a much longer commitment to "selling identity" that began with the move away from mass market to niche markets. In *Shopping for Identity: The Marketing for Ethnicity*, historian Marilyn Halter explains:

> By the early 1970s, change was permeating the cultural front and the parameters of the American marketplace were shifting quite dramatically ... Companies needed to find new ways to hook consumers on their particular brands and to make customers loyal in an increasingly competitive and saturated marketplace. Corporate industry leaders began taking a different tack, turning away from mass advertising campaigns to concentrate on segmented marketing approaches. One of the most successful of the segmenting strategies has been to target specific ethnic constituencies.[28]

Today customization is typically taken for granted as a normal feature of social life, online and offline. When you and a friend are browsing the same website, you can expect to see different advertisements, which are based on algorithms that have been following your search and consumer habits. In an experiment meant to help her avoid being followed, science and technology studies (STS) scholar Janet Vertesi tried to keep her pregnancy private from the "bots, trackers, cookies and other data sniffers online that feed the databases that companies use for targeted advertising."[29] In the end she had to forego all baby-related searches and avoid all computer-based correspondence with family and friends that could end up on the data dragnet, and she paid for all pregnancy-related products by cash or gift cards.

But, crucially, these evasive efforts marked her as someone who was likely engaged in illicit activity, and her husband was flagged for purchasing too many gift cards: "a warning sign behind the cashier informed him that the store 'has an obligation to report excessive transactions to the authorities.'" Upon further reflection, Vertesi declares: "No one should have to act like a criminal just to have some privacy from marketers and tech giants. But the data-driven path we are currently on – paved with the heartwarming rhetoric of openness, sharing and connectivity – actually undermines civic values and circumvents checks and balances."[30]

Moreover, despite all the talk of tailoring, it is never uniquely you who is hailed by such advertisements, but rather people "like you" are the crucial target. To be served under a regime of personalization, one must first be secured as a particular type of person, a social kind – the parameters of which are shaped by a variety of assumptions, racial and otherwise. This is not to say that such assumptions are automatically wrong or inherently "bad" in any straightforward sense of causing direct harm to an individual. Nor are they avoidable altogether. But rather, even as they are synthesized and tested in marketing departments, it is doubtful that such groupings and generalizations are vigorously analyzed as a basis and byproduct of deep-seated social inequities.

Despite this, one might reason that, without the ability to target different groups, we are left with false universals (think flesh-colored Band-Aids that are pinky beige, or emojis that only come in one color). Perhaps, then, a racial generalization is a step in the right direction, gesturing at least to recognizing different social identities and experiences. The optimistic way to look at discriminatory design, one could conclude, is more akin to discerning design, which may not fully account for individual nuances but nevertheless offers people a more tailored experience. Here is where we should pause. Because any time we are presented with a binary decision – bland generalization or spicy stereotype – it is important to ask what options are left out of the frame. If our choices are so narrowly defined, are they "choices" after all? By unsettling such binaries we can undertake a clear-eyed assessment of the politics and penalties of refusing racial fixes and insist upon a far-reaching imagination of what alternatives are possible.

Fixing Health

Medical historian Lundy Braun's *Breathing Race into the Machine* offers a poignant illustration of the duplicity of fixity, wherein race is used simultaneously to help and harm Black workers. She examines how "cultural notions of race became embedded in the architecture of an apparently ordinary instrument," the spirometer (a device built to assess lung function), and reviews the widespread implications of this process – from research to clinics to medical school training to insurance claims.[31] In 1999 the world's largest insulation manufacturer was busily trying to limit disability claims in a class-action lawsuit brought by 15,000 asbestos workers by drawing upon the long-standing belief among pulmonologists that racial groups differed in the capacity and the function of their lungs.

Drawing upon the widely accepted practice of "race correction . . . the idea of racial difference in lung capacity" – so normalized that there is a button for it on the spirometer that produces different measurements of normalcy by race – the company made it more difficult for Black workers to qualify for workers' compensation. Black workers were required to demonstrate worse lung function and more severe clinical symptoms than White workers owing to this feature of the spirometer, whose developer, Dr. John Hutchinson, was employed by insurance companies in the mid-1800s to minimize payouts. Such discriminatory design normalizes environmental racism – not as an aberration from "business as usual," but as a racial–economic imperative that is built in to the machine.

In this way, such medical techniques demonstrate a type of "fixing": they are health interventions that embrace a racialized conception of "problem people," and thereby influence the direction of treatment by improper means. Drawing on Derrida's notion of *pharmakon* as both cure and poison, STS scholar Anne Pollock explains that race-based drugs "have the capacity to be both beneficial and detrimental to the same person at the same time . . . Moreover, the poison that is part of the pharmakon is not separate from its efficacy, but immanent to it."[32] If we are to draw a parallel with the context of information technologies, racial fixes are better understood not as viruses but as a part of the underlying code of operating systems – often developed as solutions to particular kinds of predicaments without sufficient awareness of the problems that they help produce and preserve.

In the United States, for example, 5 percent of Americans account for nearly 50 percent of healthcare costs and 1 percent comprise 20 percent of costs, and so the practice of healthcare "hot-spotting" is a kind of market segmentation. According to this approach, which started in Camden, New Jersey, the purpose of healthcare hot-spotting is the "strategic use of data to reallocate resources to a small subset of high-needs, high-cost patients," or what they call *super-utilizers*.[33] In Camden, 13 percent of the population accounts for

80 percent of healthcare costs. In 2007 a coalition of healthcare providers started using (insurance claims) data from all three city hospitals to examine the relationship between geography, utilization, cost, and other variables. They also employ "Geographic Information Systems (GIS) technologies and spatial profiling to identify populations that are medically vulnerable ('health care's costliest 1%'),"[34] a form of techno-benevolence that blurs the line between niche tailoring and unwanted targeting.

Family physician Jeffrey Brenner, who founded the healthcare hotspotting initiative, was inspired by the work of the New York Police Department. According to Nadine Ehlers and Shiloh Krupar in "When Treating Patients Like Criminals Makes Sense," hot-spotting uses not only GIS but also the principles of racial profiling. They focus on "how attempts to lower the monetary debt incurred by hospitals – through this new form of race-based medicine – situates minorities as responsible for this debt and actually re-entrenches racial disparity" and those targeted "are often classified as 'socially disintegrated,' as dependent, and as unable to self-care."[35] The medical and economic intervention, in short, fixes people into stigmatizing categories – the very forms of classificatory stigma that restrict people's life chances and fuel health disparities in the first place.

Some may argue that stigma is a small price to pay for access to the much-needed medicine and attention. Indeed, this is the allure of tech fixes. They offer pragmatic inclusion in place of political and social transformation. *The medical means justify the social ends*, we are led to believe. But too often the means are the end. New Jim Code fixes are a permanent placeholder for bolder change. Sure, some people may live longer, but they are still living in neighborhoods and schools that those in power are less motivated to spot and fix. Medical inclusion, in short, can be a lucrative stand-in for social and political justice. To its credit, the Camden coalition has expressed commitment to a more holistic approach than most healthcare systems, attentive to the "non-medical needs that affect health: housing, mental health, substance abuse, emotional support."[36] Even so, those who adopt a hotspotting method may not necessarily embrace such a far-reaching vision.

Detecting Fixes

As the analogy with technological systems suggests, racial logics are readily embedded in social systems when underlying normative assumptions and social biases are ignored. The denial of racial–ethnic categories may very well lead to some of the most sinister and systemic forms of racism, with very little recourse. This is especially the case when people refuse to acknowledge and to challenge how such logics structure the development and deployment of technoscience and, by extension, access to resources and the rights associated with such initiatives. Likewise, as Chapter 2 argued, in thinking about the function of racialized codes within algorithms, it is important not to assume that they are simply unintended glitches.[37] The "productive" (in the generic sense of producing things, not in the normative sense of necessarily beneficial) function of race within technical systems should not be underestimated. That is, computer programs that are not "tuned in" to the racism of the humans with whom they are meant to interact are akin to children who do not speak the language of their parents.

Returning to electronic monitoring, like other forms of racial fixing, its function is to create vertical realities – surveillance and control for some, security and freedom for others.[38] Those who are not generally the target of such practices can sleep soundly in the knowledge that such technologies are being used for the greater good, even as they extend the tentacles of incarceration outside jails and prisons and into the most intimate settings of everyday life.

In tracing the connections between electronic monitoring, predictive policing, facial recognition, and more, Malkia Cyril explains that "technology is being used to expand the carceral state, allowing policing and imprisonment to stand in for civil society while seemingly neutral algorithms justify that shift ... Digital technologies extend the reach of this structural surveillance, make it persistent for some and nearly invisible to those with enough power to escape its gaze."[39] The shackles that Grace and thousands of other people must wear as a condition of their release are not simply technologies of containment. They are lucrative devices for capitalizing on the misery of others while claiming humanistic concern.

By making the duplicity and multiplicity of racial fixes visible, those who genuinely seek social justice can avoid falling under the spell of techno-benevolence, for which "revolution" is a marketing catchphrase used to entice investors. In striking contrast, we urgently need what religious studies scholar Eddie Glaude Jr. calls a "revolution of value and radical democractic awakening," which encompasses traditional areas of public concern – work, health, and education among them – and should also tackle the many discriminatory designs that codify the *value gap* between Black and White by automating *racial habits* in digital systems.[40]

5

Retooling Solidarity, Reimagining Justice

The power of the New Jim Code is that it allows racist habits and logics to enter through the backdoor of tech design, in which the humans who create the algorithms are hidden from view. In the previous chapters I explored a range of discriminatory designs – some that explicitly work to amplify hierarchies, many that ignore and thus replicate social divisions, and a number that aim to fix racial bias but end up doing the opposite. In one sense, these forms of discriminatory design – engineered inequity, default discrimination, coded exposure, and technological benevolence – fall on a spectrum that ranges from *most obvious* to *oblivious* in the way it helps produce social inequity. But, in a way, these differences are also an artifact of marketing, mission statements, and willingness of designers to own up to their impact. It will be tempting, then, to look for comparisons throughout this text and ask: "Is this approach better than that?" But in writing this book I have admittedly been more interested in connections rather than in comparisons; in how this seemingly more beneficent approach to bypassing bias in tech relates to

160

that more indifferent or avowedly inequitable approach; in entangling the seeming differences rather than disentangling for the sake of easy distinctions between good and bad tech.

On closer inspection, I find that the varying dimensions of the New Jim Code draw upon a shared set of methods that make coded inequity desirable and profitable to a wide array of social actors across many settings; it appears to rise above human subjectivity (it has impartiality) because it is purportedly tailored to individuals, not groups (it has personalization), and ranks people according to merit, not prejudice (or positioning) – all within the framework of a forward-looking (i.e. predictive) enterprise that promises social progress. These four features of coded inequity prop up unjust infrastructures, but not necessarily to the same extent at all times and in all places, and definitely not without eliciting countercodings that retool solidarity and rethink justice.

These forms of resistance are what I think of as abolitionist tools for the New Jim Code. And, as with abolitionist practices of a previous era, not all manner of *gettin' free* should be exposed. Recall that Frederick Douglass, the philosopher of fugitivity, reprimanded those who revealed the routes that fugitives took to escape slavery, declaring that these supposed allies turned the underground railroad into the *upperground* railroad.[1] Likewise, some of the efforts of those resisting the New Jim Code necessitate strategic discretion, while others may be effectively tweeted around the world in an instant.

Thirty minutes after proposing an idea for an app "that converts your daily change into bail money to free black people," Compton, California-born Black trans

King Kortney, PhD
@fakerapper

An app that converts your daily change into bail money to free black people.

2:58 PM - 23 Jul 2017

627 Retweets **1,716** Likes

🔲 56   ⟲ 627   ♡ 1.7K   ✉

Figure 5.1   Appolition
Source: Twitter @fakerapper July 23, 2017 at 2:58 p.m.

tech developer Dr. Kortney Ziegler added: "It could be called Appolition" (Figure 5.1).[2] The name is a riff on *abolition* and a reference to a growing movement toward divesting resources from policing and prisons and reinvesting in education, employment, mental health, and a broader support system needed to cultivate safe and thriving communities. Calls for abolition are never simply about bringing harmful systems to an end but also about envisioning new ones. After all, the etymology of "abolition" includes Latin root words for "destroy" (*abolere*) and "grow" (*olere*).

And, lest we be tempted to dismiss prison abolition as a far-fetched dream (or nightmare, depends), it is also worth considering how those who monopolize power and privilege already live in an abolitionist reality! As executive director of Law for Black Lives, Marbre Stahly-Butts, asserts:

There's a lot of abolitionist zones in the US. You go to the Hamptons, its abolitionist. You go to the Upper West Side, its abolitionist. You go to places in California

162

where the medium income is over a million dollars, *abolitionist*. There's not a cop to be seen. And so, the reality is that rich White people get to deal with all of their problems in ways that don't involve the police, or cages, or drug tests or things like that. The reality is that people actually know that police and cages don't keep you safe, if it's your son or your daughter.[3]

As a political movement, prison abolition builds on the work of slavery abolitionists of a previous era and tools like Appolition bring the movement into the digital arena. Days after the original tweet first circulated, Ziegler partnered with Tiffany Mikell to launch the app and began collaborating with the National Bail Out movement, a network of organizations that attempt to end cash bail and pretrial detention and to get funds into the hands of local activists who post bail. In September 2017 Ziegler was planning a kickoff event with the modest goal of enrolling 600 people. But after the launch in November the project garnered 8,000 enrollments, which landed Appolition in the top ten most innovative companies in 2018.[4]

More important for our discussion is that Appolition is a technology with an emancipatory ethos, a tool of solidarity that directs resources to getting people literally free. In fact, many White people who have signed up say that they see it as a form of reparation,[5] one small way to counteract the fact that the carceral system uses software that codes for inequity. To date, Appolition has raised $230,000, that money being directed to local organizations whose posted bails have freed over 65 people.[6] As the National Bail Out network explains, "[e]veryday an average of 700,000 people are condemned to local jails and separated from their families. A majority of them are there simply because they cannot afford to pay bail."[7]

When Ziegler and I sat on a panel together at the 2018 Allied Media Conference, he addressed audience concerns that the app is diverting even more money to a bloated carceral system. As Ziegler clarified, money is returned to the depositor after a case is complete, so donations are continuously recycled to help individuals. Interest in the app has grown so much that Appolition has launched a new version, which can handle a larger volume of donations and help direct funds to more organizations.

But the news is not all good. As Ziegler explained, the motivation behind ventures like Appolition can be mimicked by people who do not have an abolitionist commitment. He described a venture that the rapper Jay-Z is investing millions in, called Promise. Although Jay-Z and others call it a "decarceration start-up" because it addresses the problem of pretrial detention, which impacts disproportionately Black and Latinx people who cannot afford bail, Promise is in the business of tracking individuals via the app and GPS monitoring. And, whereas a county can spend up to $200 a day holding someone in jail, Promise can charge $17.[8] This is why the organization BYP100 (Black Youth Project 100) issued a warning that Promise

> helps expand the scope of what the Prison Industrial Complex is and will be in the future. The digital sphere and tech world of the 2000's [sic] is the next sector to have a stronghold around incarceration, and will mold what incarceration looks like and determine the terrain on which prison abolitionists have to fight as a result.[9]

BYP100 extends the critique of abolitionist organizations like Critical Resistance, which describes "the overlapping interests of government and industry that use surveillance, policing, and imprisonment as solutions to what are, in actuality, economic, social, and political 'problems'" under the description prison–industrial complex (PIC).[10] The Corrections Project has created a map of all these interests, with prisons and jails at the core and extending to law enforcement, prison guard unions, prison construction companies and vendors, courts, urban and rural developers, corporations, the media, and more.[11]

It is important to note that there is debate about whether "PIC" is an accurate and useful descriptor. Some prefer "*corrections* industrial complex," to draw attention to probation and surveillance as the fastest growing part of the industry. Others offer a more far-reaching critique by questioning *how industrial* and *complex* the PIC really is since the corrections arena is still overwhelmingly public – the budget is less than 1 percent of the GDP, less than 0.5 percent of the incarcerated being employed by private firms. It is also an overwhelmingly decentralized enterprise, run at the local, county, and state levels rather than masterminded by a central government entity, as is for example the Pentagon vis-à-vis the military–industrial complex.[12]

Even so, the term "PIC" has been useful as a rhetorical device for drawing widespread attention to the exponential growth of prison and policing since 1980 and for highlighting the multiple investments of a wide range of entities. Profit, in this context, is made not only in cash, but also in political power, property, TV ratings, and other resources from economic to symbolic, including the fact that many companies now invest in e-corrections as a fix for prison overcrowding.

If both Appolition and Promise apply digital tools to helping people who cannot afford bail to get out of cages, why is Promise a problem for those who support prison abolition? Because it creates a powerful mechanism that makes it easier to put people back in; and, rather than turning away from the carceral apparatus, it extends it into everyday life.

Whereas the money crowdfunded for Appolition operates like an endowment that is used to bail people out, Promise is an investment and collaborates with law enforcement. The company, which received $3 million in venture capital, is not in the business of decarceration but is part of the "technocorrections" industry, which seeks to capitalize on very real concerns about mass incarceration and the political momentum of social justice organizing. Products like Promise make it easier and more cost-effective for people to be tracked and thrown back into jail for *technical* violations. One "promise" here is to the state – that the company can keep track of individuals – and another to the taxpayer – that the company can cut costs. As for the individuals held captive, the burden of nonstop surveillance is arguably better than jail, but a digital cell is still a form of high-tech social control.

Promise, in this way, is exemplary of the New Jim Code; and it is dangerous and insidious precisely because it is packaged as social betterment. This, along with the weight of Jay Z's celebrity, will make it difficult to challenge Promise. But if this company is to genuinely contribute to decarceration, it would need to shrink the carceral apparatus, not extend it and make it more encompassing. After all, prison conglomerates such as Geo Group and CoreCivic are proving especially adept at reconfiguring their business investments, leaving prisons and detention centers and turning to tech alternatives, for instance ankle monitors and other digital tracking devices. In some cases the companies that hold lucrative government contracts to imprison asylum seekers are the same ones that the US Immigration and Customs Enforcement (ICE) hires to provide social services to these very people, as they continue to be monitored remotely.[13] While not being locked in a cage is an improvement, the alternative is a form of coded inequity and carceral control; and it is vital that people committed to social justice look beyond the shiny exterior of organizations that peddle such reforms.

A key tenet of prison abolition is that caging people works directly against the safety and well-being of communities because jails and prisons do not address the underlying reasons why people harm themselves and others – in fact they exacerbate the problem by making it even more difficult to obtain any of the support needed to live, work, and make amends for harms committed. But in the age of the New Jim Code, as BYP100 noted, this abolitionist ethos must be extended beyond the problem of caging, to our consideration of technological innovations marketed as supporting prison reform.

Coding people as "risky" kicks in an entire digital apparatus that extends incarceration well beyond the prison wall.[14] Think of it this way. Yes, it is vital to divert money away from imprisonment to schools and public housing, if we really want to make communities stronger, safer, and more supportive for all their members. But, as Critical Resistance has argued, simply diverting resources in this way is no panacea, because schools and public housing as they currently function are an *extension* of the PIC: many operate with a logic of carcerality and on policies that discriminate against those who have been convicted of crimes. Pouring money into them *as they are* will only make them more effective in their current function as institutions of social control. We have to look beyond the surface of what they say they do to what they actually do, in the same way in which I am calling on all of us to question the "do good" rhetoric of the tech industry.

For prison abolitionists, "we don't just want better funded schools (although that might be an important step). We also demand the power to shape the programs and institutions in our communities"[15] and to propose a new and more humane vision of how resources and technology are used. This requires us to consider not only the ends but also the *means*. How we get to the end matters. If the path is that private companies, celebrities, and tech innovators should cash in on the momentum of communities and organizations that challenge mass incarceration, the likelihood is that the end achieved will replicate the current social order.

Let us shift, then, from technology as an outcome to toolmaking as a practice, so as to consider the many different types of tools needed to resist coded inequity, to build solidarity, and to engender liberation. Initiatives like Appolition offer a window into a wider arena of "design justice" that takes many forms (see Appendix), some of which I will explore below. But first allow me a reflection on the growing discourse around technology and *empathy* (rather than equity or justice).

168

Selling Empathy

Empathy talk is everywhere. I have used it myself as shorthand, as a way to index the lack of social cohesion and justice, and as a gentler way to invoke the need for solidarity. Empathy is woven more and more into the marketing of tech products. I participate in a lot of conferences for primary and secondary school educators and I see how the product expos at these events promise these teachers that gadgets and software will cultivate empathy in students. Virtual reality (VR) technology in particular is routinely described as an "empathy machine" because of the way it allows us to move through someone else's world. Perhaps it does, in some cases.[16] But, as some critics emphasize, this rhetoric creates a moral imperative to sell headsets and to consume human anguish, and in the process "pain is repurposed as a site of economic production":[17]

> Imagine a VR live stream of a police killing. This, tragically, will soon cease to be science fiction: within years, you will be able to experience an extremely convincing simulation of what it's like to be murdered by a cop. Will this lead to the cop's conviction, or to meaningful criminal justice reform? Recent history suggests the answer is no. But the content will probably go viral, as its affective intensity generates high levels of user engagement. And this virality will generate revenue for the company that owns the platform.[18]

Empathy makes businesses grow. In the first quarter of 2016 alone, venture capitalists invested almost $1.2 billion in VR technologies, almost 50 percent more than in the previous quarter.[19] In 2017, following the devasting hurricane in Puerto Rico, Facebook founder Mark Zuckerberg used the company's VR app to "visit" the island as part of Facebook's partnership with the Red Cross recovery effort. While Zuckerberg was immersed in the scene, those watching the live feed saw his cartoon avatar touring through the wreckage alongside another company executive who, at one point, comments: "it's crazy to feel like you're in the middle of it."[20] In response to criticism, Zuckerberg apologized by saying:

> One of the most powerful features of VR is empathy. My goal here was to show how VR can raise awareness and help us see what's happening in different parts of the world. I also wanted to share the news of our partnership with the Red Cross to help with the recovery. Reading some of the comments, I realize this wasn't clear, and I'm sorry to anyone this offended.[21]

While some observers said the problem was that Zuckerberg's immersive experience was not reflected in the cartoonish portrayal that viewers were witnessing, others have called into question the very idea of VR as empathy-inducing. As in other "awareness-raising experiences where viewers get a firsthand view of war, sickness, or other forms of suffering,"[22] good intentions are no safeguard against harm or exploitation. As one critic observed:

> The rhetoric of the empathy machine asks us to endorse technology without questioning the politics of its construction or who profits from it . . . Do you really need to wear a VR headset in order to empathize with someone? Can't you just fucking listen to them and believe them? You need to be entertained as well? Are you sure this

isn't about *you? . . . I don't want your empathy, I want justice!*"[23]

When I ask my students to question their assumptions about various issues, I often use the analogy of "lenses" – encouraging a different lens so that we may look anew at all that we take for granted. Well, now the lenses are no longer metaphorical. But, as anthropologist John L. Jackson has noted, "seeing through another person's eyes is not the same thing as actually seeing that person. In fact, one precludes the other, by definition, unless the gaze is (tellingly) merely into a mirror."[24] *Being* the other, conceived of in this way, is an extension of what bell hooks calls "eating the other."[25] Tech designers have created actual headsets that we can don, our physical body in one world as our mind travels through another. Or is that really how it works? By simply changing what (as opposed to how) we see, do we really leave behind all our assumptions and prior experiences as we journey into virtual reality? Perhaps we overestimate how much our literal sight dictates our understanding of race and inequity more broadly?

I am reminded of a study by sociologist Osagie Obasogie, author of *Blinded by Sight*, in which he interviewed people who were blind from birth, asking them about their experiences of race. He found that, like everyone else, they had learned to "see" – that is, *perceive* – racial distinctions and hierarchies through a variety of senses and narratives that did not depend on actual sight. From this, Obasogie compels us to question two things: sight as an objective transmitter of reality and colorblindness as a viable legal framework and social ideology. *If blind people admit to seeing race, why do sighted people pretend not see it?* In his words, "our seemingly objective engagements with the world around us are subordinate to a faith that orients our visual experience and, moreover, produces our ability to see certain things. *Seeing is not believing.* Rather, to believe, in a sense, is to see."[26]

So how can we apply this lesson to the promises surrounding VR? Even as we are seeing and experiencing something different, we do not simply discard our prior perceptions of the world. One of the problems with VR is that it can present another opportunity for "poverty porn" and cultural tourism that reinforces current power dynamics between those who do the seeing and those who are watched.

Even so, what makes and will continue to make VR and other empathy machines so appealing, not just for big business but also for numerous NGOs, the United Nations, and UNICEF, which are using it to fundraise for human rights campaigns,[27] is that they seem to offer a technical fix for deep-seated divisions that continue to rip the social fabric.

For instance, there is growing buzz around using VR for "immersive career and vocational training" for prisoners to gain job and life skills prior to release.[28] At first glance, we might be tempted to count this as an abolitionist tool that works to undo the carceral apparatus by equipping former prisoners with valuable skills and opportunities. But what will the job market be like for former prisoners who have used VR? Research shows that there is widespread discrimination in the labor market, especially against African Americans convicted of a felony. And the labor market is already shaped by a technology that seeks to sort out those who are convicted of crimes, or even arrested, regardless of race. A US National Employment Law Project report shows that a staggering number of people – 65 million – "need not apply" for jobs from the numerous companies who outsource background checks to firms that, reportedly, look "just" at the facts (arrested? convicted?).[29] When such technological fixes are used by employers to make hiring decisions in the name of efficiency, there is little opportunity for a former felon, including those who have used VR, to garner the empathy of an employer who otherwise might have been willing to ponder over the circumstances of an arrest or conviction.

Given the likelihood that many of those who have been incarcerated will be discriminated against in the labor market as it currently operates, the question remains: who is actually profiting from VR-training for prisoners? And how does this technical fix subdue the call for more far-reaching aims, such as to weaken the carceral apparatus or to reimagine how the labor market operates?

In fact, VR is more likely employed to generate greater empathy for officers than, say, for people who are the object of police harassment and violence. According to a report published by a website geared to law enforcement, VR is a "public relations tool for strengthening public opinion of law enforcement because the technology allows a user to virtually walk in a cop's shoes . . . police agencies could bring VR into classrooms and community centers so the public can experience first-hand the challenges police officers face on patrol."[30] If even empathy machines are enrolled in the New Jim Code, what do abolitionist tools look like? What does an emancipatory approach to tech entail?

Rethinking Design Thinking

Now keep in mind that empathy is the first of five steps in an approach called "design thinking": empathize; define; ideate; prototype; test. Although there are different versions of this methodology, this is the one most commonly cited as the basis of "human-centered design." But, as we think about coded inequity and discriminatory design, it is vital to question *which humans* are prioritized in the process. Practically speaking, the human paying the designer's bill is the one most likely prioritized. But more people are speaking out about problems and pitfalls in the world of design, where the assumptions and methods of designers do not receive nearly as much critical engagement as they should.

Graphic designer Natasha Jen puts it bluntly in her talk "Design Thinking is Bullsh*t," urging design practitioners to avoid the jargon and buzzwords associated with their field, to engage in more self-criticism, to base their ideas on evidence, and to stop assuming that their five-step process is needed for anything and everything. On that last point, she notes a number of activities (such as surrounding a children's MRI machine with a cartoon mural) as examples of obvious ideas that do not require the input of professional designers.

If Jen is wary about the proliferation of design thinking, others are concerned with who is left out. At the 2018 meeting of the Design Research Society, the top ranked questions on Slido (an audience engagement tool that allows people to pose questions in real time) were: "Why is #DesignSoWhite?" "To do design for good don't we have to talk about the oppressive systems of white supremacy, heteropatriarchy, capitalism, we need to dismantle or transform?" "Are designers still mainly occupied with design that makes people want things? What kind of a future this implies?"[31] The panelists awkwardly ignored the questions for some twenty minutes until eventually the session ended with no response. Author of two of the questions, Sasha Costanza-Chock, a professor at the MIT, has developed the idea of "design justice" with Allied Media Network collaborators, to get us thinking more about the *process* and power dynamics of design across multiple axes of oppression.[32] They define design justice as "a field of theory and practice that is concerned with how the design of objects and systems influences the distribution of risks, harms, and benefits among various groups of people," and is focused on procedural and distributive justice:

> We have an ethical imperative to systematically advance the participation of marginalized communities in all stages of the technology design process; through this process, resources and power can be more equitably distributed.[33]

Sounds good, right? But if the "justice" used here is meant to augment dominant notions of design as a universal good, I wonder how justice itself might be altered by its proximity to design as a buzzword and brand. Is this not what we are seeing with Jay Z's Promise and other such products?

How, then, might we think critically about the assumptions of design, as well as about those of justice? In a recent workshop I participated in on "subversive design," we tried to grapple with this question. The facilitators asked participants to throw out terms and phrases that described what we thought design was:

- the expression of a value system
- how we create space
- solving a problem
- visually shaping something
- tool for maintaining power
- intentional creation
- *and more!*

As I sat there looking up at the screen, trying to think of what to add, it struck me that maybe the growing list was a problem. But, good student that I am, I still raised my hand to chime in – *design is a colonizing project*, I offered, to the extent that it is used to describe anything and everything.[34] The affirming nods and groans from the facilitators and others in the room suggested that this critique resonated with them.

What, I wonder, are the theoretical and practical effects of using design-speak to describe all our hopes, dreams, qualms, criticisms, and visions for change? What is gained and by whom in the process of submerging so much heterogeneity under the rubric of design? I can see how it might work as a way to draw out commonalities and build coalitions, as when Costanza-Chock writes: "Design justice as a theoretical framework recognizes the *universality of design* as a human activity."[35] In enrolling so many issues and experiences as design-related, maybe this could build a foundation for solidarity ... but it could also sanitize and make palatable deep-seated injustices, *contained* within the innovative practices of design.

If, in the language of the workshop, one needs to "subvert" design, this implies that a dominant framework of design reigns – and I think one of the reasons why it *reigns* is that it has managed to fold anything and everything under its agile wings. I am not the first to raise this concern.

In a recent set of essays, science and technology studies scholar Lee Vinsel warns that "design thinking is a kind of syphilis" and that its overblown claims are "boondoggle."[36] If it were just another fad, that would be one thing. The problem is how it envelops ideas and practices that have been around for a while, across a number of fields, while throwing in vague and unsubstantiated claims about the efficacy of design thinking for other fundamental institutions. Vinsel, for his part, is especially frustrated with the application of design thinking to "transform" higher education. He takes special issue with Stanford University d.school, whose executive director, Sarah Stein Greenberg, recently proscribed some "radical ideas for reinventing college." Her talk starts by discussing how lecture halls, in the way they are designed, reflect certain assumptions about learning even as they shape the very possibilities for doing so.

Vinsel's criticism includes a photo of one of my favorite pedagogues, Brazilian educator Paulo Freire, with a fictional thought bubble that reads, "Dear Sarah, The first 2 minutes of your talk is the same critique of education I made in 1968."[37] My own teaching philosophy draws heavily from Freire's *Pedagogy of the Oppressed*, in which he writes, "if the structure does not permit dialogue, the structure must be changed."[38] So ... was Freire a design thinker? Or is Greenberg a Freirian? *Or does it matter?* I would argue that how we chronicle the connection between ideas is what matters. Genealogies reflect and reproduce power relations.

Citational practices are political, especially when we start talking about "innovation" – oppressed people and places are rarely cited for their many inventions.

Lilly Irani and M. Six Silberman contend: "What if the problem is not how we design in a highly unequal world, but the very fact that we are read as designers at all? Designers are more than those who seek to move from current states to preferred ones. Designers also occupy a relatively high rung in hierarchies of 'knowledge economy' projects."[39] Irani and Silberman's query grows out of their experience as developers of Turkopticon, an activist tool for workers that aims to help "the people in the 'crowd' of crowdsourcing watch out for each other – because nobody else seems to be."[40] And what they found was that, in public depictions of their work, designers were elevated while workers were cast as being "without agency and capacity to change their situation." Even though they themselves were guided by a solidaristic relationship with the workers, the public granted them, as "designers," a higher status than to their laboring counterparts.

If design as a *branded* methodology is elevated, then other forms of *generic* human activity are diminished. As Irani and Silberman put it, "workers who powered these platforms appeared as exploited cogs in other people's plans, toiling in digital sweatshops with little creativity or agency."[41] To the extent that design as brand colonizes all things – even the brainchild behind liberatory movements gets subsumed under a single approach precisely because it is set up to encompass anything and everything – who benefits and to what end? Is this umbrella philosophy the one best suited for the violent storms we face?

Whether or not design-speak sets out to colonize human activity, it is enacting a monopoly over creative thought and praxis. Maybe what we must demand is not liberatory *designs* but just plain old liberation. *Too retro*, perhaps? And that is part of the issue – by adding "design" to our vision of social change we rebrand it, upgrading social change from "mere" liberation to something out of the box, "disrupting" the status quo. *But why?* As Vinsel queries, "would Design Thinking have helped Rosa Parks 'design' the Montgomery Bus Boycott?"[42] It is not simply that design thinking wrongly claims newness, but in doing so it erases the insights and agency of those who are discounted because they are not designers, capitalizing on the demand for novelty across numerous fields of action and coaxing everyone who dons the cloak of design into being seen and heard through the dominant aesthetic of innovation.

Along with this, my critical engagement with the various forms of discriminatory design in the previous pages needs therefore to question not only the "discriminatory" part of the equation but also the seeming goodness of design itself. In Safiya Noble's incisive words, "an app will not save us."[43] The design framework often requires us to move ahead and to treat this as progress. It is also in sync with the maintenance of capitalism, even as some might push for reforms to the labor market or for the regulation of the economy. But, in the current technological environment, the quickness with which someone can design "an app for that" marvels. As Ziegler's Appolition makes clear when contrasted with products from the growing "technocorrections" industry, the politics and purposes of design matter.

Put simply, forward movement, the ethos of design,

matters, of course, but rarely does such an approach allow us to slow down and let ourselves breathe in ways that may be useful. Elsewhere I have urged readers to consider how Eric Garner's last words, "I can't breathe," spoken as officer Daniel Pantaleo choked him to death, compel us to reflect on the epistemic and political dimensions of breathing.[44] "Under these conditions, the individual's breathing is an observed, an occupied breathing. It is a combat breathing," Fanon wrote.[45] In the breathless race for newer, faster, better technology, what ways of thinking, being, and organizing social life are potentially snuffed out? If design is treated as inherently moving forward, that is, as the solution, have we even agreed upon the problem?

Beyond Code-Switching

When people change how they speak or act in order to conform to dominant norms, we call it "code-switching." And, like other types of codes we have explored in this book, the practice of code-switching is power-laden. Justine Cassell, a professor at Carnegie Mellon's Human–Computer Interaction Institute, creates educational programs for children and found that avatars using African American Vernacular English lead Black children "to achieve better results in teaching scientific concepts than when the computer spoke in standard English." But when it came to tutoring the children for class presentations, she explained that "we wanted it [*sc.* the avatar] to practice with them in 'proper English.' Standard American English is still the code of power,[46] so we needed to develop an agent that would train them in code switching."[47] This reminds us that whoever defines the standard expression exercises power over everyone else, who is forced to fit in or else risks getting pushed out. But what is the alternative?

When I first started teaching at Princeton, a smart phone app, Yik Yak, was still popular among my students. It was founded in 2013 and allowed users to post anonymously while voting "up" and voting "down" others' posts, and was designed to be used by people within a five-mile radius. It was especially popular on college campuses and, like other social media sites, the app reinforced *and* exposed racism and anti-Black hatred among young people. As in Internet comments sections more broadly, people often say on Yik Yak what they would not say in person, and so all pretense of racial progress is washed away by spending just five minutes perusing the posts.

But the difference from other virtual encounters is that users know that the racist views on Yik Yak are held by people in close proximity – those you pass in the dorm, make small talk with in the dining hall, work with on a class project. I logged on to see what my students were dealing with, but quickly found the toxicity to consist overwhelmingly of . . . racist intellectualism, false equivalences, elite entitlement, and just plain old ignorance in peak form. White supremacy upvoted by a new generation . . . truly demoralizing for a teacher. So I had to log off.

Racism, I often say, is a form of *theft*. Yes, it has justified the theft of land, labor, and life throughout the centuries. But racism also robs us of our relationships, stealing our capacity to trust one another, ripping away the social fabric, every anonymous post pilfering our ability to build community. I knew that such direct exposure to this kind of unadulterated racism among people whom I encounter every day would quickly steal my enthusiasm for teaching. The fact is, I do not need to be constantly exposed to it to understand that we have a serious problem – exposure, as I discussed it in previous chapters, is no straightforward good. My experience with Yik Yak reminded me that we are not going to simply "age out" of White supremacy, because the bigoted baton has been passed and a new generation is even more adept at rationalizing racism.

Yik Yak eventually went out of business in 2017, but what I think of as NextGen Racism is still very much in business . . . more racially coded than we typically find in anonymous posts. Coded speech, as we have seen, reflects particular power dynamics that allow some people to impose their values and interests upon others. As one of my White male students wrote – in solidarity with the Black Justice League, a student group that was receiving hateful backlash on social media after campus protests:

> To change Yik Yak, we will have to change the people using it. To change those people, we will have to change the culture in which they – and we – live. To change that culture, we'll have to work tirelessly and relentlessly towards a radical rethinking of the way we live – and that rethinking will eventually need to involve all of us.[48]

I see this as a call to rewrite dominant cultural codes rather than simply to code-switch. It is a call to embed new values and new social relations into the world.[49] Whereas code-switching is about fitting in and "leaning in" to play a game created by others, perhaps what we need more of is to stretch out the arenas in which we live and work to become more inclusive and just.

If, as Cathy O'Neil writes, "Big Data processes codify the past. They do not invent the future. Doing that requires moral imagination, and that's something only humans can provide,"[50] then what we need is greater investment in socially just imaginaries. This, I think, would have to entail a socially conscious approach to tech development that would require prioritizing equity over efficiency, social good over market imperatives. Given the importance of training sets in machine learning, another set of interventions would require designing computer programs from scratch and training AI "like a child,"[51] so as to make us aware of social biases.

The key is that all this takes time and intention, which runs against the rush to innovate that pervades the ethos of tech marketing campaigns. But, if we are not simply "users" but people committed to building a more just society, it is vital that we demand a slower and more socially conscious innovation. The nonprofit AI research company Open AI says, as a practical model for this approach, that it will stop competing and start assisting another project if it is value-aligned and safety-conscious, because continuing to compete usually short changes "adequate safety precautions" and, I would add, justice concerns.[52]

Ultimately we must demand that tech designers and decision-makers become accountable stewards of technology, able to advance social welfare. For example, the Algorithmic Justice League has launched a Safe Face Pledge that calls on organizations to take a public stand "towards mitigating the abuse of facial recognition analysis technology. This historic pledge prohibits lethal use of the technology, lawless police use, and requires transparency in any government use"[53] and includes *radical* commitments such as "show value for human life, dignity, and rights." Tellingly, none of the major tech companies has been willing to sign the pledge to date.

Nevertheless, there are some promising signs that the innocent do-good ethos is shifting and that more industry insiders are acknowledging the complicity of technology in systems of power. For example, thousands of Google employees recently condemned the company's collaboration on a Pentagon program that uses AI to make drone strikes more effective.[54] And a growing number of Microsoft employees are opposed to the company's contract with the US Immigration and Customs Enforcement (ICE): "As the people who build the technologies that Microsoft profits from, we refuse to be complicit."[55] Much of this reflects the broader public outrage surrounding the Trump administration's policy of family separation, which rips thousands of children from their parents and holds them in camps reminiscent of the racist regimes of a previous era.

The fact that computer programmers and others in the tech industry are beginning to recognize their complicity in making the New Jim Code possible is a worthwhile development. It also suggests that design is intentional and that political protest matters in shaping internal debates and conflicts within companies. This kind of "informed refusal" expressed by Google and Microsoft employees is certainly necessary as we build a movement to counter the New Jim Code, but we cannot wait for worker sympathies to sway the industry.[56]

Where, after all, is the public outrage over the systematic terror exercised by police in Black neighborhoods with or without the aid of novel technologies? Where are the open letters and employee petitions refusing to build crime production models that entrap racialized communities? Why is there no comparable public fury directed at the surveillance techniques, from the prison system to the foster system, that have torn Black families apart long before Trump's administration? The selective outrage follows long-standing patterns of neglect and normalizes anti-Blackness as the weather, as Christina Sharpe notes, whereas non-Black suffering is treated as a disaster. This is why we cannot wait for the tech industry to regulate itself on the basis of popular sympathies.

Audits and Other Abolitionist Tools

To cultivate the ongoing practice of unflinching account-ability, a number of organizations are encouraging the development and implementation of *coded equity audits* for all new and existing technologies (see Appendix). "Auditing" is most commonly associated with the world of finance, but audit experiments have also been used to demonstrate continued discrimination in real estate and hiring practices in the post civil rights era. It is also an established methodology in the social sciences, where researchers set up field experiments that expose the per-sistence of racial discrimination in employment. "Equity audits," too, are employed in educational settings, in which teachers and administrators use established crite-ria for determining whether equity standards are being met in schools and classrooms.[57]

A recent initiative called Auditing Algorithms is developing a research community around the practice of auditing, and they released a white paper in August 2018 that outlines a way forward.[58] To date, the Data & Society Research Institute offers the most thorough elaboration of "algorithmic accountability," noting that "there are few consumer or civil rights protections that limit the type of data used to build data profiles or audit algorithmic decision-making."[59] Advancing this effort, danah boyd and M. C. Elish pose three crucial questions that are a starting point for any tech equity audit as it relates to AI systems:

- What are the unintended consequences of designing systems at scale on the basis of existing patterns in society?
- When and how should AI systems prioritize individuals over society and vice versa?
- When is introducing an AI system the right answer – and when is it not?

Crucially, such audits need to be independent and enforceable. Currently there are not even any industry-wide standards for social impact that fully account for the way in which algorithms are used to "allocate housing, healthcare, hiring, banking, social services as well as goods and service delivery."[60] Google's AI ethics principles, created in the aftermath of the controversy over the company's Pentagon contract, are a good start but focus too narrowly on military and surveillance technologies and, by relying on "widely accepted principles of international law and human rights," they sidestep the common practice of governments surveilling their own citizens. Nor do these principles ensure independent and transparent review; they follow instead a pattern current in corporate governance that maintains "internal, secret processes" that preclude public accountability.[61]

This is why the work of Stop LAPD Spying Coalition and other efforts to enact what Simone Browne calls "sousveillance . . . an active inversion of power relations that surveillance entails" are an essential part of any abolitionist toolkit.[62] In their workshop on these different approaches, organizers were clear to distinguish their efforts from carceral reforms such as police body cameras, which one presenter called "an empty reform to extend the stalker state."[63] Like Jay-Z's Promise app, these technical fixes give the illusion of progress but reinforce the power of state actors over racialized groups.

The European Union recently instituted the General Data Protection Regulation (GDPR), a law that covers many different facets of data protection and privacy. Among the provisions is the right to object to the processing of one's personal data at any time, the right not to be subject to automated decisions, and the right to *data portability*, in which the "data subject shall have the right to receive the personal data concerning him or her."[64] Even Jack Dorsey, Twitter's CEO, supports data portability: "I do believe that individuals should own their data and should have the right to have the controls over how a company might utilize that and how a service might utilize that and be able to pull it immediately."[65]

But individual-level rights such as those implemented by the European Union and espoused by tech entrepreneurs do not by themselves address the New Jim Code. In fact, a major exception built into Europe's law is that these rights do not apply if personal data are processed by "competent authorities for the purposes of the *prevention, investigation, detection or prosecution of criminal offences or the execution of criminal penalties,* including the safeguarding against and the prevention of threats to *public security.*"[66] This provision offers wide latitude for government officials to revoke data rights in an instant. It reminds us how coded inequity builds, and even deepens, existing inequities of race, class, nationality, and more. What looks like an expansion of data rights for individuals rests on the ability of governments to revoke those rights from anyone deemed a public threat.[67]

As we discussed before, automated systems are in the business of not simply "predicting" but *producing* crime. In Europe as elsewhere, already racialized and criminalized groups that try to exercise their newfound right to avoid data dragnets simply by opting out become doubly suspect: "What do you have to hide anyway?" (Recall the assumption of guilt for those who refused DNA collection by the United Kingdom's Human Provenance Pilot Project, discussed in chapter 3.) In this way, data portability, like other forms of movement, is already delimited by *race as a technology* that constricts one's ability to move freely.

Efforts to combat coded inequity cannot be limited to industry, nonprofit, and government actors, but must include community-based organizations that offer a vital set of counternarratives about the social and political dimensions of the New Jim Code. Too often, "inclusion" is limited to the visible representation of people of color and presumes that those who have been excluded want to be part of a tech future envisioned by others. As one reviewer put it, "Microsoft 'Improves' Racist Facial Recognition Software" – a win for inclusion! A loss for justice?[68]

Abolitionist toolmaking must entail the democratization of data – both its design and its application. For example, the DiscoTech ("discovering technology") model developed by the Detroit Digital Justice Coalition is a replicable approach that aims to demystify tech as a first step toward mobilizing community participation in questioning and shaping "data-driven" decisions that impact people's lives.[69]

Similarly, the Our Data Bodies (ODB) project retells stories of surveillance and data-based discrimination from the perspectives of those who are typically watched but not seen. The ODB team recently published a Digital Defense Playbook – an abolitionist tool based on in-depth interviews with community research participation in three US cities.[70] The Playbook presents some of the strategies that individuals and organizations are using; but, in the spirit of Frederick Douglass' admonishment about the upperground railroad, not everything that the team knows is exposed. Detroit-based digital justice activist Tawana Petty put it bluntly: "Let me be real, y'all gettin the Digital Defense Playbook, but we didn't tell you all their strategies and we never will, because we want our community members to continue to survive and to thrive and so . . . the stuff that's keepin' them alive, we keepin' to ourselves."[71]

If we come to terms with the fact that all data are necessarily partial and potentially biased, then we need long-term approaches that optimize for justice and equity. Timnit Gebru, computer scientist and founder of Black in AI, urges companies to give more information not just to users, but also to researchers. For any set of data, they can include "recommended usage, what the pitfalls are, how biased the data set is, etc." She says: if "I'm just taking your off-the-shelf data set or off-the-shelf model and incorporating it into whatever I'm doing, at least I have some knowledge of what kinds of pitfalls there may be. Right now we're in a place almost like the Wild West, where we don't really have many standards [about] where we put out data sets."[72]

Akin to the "organic" label on food that signals how items were sourced, I could imagine an "equity" label that demonstrates how data and machine learning programs were produced. In fact there is a Dataset Nutrition Label project that riffs off nutrition labels found on food, measuring and presenting the key ingredients of a dataset – for instance where, when, and by whom the data were produced. The project team aims to create standard quality measures that can be widely used as a prerequisite to developing more inclusive datasets.[73] As some observers have pointed out, we need to implement approaches that extend beyond the initial design. With machine learning, systems can become more discriminatory over time, as they learn to interact with humans. Thus avoiding discrimination requires that we scrutinize how "systems operate in practice."[74] This, in turn, requires transparency and accountability, which is why democratic oversight and engagement are vital.

Allied Media Network, mentioned previously, has been at the forefront of collaborating with community-based initiatives, as has the Detroit Community Tech Portal, for twenty years.[75] As the organization Stop LAPD Spying Coalition, which is engaged in participatory action research to understand community members' experiences of intensifying surveillance, the Detroit initiative crafted digital justice principles after surveying its members. Among other important shifts, "Digital justice demystifies technology to the point where we can not only use it, but create our own technologies and participate in the decisions that will shape communications infrastructure."[76] And it is not only concerned with access to technology, however important, but also with participation and common ownership designed to foster healthy communities.[77] This is also something I have come to appreciate more in my engagement with Data for Black Lives, a growing collective of organizers, scholars, data scientists, and more.[78] In the aftermath of the scandal surrounding Russia's use of social media to steer the 2016 presidential election, Data for Black Lives cofounder, Yeshimabeit Milner, wrote an open letter to Mark Zuckerberg, calling on Facebook to "commit anonymized Facebook data to a Public Data Trust, to work with technologists, advocates, and ethicists to establish a Data Code of Ethics, and to hire Black data scientists and research scientists."[79] A key tenet of the Data for Black Lives movement is that the data justice issues we are dealing with today are predicated on a much longer history of systematic injustice, in which those in power have employed data *against* Black lives. But not only that.

The history of data disenfranchisement has always been met with resistance and appropriation in which scholars, activists, and artists have sharpened abolitionist tools that employ data for liberation. In my talk at the inaugural Data for Black Lives conference in 2018, I started with an ancestral roll call to draw attention to this legacy. From W. E. B. Du Bois' modernist data visualizations – dozens of graphs, charts, and maps that visualized the state of Black life[80] – to Ida B. Wells-Barnett's expert deployment of statistics in *The Red Record* (1895), which illustrated the widespread practice of lynching and White terrorism, there is a long tradition of employing and challenging data for Black lives. But before the data there were, for Du Bois, Wells-Barnett, and many others, the political questions and commitment to Black freedom. Today this commitment continues in the work of numerous organizations that are not content with simply reforming a system that "never loved us," that is, was designed against us.

An abolitionist toolkit, in this way, is concerned not only with emerging technologies but also with the everyday production, deployment, and interpretation of data. Such toolkits can be focused on computational interventions, but they do not have to be. In fact, *narrative tools* are essential. In a recent study, a Stanford research team introduced people to shocking statistics about racial disparities in policing and incarceration and found that exposure to the data led those surveyed to become more punitive and less supportive of policies that might counteract the criminalization of Black people.[81]

Data, in short, do not speak for themselves and don't always change hearts and minds or policy. To address this phenomenon, the Stanford team encouraged researchers to offer more context, challenge stereotypical associations, and highlight the role of institutions in producing racial disparities. And while this more holistic approach to framing is vital, the problem extends well beyond retooling social science communication. It calls for a justice-oriented, emancipatory approach to data production, analysis, and public engagement as part of the broader movement for Black lives.

If, as many have argued, the rhetoric of human betterment distorts an understanding of the multifaceted interplay between technology and society, then a thoroughgoing commitment to justice has the potential to clarify and inspire possibilities for designing this relationship anew. Justice, in this sense, is not a static value but an ongoing methodology that can and should be incorporated into tech design.[82] For this reason, too, it is vital that people engaged in tech development partner with those who do important sociocultural work honing narrative tools through the arts, humanities, and social justice organizing.[83] As Kamal Sinclair – emerging media researcher and artist – posits:

> Story and narrative are the code for humanity's operating system. We have used stories to communicate knowledge, prescribe behavior, and imagine our futures since our earliest days. Story and narrative inform how we design everything from technology to social systems. They shape the norms in which we perform our identities, even perhaps the mutations of our DNA and perceptions of reality. Stories are the first step in the process of how we imagine our reality; they literally make our reality.[84]

But too often the story that dominates is the one that purports to rise above the genre, becoming *the* story of reality because it deploys the language of big data, thereby trumping all other accounts. This master narrative must be abolished – including the subplot that says "that technology is loyal to the master."[85] Abolitionist and decolonial technologies tell a different story: emancipatory designs are not only possible, they already exist.

Perhaps most importantly, abolitionist tools are predicated on solidarity, as distinct from access and charity. The point is not simply to help others who have been less fortunate but to question the very idea of "fortune": Who defines it, distributes it, hoards it, and how was it obtained? Solidarity takes interdependence seriously. Even if we do not "believe in" or "aspire to" interdependence as an abstract principle, nevertheless our lived reality and infrastructural designs connect us in seen and unseen ways. This is why, as Petty insists, oppressed people do not need "allies," a framework that reinforces privilege and power. Instead, "co-liberation" is an aspirational relationship that emphasizes linked fate.[86]

In her study of how automated decision-making impacts welfare recipients in the United States, Virginia Eubanks recounts a conversation she had with a young mother who, in 2000, alerted Eubanks to the fact that caseworkers were using electronic benefit transfer (EBT) cards to track people's spending. With prescience about the pervasive "electronic scrutiny" that now embraces many more people across the class spectrum, the young woman urged: "You should pay attention to what happens to us. You're next."[87] By deliberately cultivating a solidaristic approach to design, we need to consider that the technology that might be working just fine for some of us (now) could harm or exclude others and that, even when the stakes seem trivial, a visionary ethos requires looking down the road to where things might be headed. *We're next.*

Reimagining Technology

It is easy to get caught off guard by new "killer apps" that are developed and marketed, sometimes as "reform." It is vital, therefore, to experiment with speculative methods, so that analysts, artists, and activists alike may better anticipate and intervene in new racial formations that, like shiny new gadgets, may appear to be a kind of radical alternative but may very well entail their own logics of subjugation. Writer Arundhati Roy expresses this struggle over the future:

> One particular imagination – a brittle, superficial pretense of tolerance and multiculturalism (that morphs into racism, rabid nationalism, ethnic chauvinism, or war-mongering Islamophobia at a moment's notice) under the roof of a single overarching, very unplural economic ideology – began to dominate the discourse. It did so to such an extent that it ceased to be perceived as an ideology at all. It became the default position, the natural way to be . . . From here it was a quick, easy step to "There is no alternative."[88]

But there are many alternatives beyond the default settings. In countering the overwhelming Whiteness of the future in most popular representations of Hollywood films and science fiction texts, we can point to Afrofuturist and Chicanofuturist visions that not only center on people of color, but grapple with racism and related axes of domination.[89] This work has a lot to teach us about reimagining the default settings – codes and environments – that we have inherited from prior regimes of racial control, and how we can appropriate and reimagine science and technology for liberatory ends.[90]

Likewise, critical race studies has long urged scholars to take narrative seriously as a liberating tool, as when legal scholar Derrick Bell urges a radical assessment of reality through creative methods and racial reversals, insisting that "[t]o see things as they really are, you must *imagine* them for what they might be."[91]

195

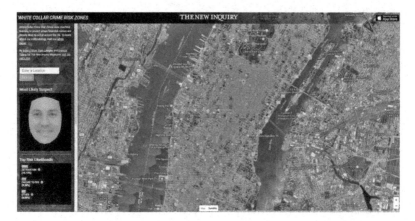

Figure 5.2 White-Collar Crime Risk Zones

Source: App created by Brian Clifton, Sam Lavigne, and Francis Tseng for *The New Inquiry Magazine*, Vol. 59, "Abolish," March 2017

Take, for instance, a parody project that begins by subverting the anti-Black logics embedded in new high-tech approaches to crime prevention (Figure 5.2). Instead of using predictive policing techniques to forecast street crime, the White-Collar Early Warning System flips the script by creating a heat map that flags city blocks where financial crimes are likely to occur.

The system not only brings into view the hidden but no less deadly crimes of capitalism and the wealthy's hoarding of resources, but includes an app that alerts users when they enter high-risk areas to encourage "citizen policing and awareness." Taking it one step further, the development team is working on a facial recognition program meant to flag individuals who are likely perpetrators, and the training set used to design the algorithm includes the profile photos of 7,000 corporate executives downloaded from the popular professional networking site LinkedIn. Not surprisingly, the "averaged" face of a criminal is White and male. In this sense, the narrative of what we consider to be a crime and of whom we consider to be a criminal is being challenged. But it remains to be seen whether such initiatives can help generate a different social order when it comes to criminalization. And creative exercises like this one are comical only if we ignore that all their features are drawn directly from actually existing proposals and practices "in the real world," including the use of facial images to predict criminality – all techniques that tend to target racialized groups.

By deliberately and inventively upsetting the techno status quo in this manner, analysts can better understand and expose the many forms of discrimination embedded in and enabled by technology. And the process of refashioning the relationship between race and technology may entail actual fashion. Hyphen-Labs, an international team of women of color who work at the intersection of technology, art, science, and futurism, experiments with a wide array of subversive designs – including earrings for recording police altercations, and visors and other clothing that prevent facial recognition.[92] This work, as I see it, recasts what counts as technoscience and whom we think of as innovators.[93]

If we take all its elements together, an emancipatory approach to technology entails an appreciation for the aesthetic dimensions of resisting the New Jim Code and a commitment to coupling our critique with creative alternatives that bring to life liberating and joyful ways of living in and organizing our world.[94]

Acknowledgments

I could not imagine finishing this book without the editorial guidance of my brilliant colleague Tamara K. Nopper. The incredible staff at Polity, especially Jonathan Skerrett and Karina Jákupsdóttir, have been patient and passionate stewards of this work over the last two years. Jonathan saw the seeds of this project buried in what I thought was a fleeting review essay – and now here we are!

Throughout, I have been boosted up by the unending awesomeness of Princeton's Department of African American Studies. Among other things, the department sponsored a book workshop that included the combined brilliance of Patricia J. Williams, Jessie Daniels, and Naomi Murakawa who pushed my thinking at a crucial stage.

It is a rare thing, I suspect, to love, respect, *and* enjoy the company of one's colleagues: Anna Arabindan-Kesson, Wendy Belcher, Wallace Best, Eddie Glaude, Reena Goldthree, Joshua Guild, Tera Hunter, Naomi Murakawa, Kinohi Nishikawa, Chika Okeke-Agulu, Imani Perry, Stacey Sinclair, Keeanga-Yamahtta Taylor,

Acknowledgments

Judith Weisenfeld, and Autumn Womack teach me that it is possible, even within old systems, to forge new ways of relating and being together.

And it is an open secret that our work would not be possible without the incomparable staff, past and present, which consists of Allison Bland, Elio Lleo, Jana Johnson, April Peters, and Dionne Worthy. For me, this cadre exemplifies the idea that technologies are not just "out there" in the world, but that we all employ social tools in our everyday interactions to tear down or build up one another. Needless to say, the freedom and encouragement I have experienced in this department show me that it is possible to build worlds within worlds. I am also deeply appreciative of the research assistance of Cierra Robson, who juggled GRE prep, senior thesis planning, and an internship at Facebook, all while working on this project *and* living her best (bicoastal) life!

A number of conversations and convenings have shaped my thinking on race and tech over the last few years – the Institute for Advanced Study School of Social Science 2016–17 cohort and especially Didier Fassin, who welcomed my question at the Harry's Bar Conversation series "Are Robots Racist?" – a ten-minute provocation turned into a two-year project; all those gathered at the inaugural conference *Data for Black Lives* at MIT Media Lab, especially Yeshimabeit Milner, Lucas Mason-Brown, Max Clermont, and Nana Younge for inviting me and the ancestors into that space; those gathered for the Data & Society Research Institute's Small Group Session, especially Joan Donovan and Mutali Nkonde, who pushed my ideas forward on a number of fronts; and all the students and colleagues

199

who raised questions during talks at the UC Berkeley Department of Sociology, University of Pennsylvania Annenberg School for Communication, Harvey Mudd Nelson Distinguished Lecture Series, and UC San Diego Science Studies Student Choice Speaker Event, especially Rachel Fox and Alanna Reyes for organizing my visit.

At Princeton I am incredibly thankful to Chloe Bakalar, Edward Felten, Melissa Lane, and Bendert Zevenbergen for inviting me to take part in a series of workshops and conferences on AI and ethics organized by the University Center for Human Values and by the Center for Information Technology Policy, and to Tithi Chattopadhyay for all her behind-the-scenes work to make these convenings happen. The latter two also contributed to the publication costs of this book, for which I am very grateful.

I received invaluable feedback from the 2018 African American Studies Faculty–Graduate Seminar participants, especially the discussants Shreya Subramani and Fatima Siwaju; from my accomplices in the writing workshop hosted by Wendy Belcher, who provided just the boost of energy I needed to finish a first draft of the manuscript over the summer; from attendees at the StudioLab "Rethinking Mass Incarceration" Design Challenge workshop, especially Sharon De La Cruz and Aatish Bhatia, who created such an important space on campus; and from students at the AI4All Summer Program, whose dynamism gives me hope! Finally, I am deeply appreciative of Princeton's Center for Digital Humanities for awarding me a faculty fellowship that gave me time to finish the book.

A number of colleagues have generously read and commented on drafts at different stages of this project.

Acknowledgments

These include David Theo Goldberg, Aaron Panofsky, Anne Pollock, Dorothy Roberts, Olga Russakovsky, John Steele, Elly Truitt, Janet Vertesi, Keith Wailoo and my dear friend, the late Lee Ann Fuji: I still have an email from October 17, 2016 where she urged me to draw the critical and normative dimensions of my discussion together by writing: "more incisive and trenchant critique of racism *in* technology and racism *by* technology is precisely what can lead to technology that can be harnessed to undo, unearth, uncover the racist practices/ attitudes/ beliefs/ structures/ hierarchies in the rest of society. In other words, as you said at your Harry's Bar talk, racist robots can be used to reflect ourselves back to us more effectively than humans can, precisely because of their machine-ness." Returning to Lee Ann's words now as I wrap up, I am reminded of how much her friendship and brilliance have guided me even after she left this earthly plane.

Finally, my *day ones*, Khalil, Malachi, Shawn, and Behin, and the wider web of kin and community who are an ongoing source of grounding and lifting, there are really no words.

Notes

Notes to Dedication

1 Toye 2016.
2 Fanon 2008, p. 179.

Notes to Introduction

1 Kaba describes "grounded hope" as a philosophy of living that must be practiced every day and that it is different from optimism and does not protect one from feeling sadness, frustration, or anger. See her "Beyond Prisons" podcast, episode 19, at https://shadowproof.com/2018/01/05/beyond-prisons-episode-19-hope-is-a-discipline-feat-mariame-kaba.
2 Brown 2015, p. 26.
3 Inevitably, my students turn the question back on me: "Tell us about your name, prof?" As I was born to an African American father and a Persian Indian mother, my parents wanted me to have a first name with Arabic origins, but one that was short enough, so English speakers wouldn't butcher it. They were mostly successful, except that my friends still call me "Ru" ... nicknames are a form of endearment after all. What I find amusing these days is getting messages addressed to "Mr. Benjamin" or

"Mr. Ruha." Since Benjamin is more often used as a mas-
culine first name, people whom I have never met routinely
switch the order in their heads and mis-gender me as a
result. I sometimes wonder whether I receive some fleeting
male privilege – more deference, perhaps. This, after all,
is the reason why some of my female students say their
parents gave them more gender-neutral names: to delay
(if not diminish) sexist assumptions about their qualifi-
cations and capacities. Similar rationale for my Black,
Asian, and Latinx students with stereotypically White-
sounding names: "My parents didn't want me to have a
hard time," "They wanted me to have a normal American
name" (where "American" is always coded "White").

4 The Apples and Norths of the world tend to experience less ridicule and more fascination, owing to their
celebrity parentage, which tell us that there is nothing
intrinsic to a "good" name, nothing that makes for it.

5 So, is the solution for those with racially stigmatized
names to code-switch by adopting names that offer more
currency on the job market? Or does this simply accommodate bias and leave it in place? In a number of informal
experiments, job seekers put this idea to the test. Jose
Zamora dropped one letter from his first name and found
that "Joe Zamora," with all the same education and
credentials, magically started hearing from employers.
Similarly, after two years of searching for a job, Yolanda
Spivey changed the name on her résumé to "Bianca
White," and suddenly her inbox was full of employers
interested in interviewing her. What stunned Yolanda
most was that, while the same résumé was posted with her
real name on the employment website, employers were
repeatedly calling "Bianca," desperate to get an interview.

6 When the study was replicated in France, another team
found that Christian-sounding names had a similar value
over and above Muslim-sounding names, and they could

not explain the difference through other factors such as experience or education.

7 Caliskan et al. 2017. Fun fact: did you know that the words "algorithm" and "algebra" come from a Persian astronomer and mathematician, Muhammad Ibn Musa al-Khwarizmi, whose last name was Latinized as Algorithmi? I suspect, given how his name would likely trigger surveillance systems today, he would cheer on algorithmic audits that are trying to prevent such biased associations!

8 I'm thinking of Browne's (2015) "racializing surveillance," Broussard's (2018) "technochauvinism," Buolamwini's (2016) "coded gaze," Eubanks' (2018) "digital poorhouse," Noble's (2018) "algorithms of oppression and technological redlining," or Wachter-Boettcher's (2017) "algorithmic inequity" (among other kindred formulations) as "cousin concepts" related to the New Jim Code.

9 O'Neil 2016, p. 23.

10 Another example is Wilmer Catalan-Ramirez, an undocumented Chicago resident who was listed without his knowledge in the city's gang database as a member of two *rival* gangs (Saleh 2018).

11 See the CalGang Criminal Intelligence System report at http://www.voiceofsandiego.org/wp-content/uploads/2016/08/CalGangs-audit.pdf. See also Harvey 2016.

12 Harvey 2016.

13 Muhammad 2011, p. 20, emphasis added; see also Zuberi 2003.

14 Wacquant 2017, p. 2.

15 Wacquant 2017; emphasis added.

16 Sweeney 2013.

17 boyd and Elish 2018.

18 Baldwin 1998, p. 723.

19 In her letter to Zuckerberg, Milner (2018) continues:

"Histories of redlining, segregation, voter disenfranchisement and state sanctioned violence have not disappeared, but have been codified and disguised through new big data regimes."

20 This refers to a classic line in the film *Wizard of Oz* in which Oz attempts to conceal his machinations: "Pay no attention to the man behind the curtain."
21 boyd and Elish 2018.
22 Alexander 2018.
23 Frenkel et al. 2018.
24 Cohen 2017.
25 Gelin 2018.
26 Liao 2018.
27 Talk by Christina Colclough at the AI Ethics conference, March 10, 2018, Princeton University, sponsored by the Center for Information Technology Policy and the University Center for Human Values. See also http://www.thefutureworldofwork.org.
28 Monahan and Palmer 2009, p. 617.
29 Hart 2018.
30 Thompson and Lapowsky 2018.
31 Twitter @kevinroose, November 15, 2018, 3:33 p.m.
32 Twitter @katecrawford, November 15, 2018, 4:37 p.m.
33 Solon 2018.
34 Streitfeld 2019.
35 Weller 2017.
36 Lebowitz 2018.
37 Hoyle 2018.
38 Of John Lilly, a Silicon Valley-based venture capitalist, a *New York Times* article reports: "he tries to help his 13-year-old son understand that he is being manipulated by those who built the technology. 'I try to tell him somebody wrote code to make you feel this way – I'm trying to help him understand how things are made, the values that are going into things and what people are

doing to create that feeling,' Mr. Lilly said" (Bowles 2018).

39 Roberts 2018. Data journalist Meredith Broussard calls this "technochauvinism," which she describes as the "belief that tech is always the solution ... Somehow, in the past two decades, many of us began to assume that computers get it right and people get it wrong" (Broussard 2018, p. 7–8).

40 See Bridges' (2017) analysis of the "poverty of privacy rights."

41 Edelman 2018.

42 Echoing the concerns of their Silicon Valley counterparts, Brooklyn parents expressed worry about the "wealth of information on each student, from age, ethnicity, and extracurricular activities, to grades, test scores and disciplinary penalties" (Edelman 2018).

43 Baldwin and Kenan 2011, p. 158. See also DuBois (1935) on Whiteness as a "public and psychological wage" for the White working class, Roediger (2007) on the "wages of Whiteness," and Lewis (2004) on "hegemonic Whiteness".

44 See https://www.wired.com/story/algorithms-netflix-tool-for-justice/?BottomRelatedStories_Sections_2.

45 "#OscarsSoWhite also known as Oscars So White or Oscar Whitewash, is a hashtag used to protest the under-representation of people of color in the annual Academy Award nominations. The hashtag came into use during the 2015 award cycle, and re-appeared in 2016" (from https://knowyourmeme.com/memes/oscars-so-white).

46 Williams 2015.

47 Sieczkowski 2012.

48 King 2006.

49 Cresci 2015.

50 N-Tech Lab 2015.

51 See https://ntechlab.com.

52 N-Tech Lab 2015; in fact, in April 2018 China made headlines for apprehending a suspect at a concert with nearly 60,000 people in attendance with the help of a similar program; see https://www.washingtonpost.com/news/worldviews/wp/2018/04/13/china-crime-facial-recognition-cameras-catch-suspect-at-concert-with-60000-people.

53 In "The Algorithmic Rise of the 'Alt-Right,'" Daniels writes: "There are two strands of conventional wisdom unfolding in popular accounts of the rise of the alt-right. One says that what's really happening can be attributed to a crisis in White identity: the alt-right is simply a manifestation of the angry White male who has status anxiety about his declining social power. Others contend that the alt-right is an unfortunate eddy in the vast ocean of Internet culture. Related to this is the idea that polarization, exacerbated by filter bubbles, has facilitated the spread of Internet memes and fake news promulgated by the alt-right. While the first explanation tends to ignore the influence of the Internet, the second dismisses the importance of White nationalism. I contend that we have to understand both at the same time" (Daniels 2018, p. 61).

54 The term for the specific form of anti-Black racist mysogyny that Black women experience is "mysogynoir" (Bailey and Trudy 2018).

55 Daniels 2017.

56 Thompson 2018a.

57 Wacquant 2005.

58 Taylor 2016.

59 Visit https://www.youtube.com/watch?v=9tucY7Jhhs4.

60 These remarks were made by an audience member at the Data for Black Lives conference at MIT Media Lab in Cambridge, MA on January 12, 2019.

61 Hardy 2016.

62 This turn is what scholars refer to as neoliberalism – "a

peculiar form of reason that configures all aspects of existence in economic terms" (Brown 2015, p. 17).

63 Thompson 2018b.

64 I am indebted to legal scholar Patricia Williams for underscoring this point: personal communication, November 9, 2018.

65 Weheliye 2014, p. 3.

66 Wynter 2003.

67 paperson 2017, p. 12.

68 This formulation is inspired by Jarmon 2013.

69 Pasquale 2014, p. 3.

70 Coleman 2009; Chun 2009.

71 Perry (2011, p. 22) writes: "Americans have a long tradition of reconciling inconsistencies between professed values and cultural practices ... Therefore, we do not experience cognitive dissonance when such inconsistencies arise; rather, we cultivate explanations that allow them to operate in tandem."

72 Morgan 1975; Smedley 2007.

73 Perry 2018, p. 45.

74 Such care is often articulated in terms of the "precautionary principle" as a way to manage the uncertainties associated with technoscience, though too often it gets limited to questions of ethics and safety rather than extending to issues of politics and democracy. As adrienne maree brown (2017, p. 87) explains, "we have to decentralize our idea of where solutions and decisions happen, where ideas come from."

75 Turan 2009.

76 Moore 2011.

77 See D'Ignazio and Klein (2019) for a discussion of "data feminism" where the focus is not just on gender but on power more broadly.

78 As Toni Cade Bambara (1970, p. 110) famously cautioned in a different context, "[n]ot all speed is movement."

79 Braun 2014.
80 Daly 2014.
81 Daly 2014.
82 Marche 2012.
83 Kurzgesagt 2016.
84 Turse 2016.
85 Ridley 2015.
86 Castells 2009, p. 5.
87 Van Dijk 2006.
88 See Daniels 2013. Daniels also says: "According to the Pew Research Center's Internet & American Life Project ... African–Americans and English-speaking Latinos continue to be among the most active users of the mobile web. Cell phone ownership is higher among African Americans and Latinos than among Whites (87 percent versus 80 percent) and minority cell phone owners take advantage of a much greater range of their phones' features compared with white mobile phone users" (2013, p. 698).
89 Everett 2002, p. 133.
90 "Though rarely represented today as full participants in the information technology revolution, Black people are among the earliest adopters and comprise some of the most ardent and innovative users of IT (information technology). It is too often widespread ignorance of African Diasporic people's long history of technology adoption that limits fair and fiscally sound IT investments, policies and opportunities for Black communities locally and globally. Such racially aligned politics of investment create a self-fulfilling-prophesy or circular logic wherein the lack of equitable access to technology in Black communities produces a corresponding lack of technology literacy and competencies" (from http:// international.ucla.edu/africa/event/1761, the home page of AfroGEEKS: From Technophobia to Technophilia).

91 Nakamura 2002, pp. 22–3.
92 Nelson 2002, p. 1.
93 Nakamura 2002; 2008.
94 Nelson 2002, p. 1.
95 Noble 2018, p. 5; Browne 2015, p. 7.
96 Browne 2015, pp. 8–9.
97 See Jasanoff (2004, p. 3) for an elaboration on co-production: co-production is a "shorthand for the proposition that the ways in which we know and represent the world (both nature and society) are inseparable from the ways in which we choose to live in it. Knowledge and its material embodiments [e.g. technology] are at once products of social work and constitutive of forms of social life; society cannot function without knowledge any more than knowledge can exist without appropriate social supports. Scientific knowledge, in particular, is not a transcendent mirror of reality. It both embeds and is embedded in social practices, identities, norms, conventions, discourses, instruments and institutions – in short, in all the building blocks of what we term the *social*. The same can be said even more forcefully of technology" (p. 3).
98 I am inspired here by paperson's (2017, p. 5) discussion of "hotwiring" settler colonial technologies: "Instead of settler colonialism as an ideology, or as history, you might consider settler colonialism as a set of technologies – a frame that could help you to forecast colonial next operations and to plot decolonial directions . . . Technologies mutate, and so do these relationships."
99 Samatar 2015; I am indebted to Fatima Siwaju, whose question about methodology during the 2018 African American Studies Faculty-Graduate Seminar prompted me to elaborate my thinking here.
100 Jackson 2013, p. 16.
101 Jackson 2013, p. 14.

102 Jackson 2013, p. 153.

103 The concept "imperialist White supremacist capitalist patriarchy" was coined by bell hooks (2015); it was intended to pick out the interlocking systems of domination also theorized by Crenshaw (1991) and Collins (1990).

Notes to Chapter 1

1 Visit Beauty.AI First Beauty Contest Judged by Robots, at http://beauty.ai.

2 Pearson 2016b.

3 Pearson 2016b.

4 Levin 2016.

5 Both Harcourt quotations are from Levin 2016.

6 See http://beauty.ai.

7 See https://machinelearningmastery.com/what-is-deep-learning.

8 Metz 2013.

9 Field note, Jack Clark's Keynote Address at the Princeton University AI and Ethics Conference, March 10, 2018.

10 The flip side of personalization is what Eubanks (2018) refers to as an "empathy override." See also Edes 2018.

11 Fox 2012, n.p.

12 "Homelessness is not a systems engineering problem, it's a carpentry problem" (Eubanks 2018, p. 125).

13 The term "uncanny valley" was coined by Masahiro Mori in 1970 and translated into English by Reichardt (1978).

14 But it is worth keeping in mind that many things dubbed "AI" today are, basically, just statistical predictions rebranded in the age of big data – an artificial makeover that engenders more trust as a result. This point was made by Arvind Narayanan in response to a Microsoft case study at a workshop sponsored by the Princeton University Center for Human Values and Center for Informational Technology Policy, October 6, 2017.

15 Truitt 2016.
16 Richardson 2015, p. 5.
17 Richardson 2015, p. 2.
18 As Imani Perry (2018, p. 49) explains, "Mary Shelley's *Frankenstein* provided a literary example of the domestic anxiety regarding slavery and colonialism that resulted from this structure of relations ... Frankenstein's monster represented the fear of the monstrous products that threatened to flow from the peculiar institutions. The novel lends itself to being read as a response to slave revolts across the Atlantic world. But it can also be read as simply part of anxiety attendant to a brutal and intimate domination, one in which the impenetrability of the enslaved was already threatening."
19 Richardson 2015, p. 2.
20 Everett 2009, p. 1.
21 Binder 1957.
22 These passages come from a PoliceOne report that cautions us: "as wonderful an asset as they are, they cannot provide a complete picture. The camera eye can only see so much, and there are many critical elements of information that may go undiscovered or unrecognized ... Throwable robots provide such an advance in situational awareness that it can be easy to forget that our understanding of the situation is still incomplete" (visit https://www.policeone.com/police-products/police-technology/robots/articles/320406006–5-tactical-considerations-for-throwable-robot-deployment).
23 Rorty 1962.
24 Daniels 2015, p. 1379. See also Crain et al. 2016; Gajjala 2004; Hossfeld 1990; Pitti 2004; Shih 2006.
25 Nakamura 2002, p. 24.
26 Daniels 2013, p. 679.
27 Noble and Tynes 2016.
28 Field note from the Princeton University Center for

Human Values and Center for Informational Technology
Policy Workshop, October 6, 2017.

29 The notion of "racist robots" is typically employed in
popular discourse around AI. I use it as a rhetorical
device to open up a discussion about a range of contemporary technologies, most of which are not human-like
automata of the kind depicted in films and novels. They
include forms of automation integrated in everyday life,
like soap dispensers and search engines, bureaucratic
interventions that seek to make work more efficient, as
in policing and healthcare, and fantastical innovations
first imagined in science fiction, such as self-driving cars
and crime prediction techniques.

30 McWhorter 2016.

31 Field note from the Princeton University Center for
Human Values and Center for Informational Technology
Policy Workshop, October 6, 2017.

32 The famed android Lieutenant Commander Data of
the hit series *Star Trek* understood well the distinction
between inputs and outputs, intent and action. When a
roughish captain of a small cargo ship inquired whether
Data had ever experienced love, Data responded: "The
act or the emotion?" And when the captain replied that
they're both the same, Data rejoined: "I believe that
statement to be inaccurate, sir." Just as loving behavior
does not require gushing Valentine's Day sentiment, so
too can discriminatory action be fueled by indifference
and disregard, and even by good intention, more than by
flaming hatred.

33 Baldwin 1998, p. 129.

34 See https://www.nclc.org/images/pdf/credit_discrimina
tion/InsuranceScoringWhitePaper.pdf.

35 Policeone.com, at https://www.policeone.com/police-
products/police-technology/robots.

36 This is brought to life in the 2016 HBO series *Silicon*

Valley, which follows a young Steve Jobs-type of character, in a parody of the tech industry. In a segment at TechCrunch, a conference where start-up companies present their proof of concept to attract venture capital investment, one presenter after another exclaims "we're making the world a better place" with each new product that also claims to "revolutionize" some corner of the industry. See https://longreads.com/2016/06/13/silicon-valley-masterfully-skewers-tech-culture.

37 McWhorter 2016.
38 Sociologist Eduardo Bonilla-Silva (2006) argues that "if racism is systemic, this view of 'good' and 'bad' whites distorts reality" (p. 132). He quotes Albert Memmi saying: "There is a strange enigma associated with the problem of racism. No one, or almost no one, wishes to see themselves as racist; still, racism persists, real and tenacious" (Bonilla-Silva 2006, p. 1).
39 Dobush 2016.
40 Perry explains how racial surveillance does not require a "bogeyman behind the curtain; it is a practice that emerges from our history, conflicts, the interests of capital, and political expediency in the nation and the world ... Nowhere is the diffuse and individuated nature of this practice more apparent than in the fact that over-policing is not limited to White officers but is instead systemic" (Perry 2011, p. 105).
41 Calling for a post-intentional analysis of racism, Perry argues that intent is not a good measure of discrimination because it "creates a line of distinction between 'racist' and 'acceptable' that is deceptively clear in the midst of a landscape that is, generally speaking, quite unclear about what racism and racial bias are, who [or what] is engaging in racist behaviors, and how they are doing so" (Perry 2011, p. 21).
42 Schonbrun 2017.

43 Field note from the Princeton University Center for Human Values and Center for Informational Technology Policy Workshop, October 6, 2017.

44 Field note from the Princeton University Center for Human Values and Center for Informational Technology Policy Workshop, October 6, 2017.

45 Richardson 2015, p. 12.

46 Richardson 2015, p. 12; see also Helmreich 1998.

47 See s.v. "stereotype" at https://www.etymonline.com/word/stereotype (Online Etymology Dictionary).

48 "It is to say, though, that all those inhabiting subject positions of racial power and domination – notably those who are racially White in its various formulations in different racially articulated societies – project and extend racist socialities by default. But the default is not the only position to occupy or in which to invest. One remains with the default because it is given, the easier to inhabit, the sociality of thoughtlessness" (Goldberg 2015, pp. 159–60).

49 Tufekci 2015, p. 207.

50 Haraway 1991, p. 164.

51 Haraway 1991, p. 164.

52 This potential explains the name of the provocative TV series *Black Mirror*.

53 According to Feagin and Elias (2013, p. 936), systemic racism refers to "the foundational, large-scale and inescapable hierarchical system of US racial oppression devised and maintained by whites and directed at people of colour . . . [It] is foundational to and engineered into its major institutions and organizations."

54 Wachter-Boettcher 2017, p. 200. On the same page, the author also argues that "[w]e'll only be successful in ridding tech of excesses and oversights if we first embrace a new way of seeing the digital tools we rely on – not as a wonder, or even as a villain, but rather as

a series of choices that designers and technologists have made. Many of them small: what a button says, where a data set comes from. But each of these choices reinforces beliefs about the world, and the people in it."

55 Botsman 2017.
56 Nguyen 2016.
57 Morris 2018.
58 State Council 2014.
59 State Council 2014.
60 Tufekci 2017, p. 128.
61 Nopper 2019, p. 170.
62 Hacking 2007.

Notes to Chapter 2

1 Merriam-Webster Online, n.d.
2 Personal interview conducted by the author with Princeton digital humanities scholar Jean Bauer, October 11, 2016.
3 See references to "digital gentrification" in "White Flight and Digital Gentrification," posted on February 28 at https://untsocialmedias13.wordpress.com/2013/02/28/white-flight-and-digital-gentrification by jalexander716.
4 Sampson 2009.
5 As Noble (2018, p. 10) writes, "[a]lgorithmic oppression is not just a glitch in the system but, rather, is fundamental to the operating system of the web."
6 Russell and Vinsel 2016.
7 See the conference "Dismantling Predictive Policing in Los Angeles," May 8, 2018, at https://stoplapdspying.org/wp-content/uploads/2018/05/Before-the-Bullet-Hits-the-Body-May-8-2018.pdf.
8 "Dismantling predictive policing in Los Angeles," pp. 38–9.
9 Ferguson 2017.
10 Angwin et al. 2016.

11 According to Sharpe (2016, p. 106), "the weather necessitates changeability and improvisation," which are key features of innovative systems that adapt, in this case, to postracial norms where racism persists through the absence of race.

12 Meredith Broussard, data journalist and author of *Artificial Unintelligence*, explains: "The fact that nobody at Northpointe thought that the questionnaire or its results might be biased has to do with technochauvinists' unique worldview. The people who believe that math and computation are 'more objective' or 'fairer' tend to be the kind of people who think that inequality and structural racism can be erased with a keystroke. They imagine that the digital world is different and better than the real world and that by reducing decisions to calculations, we can make the world more rational. When development teams are small, like-minded, and not diverse, this kind of thinking can come to seem normal. However, it doesn't move us toward a more just and equitable world" (Broussard 2018, p. 156).

13 Brayne 2014.

14 As Wang (2018, p. 236) puts it, "the rebranding of policing in a way that foregrounds statistical impersonality and symbolically removes the agency of individual officers is a clever way to cast police activity as neutral, unbiased, and rational. This glosses over the fact that using crime data gathered by the police to determine where officers should go simply sends police to patrol the poor neighborhoods they have historically patrolled when they were guided by their intuitions and biases. This 'new paradigm' is not merely a reworking of the models and practices used by law enforcement, but a revision of the police's public image through the deployment of science's claims to objectivity."

15 I am indebted to Naomi Murakawa for highlighting for

me the strained way in which scholars and criminologists tend to discuss "unwarranted disproportion," as if the line between justified and unjustified is self-evident rather than an artifact of racist policing, with or without the aid of crime prediction software. See Murakawa 2014.

16 Wang 2018, p. 241.
17 Wang 2018, p. 237.
18 From scifiquotes.net, http://scifiquotes.net/quotes/123_ Dont-Worry-About-the-Vase; emphasis added.
19 Collins 1990, p. 227.
20 Collins 1990, p. 230.
21 Goodyear 2013.
22 Goyette 2014.
23 Associated Press 2006.
24 Daniels 2013, p. 709.
25 Golash-Boza 2016.
26 Feagin and Elias, 2013, p. 936.
27 Bonilla-Silva 2006, p. 9.
28 Hamilton and Ture 1967, p. 38. Scholar of African American studies Keeanga-Yamahtta Taylor describes the term "institutional racism" as prescient, noting that "it is the outcome that matters, not the intentions of the individuals involved" (Taylor 2016, p. 8).
29 Omi and Winant 1994, pp. 137–8.
30 Sinclair 2004, p. 1; cf. Daniels 2013, p. 696.
31 Daniels 2009, p. 2.
32 Daniels 2009, p. 4.
33 Winner 1980.
34 Helm 2016.
35 Pearson 2016a.
36 See "How search algorithms work," https://www. google.co.uk/insidesearch/howsearchworks/algorithms. html.
37 See Chiel 2016; in its own defense, the company explained

thus: "'Our image search results are a reflection of content from across the web, including the frequency with which types of images appear and the way they're described online,' a spokesperson told the Mirror. This means that sometimes unpleasant portrayals of sensitive subject matter online can affect what image search results appear for a given query. These results don't reflect Google's own opinions or beliefs – as a company, we strongly value a diversity of perspectives, ideas and cultures."

38 Roberts 2018.
39 Sociologist Zeynep Tufekci (2019) puts it thus: "These companies – which love to hold themselves up as monuments of free expression – have attained a scale unlike anything the world has ever seen; they've come to dominate media distribution, and they increasingly stand in for the public sphere itself. But at their core, their business is mundane: They're ad brokers. To virtually anyone who wants to pay them, they sell the capacity to precisely target our eyeballs. They use massive surveillance of our behavior, online and off, to generate increasingly accurate, automated predictions of what advertisements we are most susceptible to and what content will keep us clicking, tapping, and scrolling down a bottomless feed."
40 Chiel 2016.
41 Kirchner 2015a.
42 Bertrand and Mullainathan 2003.
43 Pearson 2016a.
44 Caliskan et al. 2017, p. 186.

Notes to Chapter 3

1 Bowles 2016, "wzamen0. 'HP computers are racist,'" YouTube video, 2:15. Dec 10, 2009. https://www.you tube.com/watch?v=t4DT3tQqgRM&feature=youtube.
2 Merriam-Webster Online, n.d., s.v. "exposure."

3 "Racial Sensitivity," YouTube link, originally aired on April 8, 2009.

4 "Racial Sensitivity," YouTube link, originally aired on April 8, 2009.

5 "Racial Sensitivity," YouTube link, originally aired on April 8, 2009.

6 "Top 100 sitcom episodes of all time, No. 54: 'Racial Sensitivity,' *Better off Ted*," https://robertdavidsullivan. typepad.com/my_weblog/2012/04/top-100-sitcom-epi sodes-of-all-time-no-54-racial-sensitivity-better-off-ted. html.

7 The episode represents the ludicrous logic of *racial capitalism*, which Melamed aptly calls a "technology of *antirelationality* . . . Accumulation under capitalism is necessarily expropriation of labor, land, and resources. But it is also something else . . . the production of social separateness – the disjoining or deactiving of relations between human beings (and humans and nature) [and humans and technology!] – needed for capitalist expropriation of work" (Melamed 2015, p. 78).

8 See Joy Buolamwini at Algorithmic Justice League 2017, "The coded gaze," www.ajlunited.org/the-coded-gaze.

9 Samatar 2015.

10 Hargreaves and Hamilton 2001; Poole 1997.

11 Gidley 1992.

12 Wells 1996, p. 103.

13 Roth 2009, p. 131.

14 Samatar 2015.

15 Brown 2017.

16 To learn more about the campaign, visit http://yabablay. com/pretty-period/; see also Blay 2011.

17 Mingus 2011.

18 Roth 2009, p. 168.

19 Roth 2009, p. 169.

20 Roth 2009, p. 119.

21 Roth 2009, p. 121.

22 Unterhalter 1972, p. 109.

23 Massie, *Loosing the Bonds*, p. 272, quoted in Morgan 2006, p. 525.

24 Morgan 2006.

25 Sturken and Cartwright 2017, p. 357.

26 Quoted in Smith 2013.

27 Bowles 2016.

28 Bowles 2016.

29 Avle and Lindtner 2016.

30 Poole 1997, p. 18.

31 Poole notes: "it is almost too easy to consign all images to the task of reproducing (or perhaps even producing) imperial, racial, and sexual ideologies. The more challenging task is to think about the ways in which aesthetics and the 'open code' of visual images occasionally disrupt the powerful hold that imperial discourse has over our imaginations" (1997, p. 17).

32 Plenke 2015a.

33 Soep 2010.

34 Garvie and Frankle 2016.

35 Garvie and Frankle 2016.

36 Garvie and Frankle 2016.

37 Garvie and Frankle 2016.

38 I am indebted to legal scholar Patricia Williams for this latter insight: personal communication, November 9, 2018.

39 For California, visit https://www.npr.org/sections/thetwo-way/2013/07/09/200444613/californias-prison-sterilizations-reportedly-echoes-eugenics-era; for Tennessee, visit https://www.washingtonpost.com/news/morning-mix/wp/2017/11/21/tenn-judge-reprimanded-for-offering-reduced-jail-time-in-exchange-for-sterilization/?utm_term=.684fb785a1c6. See also Roberts 1998.

40 "DNA dreaming," posted by Jessica Cussins on January

13, 2014 at https://www.geneticsandsociety.org/biopo
litical-times/dna-dreaming.

41 As disability justice activist Mia Mingus (2011) explains,
"[a]bleism cuts across all of our movements because
ableism dictates how bodies should function against
a mythical norm – an able-bodied standard of White
supremacy, heterosexism, sexism, economic exploitation, moral/religious beliefs, age and ability." See also
Schalk 2018.

42 See Bliss 2018; Duster 2005; Keel 2018; Koenig et al.
2008; Panofsky 2014; Richardson and Stevens 2015;
Roberts 2012; TallBear 2013; Wailoo et al. 2012.

43 See the whole article at https://www.insidehighered.com/
blogs/just-visiting/why-we-shouldnt-embrace-genetics-
education.

44 Hacking 2006. A few paragraphs from this *London
Review of Books* article can be found at https://www.
lrb.co.uk/v28/n16/ian-hacking/making-up-people.

45 Rietveld et al. 2013.

46 Quotation from https://www.imdb.com/title/tt0119177/
quotes.

47 Carrington 2016 explains: "The Whiteness of science fiction names both the overrepresentation of White people
among the ranks of SF authors and the overrepresentation
of White people's experiences within SF texts" (p. 16) and,
I would add, with film and other media representations.
See also https://www.opendemocracy.net/transformat
ion/andr-carrington/whiteness-of-science-fiction.

48 As such, "reproductive justice extends well beyond the
body – so often the site of trauma and exploitation – to
encompass the full range of life-affirming practices that
implicate the body politic writ large" (Benjamin 2018,
p. 44).

49 Visit the movement's website at https://policy.m4bl.
org.

50 Shultz 2016.
51 Shultz 2016.
52 Sankar 2010, p. 52.
53 M'Charek 2013.
54 See also Bliss (2012) for an incisive analysis of Ancestry Informative Markers.
55 Foucault 1991 [1975], p. 108; emphasis added.
56 See https://supreme.justia.com/cases/federal/us/392/1; emphasis added.
57 Stop LAPD Spying Coalition 2013, p. 7.
58 Kirchner 2015b.
59 Rusert 2017, pp. 65–6. See also Nelson 2013 and 2016.
60 Visit the Media Matters blog at https://www.mediama tters.org/blog/2015/03/24/video-what-happens-when-local-news-over-represe/203010, posted on March 24, 2015 by Daniel Angster.
61 Brock 2012.
62 Buolamwini 2016. See also Buolamwini and Gebru 2018.
63 Chutel 2018.
64 Rusert 2017, p. 26.
65 Rusert 2017, p. 26.
66 Baderoon 2011, p. 71.
67 Baderoon 2011, p. 75; emphasis added.
68 "Stop LAPD Spying: They Still Lie," YouTube video, https://www.youtube.com/watch?v=tDYwvT_jPBo.
69 See https://stoplapdspying.org/wp-content/uploads/20 13/04/PEOPLES-AUDIT-UPDATED-APRIL-2–2013-A. pdf.
70 Roy 2014, p. 43.
71 "While genetic ancestry testing concentrates on tracing the genes of ancestors in contemporary human bodies, isotope testing is based on the way that the different environments in which an individual lives may leave distinctive traces in her or his body. The proportions of

different isotopes of various chemical elements present in the environment vary from one locality to another. These elements are ingested in food and drinking water and are incorporated, over time, into body tissues. Consequently, assuming that a person consumes local food, water and air, the proportions of different isotopes present in her or his tissues will mirror those in the place where s/he lives. Moreover, because different tissues are laid down at different times in a person's life, they embody a record of the person's diet, and her or his movements over time" (Tutton et al. 2014, p. 8).

72 Letter dated September 9, 2011, provided by journalist John Travis.

73 "Nationality Swapping Isotope Analysis and DNA Testing" protocol. Available upon request. The proposed language in the asylum report is as follows: "You did not give a reasonable explanation for failing to provide samples. It is considered that a person in genuine need of international protection would assist the authorities of a safe country in establishing the validity of his/her application for asylum. Your failure to do so undermines your claim to be a refugee."

74 "DNA-based ancestry testing companies and organisations make claims about individual ancestries, or indeed the nature of human ancestry in general, that are misleading and misrepresent the underlying uncertainties. By telling somebody that they 'come from' some particular ethnic, racial or national group, they also tend to reinforce the notion that these categories have long-term genetic validity, when in fact each of us has many ancestral lineages, and the prevalence of migration means that they are likely to tell many different stories. DNA tests, and claims based on them, are sometimes used in documentaries to tell stories about the origins of specific individuals. This panders to the public desire

for a good story but also to outdated notions of race, ethnicity and ancestry, while scholars who point out flaws and limitations of the methods employed are usually ignored" (Balding et al. 2010, p. 61).

75 Travis 2009.
76 Travis 2009.
77 Travis 2009.
78 Both quotations from Montgomery are taken from Silverstein n.d.
79 "The true country of origin of an applicant must be assessed by reviewing and weighing up all of the available evidence – including documentary evidence, knowledge of the country in question, the language analysis report and the isotope and DNA test results." From *Nationality Swapping Isotope Analysis and DNA Testing* (UKBA's Human Provenance Pilot Project at https://www.gov.uk/government/publications/ukba-s-human-provenance-pilot-project; see Silverstein n.d.).
80 Travis 2009.
81 Travis 2009.
82 Tutton et al. 2014, p. 739.
83 Tutton et al. 2014.
84 kracktivist 2013.
85 Chowdhury 2017.
86 Chakraborty 2017.
87 Chakraborty 2017.
88 Chakraborty 2017.
89 Roy 2014, pp. 30–1.
90 "What next? Compulsory blood donations? Mandatory vasectomy after 50? Forcing organ donations? Specifying the number of children one can or cannot have? Menstrual scanners in places of worship (as someone had jokingly suggested during the Sabarimala debate)?" (Chakraborty 2017).
91 Taylor 2016.

92 Rivero 2016.
93 Rivero 2016.
94 Rivero 2016.
95 Rivero 2016.

Notes to Chapter 4

1 Gogolak 2015.
2 Burnett 2015.
3 Keane 2018.
4 Burnett 2015.
  Carney 2012, pp. 279–305.
5 Kilgore 2015, p. 4.
6 Colaneri 2016.
7 For a general impression, visit the website of the Center for Media Justice at https://centerformediajustice.org.
8 Kilgore 2014.
9 Kilgore 2015, p. 15.
10 In Philadelphia, to "figure out which inmates could be safely released, the city will start using a machine learning-based risk assessment tool: a computer algorithm that uses data on the history of other defendants to determine the likelihood someone will skip mandatory court dates or be arrested again while waiting for trial" (Colaneri 2016).
11 See Pollock (2012, p. 174) for an elaboration of the multiple valences of "fixed" in the context of Black heart failure: one gets things fixed "by rendering race identifiably stable, by focusing attention upon it, and by promising easy repair. . . . One aspect of this process is that race is a difference that is imagined to be fixed enough for action, but that is at the same time potentially able to be medically mitigated." See also M'Charek (2013, p. 424): "The challenge in studying race is to denaturalize without dematerializing it, and to simultaneously attend to materiality without fixing race."

12 Murray 2018.
13 Finn 2017, p. 2.
14 Buranyi 2018a.
15 Dastin 2018.
16 Buranyi 2018b.
17 Littman 2002.
18 Fryer and Levitt 2004.
19 Maltais 2017; see also the posts archived at http:// blackquotidian.com/anvc/black-quotidian/april-22-19 50.
20 See Seamster and Charron-Chénier's (2017) discussion of predatory inclusion.
21 Donovan et al. 2018.
22 Bell and Hartmann 2007.
23 hooks 1992.
24 Berrey 2015, p. 7.
25 Fujii 2017.
26 Leong 2012, p. 2156.
27 Visit https://www.youtube.com/watch?v=J-GVd_HLlps.
28 Halter 2000, p. 5.
29 Vertesi 2014.
30 Vertesi 2014.
31 Braun 2014, p. xv.
32 Pollock, quoted in Sismondo and Greene 2015.
33 See Healthcare Hotspotting at https://hotspotting.cam denhealth.org.
34 Krupar and Ehlers 2017, p. 31.
35 As quoted in Ehlers and Hinkson 2017, p. 4.
36 See Healthcare Hotspotting at https://hotspotting.cam denhealth.org.
37 Legal scholar and historian Jonathan Kahn (2017), for example, studied the use of neuroscience to identify areas of the brain responsible for implicit bias.
38 Wacquant 2009.
39 Cyril 2016.

40 Glaude 2017, p. 9. The value gap, Glaude explains, is "the belief that white people are valued more than others"; and racial habits are "those things we do, without thinking, that sustain the value gap" (p. 6).

Notes to Chapter 5

1 Sharpe 2014.
2 Twitter @fakerapper July 23, 2017 at 3:24 p.m.
3 Stahly-Butts continues: "It's when we have Black and Brown folks, low-income folks, then all of sudden 'safety' means something else. And so, I think, calling the bluff. Actually, you know that for your child, you don't think a cop makes them more safe. That's just for someone else's child . . . And what we know about rich White communities, there's drug issues there, there's sexual assault there, all those things exist in the Hamptons, but there are not cops on every block, there are not big lights that shine in your window every night . . . And so actually we have the tools." Panel comments from Data for Black Lives, January 12, 2019.
4 See "Appolition" on the website of Fast Company at https://www.fastcompany.com/company/appolition.
5 This is a point Ziegler made on a panel we sat on together at Allied Media Conference, June 16, 2018.
6 See https://motherboard.vice.com/en_us/article/d3wvkk/ this-app-is-helping-black-organizers-bail-people-out-of-jail.
7 Twitter @BLM5280 May 11, 2018 at 9:44 p.m.
8 Dickey 2018.
9 BYP100 Staff 2018. See also, Carruthers 2018.
10 See "What is the PIC?" posted on the blog of Prison Culture on October 12, 2010, at http://www.usprison-culture.com/blog/what-is-the-pic.
11 The Corrections Project Map is available at http://i1.wp. com/correctionsproject.com/wordpress/wp-content/up

loads/2015/07/whatIsPIC-e1437215871385.jpg. For a wider picture, visit the website of Prison Maps at http://correctionsproject.com/prisonmaps/index.htm.

12 Visit sociologist and prison abolitionist Mariame Kaba's website for a summary of these critiques and for an exchange between Kaba and sociologist Loïc Wacquant, at http://www.usprisonculture.com/blog/2010/09/15/speaking-for-himself-professor-loic-wacquant-corrects-my-characterization-of-his-critique-of-the-concept-of-the-prison-industrial-complex/; see also, https://www.counterpunch.org/2015/08/10/do-we-need-to-rethink-the-prison-industrial-complex.

13 Burnett 2015.

14 Rollins 2017.

15 See http://criticalresistance.org/wp-content/uploads/2012/06/Ab-Toolkit-Part-2.pdf, p. 1.

16 Visit the website Making a New Reality, https://makinganewreality.org

17 Tarnoff 2017.

18 Tarnoff 2017.

19 https://www.digi-capital.com/news/2016/04/arvr-investment-hits-1-7-billion-in-last-12-months/

20 Matney 2017.

21 Matney 2017.

22 Robertson 2017.

23 Yang 2017.

24 Jackson 2013, p. 15.

25 hooks 1992.

26 Obasogie 2014, p. xvii.

27 *Clouds over Sidra*, a virtual reality film shot in a Syrian refugee camp, depicts a day in the life of 12-year-old-girl who lives there. It helped raise $3.8 billion, which was well over their fundraising goal, leading many other NGOs to create VR experiences for a wide range of causes. However, the creator of *Clouds over Sidra* and

others caution that not all these films have been successful, because without good storytelling the VR headset is insufficient for drawing people into an experience. Visit Voices of VR Podcast at http://voicesofvr.com/vr-as-the-ultimate-empathy-machine-with-the-uns-gabo-arora.

28 Oremus 2016.
29 See https://www.nelp.org/wp-content/uploads/2015/03 /65_Million_Need_Not_Apply.pdf. I am indebted to Tamara K. Nopper for highlighting this point.
30 Zercoe 2017.
31 Twitter @thisisDRS June 26, 2018 at 5:25 a.m.
32 Costanza-Chock 2018.
33 Costanza-Chock 2018.
34 Consider that, "[u]nder Western modernity, becoming 'free' means becoming a colonizer, and because of this, 'the central contradiction of modernity is freedom'" (paperson 2017, p. 7, quoting Ruthie Wilson Gilmore).
35 Costanza-Chock 2018; emphasis added.
36 Vinsel 2017; 2018.
37 From Vinsel's blog at https://blog.usejournal.com/the res-so-little-there-there-a-response-to-the-stanford-d-sc hool-s-defense-of-design-thinking-3cac35a1a365.
38 Freire 1990, p. 54.
39 Irani and Silberman 2016.
40 Quotation from Turkopticon's home page at https:// turkopticon.ucsd.edu.
41 Irani and Silberman 2016.
42 Quotation from a blog posted by Vinsel on July 14, 2018 on the website of Noteworthy: The Journal Blog at https://blog.usejournal.com/theres-so-little-there-there -a-response-to-the-stanford-d-school-s-defense-of-des ign-thinking-3cac35a1a365.
43 Noble 2018, p. 165.
44 Kimberly Bain, PhD candidate in English at Princeton

University, is examining this topic in much more depth in her dissertation "Black Breath: A Theory and Praxis."

45 Fanon 1994, p. 65.

46 Sociologist Zeynep Tufekci, author of *Twitter and Tear Gas* (Tufekci 2017), described a personal experience of digital intelligibility in her email newsletter of March 20, 2017 on the subject "On Immigration, Algorithms, and Cures: Who Really Belongs?" (available upon request). She said that she "spoke in English into the tiny icon, only to be constantly misunderstood. I would say 'how to best' and Siri would happily type 'octopus.' I said the 'tech press,' and Siri worrisomely transcribed it as 'depress.' 'An op-ed' got typed up as 'enough.' I felt like I had turned into a fortune teller, reading coffee grounds, as I tried to decipher meaning in Siri's interpretation of my accent."

47 Quoted in Hardy 2016.

48 Rivitz 2015.

49 For example, see Munger 2016; also visit the site of *Washington Post* at https://www.washingtonpost.com/news/monkey-cage/wp/2016/11/17/this-researcher-programmed-bots-to-fight-racism-on-twitter-it-worked, where one can read: "This researcher programmed bots to fight racism on Twitter. It worked."

50 O'Neil 2016, p. 204.

51 See Tanz 2016.

52 See also a charter by Open AI, a nonprofit AI research company, at https://blog.openai.com/openai-charter.

53 Visit AJL Safe Face Pledge, https://www.safefacepledge.org.

54 Visit https://www.nytimes.com/2018/04/04/technology/google-letter-ceo-pentagon-project.html.

55 Frenkel 2018.

56 Benjamin 2016a.

57 See the report *Equity Audits* at https://maec.org/

wp-content/uploads/2016/04/MAEC-Equity-Audit-1.
pdf; see also Skrla et al. 2004.

58 See http://auditingalgorithms.science.

59 Quoted from the report *Algorithmic Accountability: A
Primer*, prepared by Data & Society in 2018, at https://
datasociety.net/wp-content/uploads/2018/04/Data_
Society_Algorithmic_Accountability_Primer_FINAL-4.
pdf.

60 Quoted from the same report.

61 Eckersley 2018.

62 Browne 2015, p. 19.

63 Fieldnotes, Allied Media Conference, June 16, 2018.

64 See Article 20 ("Right to data portability") of the General
Data Protection Regulation (GDPR) "applicable as of
May 25th, 2018 in all member states to harmonize data
privacy laws across Europe," https://gdpr-info.eu/art-
20-gdpr.

65 Thompson 2018a.

66 See Article 2 of the GDPR, at https://gdpr-info.eu/art-2-
gdpr.

67 See the same article.

68 This is the title of an article published by Patrick Lucas
Austin in 2018 on the website of Gizmodo: see https://
gizmodo.com/microsoft-improves-racist-facial-recogniti
on-software-1827141398.

69 Visit the website https://www.alliedmedia.org/ddjc/dis
cotech.

70 Visit the ODB website at https://www.odbproject.org.

71 Petty's comments are from Data for Black Lives, Jan 13,
2019, "What is a Movement Scientist?" panel.

72 Snow 2018.

73 The Dataset Nutrition Label Project is based at the
Berkman Klein Center at Harvard University and
Massachusetts Institute of Technology Media Lab,
http://datanutrition.media.mit.edu.

74 Quoted from the abstract of Kim 2017 (the abstract can be accessed at https://papers.ssrn.com/sol3/papers.cfm? abstract_id=3093982).

75 Visit the website of the Detroit Community Project at http://www.detroitcommunitytech.org.

76 Quoted from the Detroit Digital Justice Coalition website at https://www.alliedmedia.org/ddjc/principles.

77 The question of ownership is also taken up in the growing movement around platform cooperativism, which counteracts platform capitalism that allows tech companies to offer "free" services in exchange for users' valuable information. See https://platform.coop/about; also Scholz and Schneider 2016.

78 Data for Black Lives, n.d. Another tool presented at the 2019 Data for Black Lives was the Community Based System Dynamics approach. This is a "participatory method for involving communities in the process of understanding changing systems from the endogenous or feedback perspective" (Hovmand 2014, p. 1). See also Richardson (2011): "System dynamics is the use of informal maps and formal models with computer simulation to uncover and understand endogenous sources of system behaviour" (p. 241).

79 Milner 2018.

80 Rusert and Brown 2018.

81 Hetey and Eberhardt 2018.

82 As Jafari Naimi and colleagues powerfully contend, "we develop the value *justice* by testing and observing the work that the justice hypothesis does in various situations, and we recognize situations as just or unjust through reference to this learning" (Jafari Naimi et al. 2015, p. 101).

83 As Imani Perry (2018) posits in *Vexy Thing*, art "answers these questions when facts cannot. Its function is to incite our imaginations, to add to the collage of our

thoughts, to know and become part of the shaping of our worlds and therefore ought not to be treated as passive commitments, adulation, or artifacts for fandom" (p. 233). See also, Imarisha and brown 2015.

84 Sinclair 2018.

85 paperson 2017, p. 6.

86 Petty in Leon's (2016) paraphrase.

87 Eubanks 2018, p. 9.

88 Roy 2014, p. 25.

89 Anderson and Jones 2016; Bell 1992; Butler 1993; Du Bois 1920; Carrington 2016; Hopkinson 1998; Imarisha and brown 2015; Ramirez 2008, Thomas 2000; Womack 2015.

90 Rusert 2017; Eglash et al. 2004.

91 Bell 1995, p. 898.

92 Visit http://www.hyphen-labs.com.

93 This speaks to Kavita Philip and colleagues' notion of "postcolonial computing – designers, planners, makers, the objects they shape, and a range of diverse users in the same analytic frame, all part of an assemblage [that] includes not only the dreams of design but the messiness of manufacture as well" (Philip et al. 2012, p. 6).

94 For the aesthetic and joyful dimensions of social movement organizing, see BYP100's "The Black Joy Experience" album at https://itunes.apple.com/us/alb um/the-black-joy-experience/1440152666.

Appendix

Tech and Social Justice Initiatives

A People's Guide to AI: This is a comprehensive beginner's guide to understanding AI and other data-driven tech. The guide uses a popular education approach to explore and explain AI-based technologies so that everyone – from youths to seniors and from non-techies to experts – has the chance to think critically about the kinds of futures automated technologies can bring. https://www.alliedmedia.org/peoples-ai.

Algorithmic Justice League: This organization aims to highlight algorithmic bias through media, art, and science; provide space for people to voice concerns and experiences with coded bias; and develop practices for accountability during the design, development, and deployment of coded systems. https://www.ajlunited.org.

Allied Media Projects: The Allied Media Network is a nonprofit organization committed to supporting, through hosted conferences and project sponsorship, the communication media sector in creating a more "just, creative and collaborative world" that is dedicated to social justice. https://alliedmedia.org.

Center for Media Justice: Aims to build a powerful movement for a more just and participatory media and digital world – with racial equity and human rights for all. https://centerformediajustice.org.

Chupadados: This project gathers stories from across Latin America about the mass collection and processing of data that governments, businesses, and we ourselves carry out to monitor our cities, homes, wallets, and bodies. https://chupadados.codingrights.org/es/introducao.

ColorCoded: A tech learning space that centers on historically excluded people in the co-teaching, co-creation, and co-ownership of new technologies. https://colorcoded.la.

Data for Black Lives: A group of multidisciplinary organizers who aim to use data to create concrete and measurable change in the lives of Black people. By convening an annual conference, the group speaks to data scientists, policy makers, researchers, students, parents, and more, in order to "chart out a new future for data science." http://d4bl.org/about.html.

Design Justice: Design Justice network members rethink design processes, center people who are normally marginalized by design, and use collaborative, creative practices to address the deepest challenges our communities face. http://designjusticenetwork.org.

Equality Labs: A South Asian organization that works for the end of caste oppression using community-based research, technology, and art, including an Internet Security and Digital Security initiative. https://www.equalitylabs.org.

Appendix

Equitable Internet Initiative: The program's mission is to ensure that more Detroit residents have the ability to leverage online access and digital technology for social and economic development. https://detroitcommunitytech.org/eii.

#MoreThanCode: This is a "participatory action research project intended to better understand the types of work currently being done with technology for social justice (and more broadly, in the public interest), as well as the pathways people take into this work." https://morethancode.cc/about.

For a Comprehensive List of Organizations, visit #MoreThanCode at https://morethancode.cc/orglist/

Fairness, Accountability, and Transparency Initiatives

Auditing Algorithms: An organization tasked with the goal of producing documentation "that will help to define and develop the emerging research community for algorithm auditing." http://auditingalgorithms.science.

AMC Fairness, Accountability, and Transparency: A multi-disciplinary conference that brings together researchers and practitioners interested in fairness, accountability, and transparency in socio-technical systems. https://fatconference.org.

Statements

Data & Society "Algorithmic Accountability" Statement: This statement seeks to help assign "responsibility for harm when algorithmic decision-making results in discriminatory and inequitable outcomes." https://

datasociety.net/output/algorithmic-accountability-a-primer.

Data for Black Lives letter to Zuckerberg: Urges Zuckerberg to "1. Commit anonymized Facebook Data to a Public Trust. 2. Work with technologists, advocates, and ethicists to establish a Data Code of Ethics. 3. Hire Black data scientists and research scientists." https://medium.com/@YESHICAN/an-open-letter-to-facebook-from-the-data-for-black-lives-movement-81e693c6b46c.

Digital Citizens' Bill of Rights: A bill proposed by Congressman Darell Issa outlining the rights people have in the digital sphere. For his first draft, the congressman publicly published the bill, asking for input from all to "help [get] this right." http://keepthewebopen.com/digital-bill-of-rights.

Equitable Open Data: A set of guidelines for advancing "equitable practices for collecting, disseminating and using open data." https://www.alliedmedia.org/news/2017/01/13/guidelines-equitable-open-data.

Principles of a Feminist Internet: Statement by the Association of Progressive Communications. https://www.apc.org/en/pubs/feminist-principles-internet-version-20.

Science for the People Statement: Calls for "pickets at Microsoft, Amazon, and Salesforce offices and stores to protest these companies' contracts with ICE." https://scienceforthepeople.org.

Tech Workers Coalition Community Guide: "seeks to redefine the relationship between tech workers and Bay Area communities. Through activism, civic engagement, direct action, and education, we work in solidarity with existing movements towards social justice and economic inclusion." https://techworkers-coalition.org/community-guide.

Statement on Project Maven by Google employees opposing the company's contract with the Department of Defense for Project Maven, a research initiative to develop computer vision algorithms that can analyze drone footage. https://static01.nyt.com/files/2018/technology/googleletter.pdf.

#NoTechForICE, petition against tech company contracts with ICE.

#TechWontBuildIt Statement by Amazon employees against the company's facial recognition contracts with law enforcement.

References

Alexander, Michelle. 2012. *The New Jim Crow: Mass Incarceration in the Age of Colorblind Racism*. New York: New Press.

Alexander, Michelle. 2018. "The newest Jim Crow." *New York Times*, November 8. https://www.nytimes.com/2018/11/08/opinion/sunday/criminal-justice-reforms-race-technology.html.

Anderson, D. 2018. "This app is helping black organizers bail people out of jail." *Motherboard*, February 8. https://motherboard.vice.com/en_us/article/d3wvkk/this-app-is-helping-black-organizers-bail-people-out-of-jail.

Anderson, Reynaldo, and Charles E. Jones. 2016. *Afrofuturism 2.0: The Rise of Astro-Blackness*. Lanham, MD: Lexington Books.

Angwin, Julia, Jeff Larson, Surya Mattu, and Lauren Kirchner. 2016. "Machine bias." *ProPublica*, May 23. https://www.propublica.org/article/machine-bias-risk-assessments-in-criminal-sentencing.

Associated Press. 2006. "Clippers owner sued by US Department of Justice." ESPN.com, August 7.

http://www.espn.com/nba/news/story?id=25427
41.

Avle, Seyram, and Silvia Lindtner. 2016. "Design(ing) 'here' and 'there': Tech entrepreneurs, global markets, and reflexivity in design processes." In *Proceedings of the 2016 CHI Conference on Human Factors in Computing Systems*, pp. 2233–45. https://static1.squarespace.com/static/52842f7de4b0b6141ccb7766/t/5736b0cc9f72666330240478/1463201999607/p2233-avle-Lindtner.pdf.

Baderoon, Gabeba. 2011. "Baartman and the private: How can we look at a figure that has been looked at too much?" In *Representation and Black Womanhood*, edited by N. Gordon-Chipembere, pp. 65–83. New York: Palgrave.

Bailey, Moya, and Trudy. 2018. "On Misogynoir: Citation, erasure, and plagiarism." *Feminist Media Studies* 18 (4), 762–8.

Balding, D., M. Weale, M. Richards, and M. Thomas. 2010. "Genetic and isotopic analysis and the UK border agency." *Significance* 7, 58–61.

Baldwin, James. 1998. *James Baldwin: Collected Essays*. New York: Library of America.

Baldwin, James and Randall Kenan. 2011. *The Cross of Redemption: Uncollected Writings*. New York: Vintage International.

Bambara, Toni Cade, ed. 1970. *The Black Woman: An Anthology*. New York: New American Library.

Barrowman, Nick. 2018. "Why data is never raw: On the seductive myth of information free of human judgement." *New Atlantis* 56, 129–35.

Becker, H. S. 1963. *Outsiders: Studies in the Sociology of Deviance*. London: Free Press of Glencoe.

References

Bell, Derrick A. 1992. "The space traders." https://whg-betc.com/the-space-traders.pdf.

Bell, Derrick A. 1995. "Who's afraid of critical race theory?" *University of Illinois Law Review*, 893–910. doi: 10.2304/power.2009.1.1.125

Bell, Joyce M., and Douglas Hartmann. 2007. "Diversity in everyday discourse: The cultural ambiguities and consequences of 'happy talk.'" *American Sociological Review* 72, 895–914.

Benjamin, Ruha. 2016a. "Informed refusal: Toward a justice-based bioethics." *Science, Technology, and Human Values* 41, 967–90.

Benjamin, Ruha. 2016b. "Innovating inequity: If race is a technology, postracialism is the genius bar." *Ethnic and Racial Studies* 39 (13), 1–8.

Benjamin, Ruha. 2018. "Black afterlives matter: Cultivating kinfulness as reproductive justice." In *Making Kin, not Population*, edited by Adele Clarke and Donna Haraway, pp. 41–66. Chicago, IL: Prickly Paradigm Press.

Benjamin, Ruha. 2019. *Captivating Technology: Race, Carceral Technoscience, and Liberatory Imagination in Everyday Life*. Durham, NC: Duke University Press.

Berrey, Ellen. 2015. *The Enigma of Diversity: The Language of Race and the Limits of Racial Justice*. London: University of Chicago Press.

Bertrand, Marianne, and Sendhil Mullainathan. 2003. "Are Emily and Greg more employable than Lakisha and Jamal? A field experiment on labor market discrimination." National Bureau of Economic Research. https://www.nber.org/papers/w9873.pdf.

Binder, O. O. 1957. "You'll own 'slaves' by 1965."

References

Mechanix Illustrated, January. http://blog.modern-mechanix.com/youll-own-slaves-by-1965.

Black Youth Project Staff. 2018. "How Jay-Z & other venture capitalists are creating new problems in the name of social justice." Black Youth Project, March 28. http://blackyouthproject.com/how-jay-z-other-venture-capitalists-are-creating-new-problems-in-the-name-of-social-justice.

Bland, Allison (alliebland). Twitter, 2013, November 19.

Blay, Yaba. 2011. "Skin bleaching and global White supremacy: By way of introduction." *Journal of Pan African Studies* 4 (4), 4–46.

Bliss, Catherine. 2012. *Race Decoded: The Genomic Fight for Social Justice*. Palo Alto, CA: Stanford University Press.

Bliss, Catherine. 2018. *Social by Nature: The Promise and Peril of Sociogenomics*. Palo Alto, CA: Stanford University Press.

Bonilla-Silva, Eduardo. 2006. *Racism without Racists: Colorblind Racism and the Persistence of Racial Inequality in the United States*, 2nd edn. New York: Rowman & Littlefield.

Botsman, Rachel. 2017. "Big data meets Big Brother as China moves to rate its citizens." *Wired UK*, October 21. http://www.wired.co.uk/article/chinese-government-social-credit-score-privacy-invasion.

Bowker, Geoffrey. 2006. *Memory Practices in the Sciences*. Cambridge, MA: MIT Press.

Bowles, Nellie. 2016. "'I think my blackness is interfering': Does facial recognition show racial bias?" *Guardian*, April 7. https://www.theguardian.com/technology/2016/apr/08/facial-recognition-technology-racial-bias-police.

References

Bowles, Nellie. 2018. "A dark consensus about screens and kids begins to emerge in Silicon Valley." *New York Times*, October 26. https://www.nytimes.com/2018/10/26/style/phones-children-silicon-valley.html.

boyd, danah, and M. C. Elish. 2018. "Don't believe every AI you see." The Ethical Machine. November 13. https://ai.shorensteincenter.org/ideas/2018/11/12/dont-believe-every-ai-you-see-1.

boyd, danah, Karen Levy, and Alice Marwick. 2014. "The networked nature of algorithmic discrimination." In *Data and Discrimination: Collected Essays*, edited by Gangadharan and Eubanks, pp. 43–57. Open Technology Institute. http://www-personal.umich.edu/~csandvig/research/An%20Algorithm%20Audit.pdf.

Braun, Lundy. 2014. *Breathing Race into the Machine: The Surprising Career of the Spirometer from Plantation to Genetics*. Minneapolis: University of Minnesota Press.

Brayne, Sarah. 2014. "Surveillance and systems avoidance." *American Sociological Review* 79 (3), 367–91.

Bridges, Khiara M. 2017. *The Poverty of Privacy Rights*. Palo Alto, CA: Stanford University Press.

Brock, Andre. 2012. "From the blackhand side: Twitter as a cultural conversation." *Journal of Broadcasting and Electronic Media* 56 (4), 529–49.

Broussard, Meredith. 2018. *Artificial Unintelligence: How Computers Misunderstand the World*. Cambridge, MA: MIT Press.

Brown, Adrienne R. 2017. *The Black Skyscraper: Architecture and the Perception of Race*. Baltimore, MD: Johns Hopkins University Press.

brown, adrienne maree. 2017. *Emergent Strategy: Shaping Change, Changing Worlds*. Oakland, CA: AK Press.

Brown, Wendy. 2015. *Undoing the Demos: Neoliberalism's Stealth Revolution*. New York: Zone Books.

Browne, Simone. 2015. *Dark Matters: On the Surveillance of Blackness*. Durham, NC: Duke University Press.

Buolamwini, Joy. 2016. "The Algorithmic Justice League." Medium Corporation, December 14. https://medium.com/mit-media-lab/the-algorithmic-justice-le ague-3cc4131c5148.

Buolamwini, Joy, and Timnit Gebru. 2018. "Gender shades: Intersectional accuracy disparities in commercial gender classification." *Proceedings of Machine Learning Research* 81, 1–15.

Buranyi, Stephen, 2018a. "'Dehumanising, impenetrable, frustrating': The grim reality of job hunting in the age of AI." *Guardian*, March 4. https://www.the guardian.com/inequality/2018/mar/04/dehumanising -impenetrable-frustrating-the-grim-reality-of-job-hun ting-in-the-age-of-ai.

Buranyi, Stephen, 2018b. "How to persuade a robot that you should get the job." *Guardian*, March 3. https://www.theguardian.com/technology/2018/mar/ 04/robots-screen-candidates-for-jobs-artificial-intellig ence.

Burnett, Joshua. 2015. "As asylum seekers swap prison beds for ankle bracelets, same firm profits." NPR, November 13. https://www.npr.org/2015/11/13/455 790454/as-asylum-seekers-swap-prison-beds-for-ank le-bracelets-same-firm-profits.

References

Butler, Octavia E. 1993. *Parable of the Sower*. New York: Warner Books.

Caliskan, Aylin, Joanna J. Bryson, and Arvind Narayanan. 2016. "Semantics derived automatically from language corpora contain human-like biases." https://arxiv.org/abs/1608.07187.

Caliskan, Aylin, Joanna J. Bryson, and Arvind Narayanan. 2017. "Semantics derived automatically from language corpora contain human-like biases." *Science* 356.6334: 183–6.

Carney, M., 2012. "Correction through omniscience: Electronic monitoring and the escalation of crime control." *Washington University Journal of Law & Policy* 40, 279–305.

Carrington, André. 2016. *Speculative Blackness: The Future of Race in Science Fiction*. Minneapolis: University of Minnesota Press.

Carruthers, Charlene. 2018. *Unapologetic: A Black, Queer, and Feminist Mandate for Radical Social Movements*. New York: Beacon Press.

Castells, Manuel. 2009. *The Rise of the Network Society*, 2nd edn. Oxford: Wiley Blackwell.

Chakraborty, Angshukanta. 2017. "With Aadhaar, government shows it wants to push India down a dark hole." *Daily O*, May 5. https://www.dailyo.in/politics/aadhaar-card-pan-link-uid-surveillance-privacy-biometrics/story/1/17033.html.

Chiel, Ethan. 2016. "'Black teenagers' vs. 'White teenagers': Why Google's algorithm displays racist results." *Splinter News*, June 10. https://splinternews.com/black-teenagers-vs-white-teenagers-why-googles-algori-1793857436.

Chowdhury, Shreya R. 2017. "By making Aadhaar

mandatory, Delhi's government schools are shutting their doors to migrant children." *Scroll.in*, April 16. https://scroll.in/article/834418/by-making-aadhaar-mandatory-delhis-government-schools-are-shutting-their-doors-to-migrant-children.

Chun, Wendy Hui Kyong. 2009. "Introduction: Race and/as technology: Or how to do things with race." *Camera Obscura* 24 (1/70), 7–35.

Chutel, Linsey. 2018. "China is exporting facial recognition software to Africa, expanding its vast database." Quartz, May 25. https://qz.com/africa/1287675/china-is-exporting-facial-recognition-to-africa-ensuring-ai-dominance-through-diversity.

Cohen, Michael J. 2017. "A Stanford study finds the tech elite aren't libertarians at all – just a strange breed of liberals." Quartz, September 6. https://qz.com/1070846/a-stanford-study-finds-silicon-valley-techies-arent-libertarians-like-peter-thiel-at-all-just-a-strange-breed-of-liberals-that-favor-democrats-and-the-democratic-party.

Colaneri, Katie. 2016. "$3.5 million grant to help Philly cut inmate population, launch other prison reforms." WHYY, April 13. https://whyy.org/articles/35-million-grant-to-help-philly-cut-inmate-population-launch-other-reforms.

Coleman, Beth. 2009. "Race as technology." *Camera Obscura* 24 (1/70), 177–207.

Collins, Patricia Hill. 1990. *Black Feminist Thought: Knowledge, Consciousness, and the Politics of Empowerment*. New York: Routledge.

Costanza-Chock, Sasha. 2018. "Design justice: Towards an intersectional feminist framework for design theory and practice." *Proceedings of the Design Research*

References

Society. https://papers.ssrn.com/sol3/papers.cfm?abstract_id=3189696.

Crain, Marion, Winifred Poster, and Miriam Cherry. 2016. *Invisible Labor: Hidden Work in the Contemporary World.* Berkeley: University of California Press.

Crenshaw, Kimberlé. 1991. "Mapping the margins: Intersectionality, identity politics, and violence against women of color." *Stanford Law Review* 43 (6), 1241–99.

Cresci, Elena. 2015. "IBM pulls #HackAHairDryer campaign admitting it 'missed the mark.'" *Guardian,* December 7. http://www.hitc.com/en-gb/2015/12/08/ibm-pulls-hackahairdryer-campaign-admitting-it-missed-the-mark.

Cyril, Malkia. 2016. "E-carceration: Race, technology, and the future of policing and prisons in America." https://centerformediajustice.org/2016/11/16/e-carceration.

Daly, Michael. 2014. "The day Ferguson cops were caught in a bloody lie." Huffington Post, August 15. https://www.huffingtonpost.com/2014/08/15/the-day-ferguson-cops-wer_n_5681363.html.

Daniels, Jessie. 2009. *Cyber Racism : White Supremacy Online and the New Attack on Civil Rights.* Lanham, MD: Rowman & Littlefield.

Daniels, Jessie. 2013. "Race and racism in Internet studies: A review and critique." *New Media & Society* 15, 695–719.

Daniels, Jessie. 2015. "My brain-database doesn't see skin color: Colorblind racism in the tech industry and in theorizing the web." *American Behavioral Scientist* 59 (11), 1377–93.

References

Daniels, Jessie. 2017. "Twitter and white supremacy, a love story." *Dame*, October 19.

Daniels, Jessie. 2018. "The algorithmic rise of the 'alt-right.'" *Contexts* 17 (1), 60–5.

Dastin, Jeffrey. 2018. "Amazon scraps secret AI recruiting tool that showed bias against women." *Reuters*, October 9. https://www.reuters.com/article/ us-amazon-com-jobs-automation-insight/amazon-scr aps-secret-ai-recruiting-tool-that-showed-bias-again st-women-idUSKCN1MK08G.

Data 4 Black Lives. n.d. Website. http://d4bl.org.

Dickey, Megan Rose. 2018. "Jay-Z's Roc Nation and First Round Capital invest $3 million in bail reform startup Promise." TechCrunch, March 19. https:// techcrunch.com/2018/03/19/jay-zs-roc-nation-and-fir st-round-capital-invest-3-million-in-bail-reform-start up-promise.

D'Ignazio, Catherine, and Lauren Klein. 2019. *Data Feminism*. Cambridge, MA: MIT Press.

Dobush, Grace. 2016. "White men dominate Silicon Valley not by accident, but by design." Quartz, March 16. https://qz.com/641070/white-men-dominate-silic on-valley-not-by-accident-but-by-design.

Donovan, Joan, Robyn Caplan, Lauren Hanson, and Jeanna Matthews. 2018. "Algorithmic accountability: A primer." https://datasociety.net/wp-content/ uploads/2018/04/Data_Society_Algorithmic_Accou ntability_Primer_FINAL.pdf

Du Bois, W. E. B. 1920. "The comet." Chapter 10 in W. E. B. Du Bois, *Darkwater: Voices from within the Veil*. New York: Harcourt, Brace. http://www. gutenberg.org/files/15210/15210-h/15210-h.htm#Ch apter_X.

References

Du Bois, W. E. B. 1998 [1935]. *Black Reconstruction in America, 1860–1880*. New York: Free Press.

Duster, Troy. 2005. "Race and reification in science." *Science* 307 (5712), 1050–1.

Eckersley, Peter, 2018. "How good are Google's new AI ethics principles?" Electronic Frontier Foundation, June 7. https://www.eff.org/deeplinks/2018/06/how-good-are-googles-new-ai-ethics-principles.

Edelman, Susan. 2018. "Brooklyn students hold walkout in protest of Facebook-designed online program." *New York Post*, November 10. https://nypost.com/2018/11/10/brooklyn-students-hold-walkout-in-pro test-of-facebook-designed-online-program.

Edes, Alyssa. 2018. "'Automating inequality': Algorithms in public services often fail the most vulnerable." NPR, February 19. https://www.npr.org/sections/alltechconsidered/2018/02/19/586387119/automating-inequality-algorithms-in-public-services-often-fail-the-most-vulnerab.

Eglash, Ron, Jennifer L. Croissant, Giovanna Di Chiro, and Rayvon Fouché, eds. 2004. *Appropriating Technology: Vernacular Science and Social Power*. Minneapolis: University of Minnesota Press.

Ehlers, Nadine, and Leslie Hinkson, eds. 2017. "Introduction." *Subprime Health: The American Health-Care System and Race-Based Medicine*, pp. 31–54. Minneapolis: University of Minnesota Press.

Eubanks, Virginia. 2018. *Automating Inequality: How High-Tech Tools Profile, Police, and Punish the Poor*. New York: St. Martin's Press.

Everett, Anna. 2002. "The revolution will be digitized: Afrocentricity and the digital public sphere." *Social Text* 20, 125–46.

References

Everett, Anna. 2009. *Digital Diaspora: A Race for Cyberspace*. Albany, NY: SUNY Press.

Fanon, Frantz. 1994. *A Dying Colonialism*. New York: Grove.

Fanon, Frantz. 2008. *Black Skin, White Masks*. New York: Grove.

Feagin, Joe, and Sean Elias. 2013. "Rethinking racial formation theory: A systemic racism critique." *Ethnic and Racial Studies* 36, 931–60.

Ferguson, Andrew Guthrie. 2017. *The Age of Big Data Policing: Surveillance, Race, and the Future of Law Enforcement*. New York: NYU Press.

Finn, Ed. 2017. *What Algorithms Want: Imagination in the Age of Computing*. Cambridge, MA: MIT Press.

Foucault, Michel. 1991 [1975]. *Discipline and Punish: The Birth of the Prison*. New York: Vintage Books.

Fox, Cybelle. 2012. *Three Worlds of Relief: Race, Immigration, and the American Welfare State from the Progressive Era to the New Deal*. Princeton, NJ: Princeton University Press.

Freire, Paulo. 1990. *Pedagogy of the Oppressed*, 20th anniversary edn. New York: Continuum.

Frenkel, Sheera. 2018. "Microsoft employees protest ICE, as tech industry mobilizes over immigration." *New York Times,* June 19. https://www.nytimes.com/2018/06/19/technology/tech-companies-immigration-border.html.

Frenkel, Sheera, Nicholas Confessore, Cecilia Kang, Matthew Rosenberg, and Jack Nicas. 2018. "Delay, deny and deflect: How Facebook's leaders fought through crisis." *New York Times*, November 14. https://www.nytimes.com/2018/11/14/technology/facebook-data-russia-election-racism.html.

Fryer, Roland G., and Stephen D. Levitt. 2004. "The causes and consequences of distinctively black names." *Quarterly Journal of Economics* 119 (3): 767–805.

Fujii, Lee Ann. 2017. "The real problem with diversity in political science." Duck of Minerva, April 27. http://duckofminerva.com/2017/04/the-real-problem-with-diversity-in-political-science.html.

Gajjala, Radhika. 2004. *Cyber Selves: Feminist Ethnographies of South Asian Women.* Walnut Creek, CA: Alta Mira Press.

Garvie, Clare, and Jonathan Frankle. 2016. "Facial-recognition software might have a racial bias problem." *Atlantic*, April 7. https://www.theatlantic.com/technology/archive/2016/04/the-underlying-bias-of-facial-recognition-systems/476991.

Gelin, Martin. 2018. "Silicon Valley's libertarians are trading blows with California Democrats in a fight for the left." Quartz, March 1. https://qz.com/1219254/california-democrats-are-trading-blows-with-silicon-valleys-libertarians-in-a-fight-for-the-left.

Gidley, Mark, ed. 1992. *Representing Others: White Views of Indigenous Peoples.* Exeter: University of Exeter Press.

Glaude, Eddie S., Jr. 2017. *Democracy in Black: How Race Still Enslaves the American Soul.* New York: Broadway Books.

Gogolak, E. C. 2015. "Ankle monitors weigh on immigrant mothers released from detention." *New York Times*, November 15. https://www.nytimes.com/2015/11/16/nyregion/ankle-monitors-weigh-on-immigrant-mothers-released-from-detention.html.

References

Golash-Boza, Tanya. 2016. "A critical and comprehensive sociological theory of race and racism." *Sociology of Race and Ethnicity* 2 (2), 129–41.

Goldberg, David T. 2015. *Are We All Postracial Yet?* Cambridge: Polity.

Goodyear, Dana. 2013. "Paula Deen's ugly roots." *New Yorker*, June 29. https://www.newyorker.com/culture/culture-desk/paula-deens-ugly-roots.

Goyette, Braden. 2014. "LA clippers owner Donald Sterling's racist rant caught on tape: Report." Huffington Post, April 29. https://www.huffingtonpost.com/2014/04/26/donald-sterling-racist_n_5218572.html.

Hacking, Ian. 2006. "Making up people." *London Review of Books* 28 (16–17): 23–26.

Hacking, Ian. 2007. "Kinds of people: Moving targets." *Proceedings of the British Academy, vol. 151: 2006 Lectures.* Oxford: Oxford University Press, pp. 285–317.

Halter, Marilyn. 2000. *Shopping for Identity: The Marketing of Ethnicity.* New York: Schocken.

Hamilton, Charles V., and Kwame Ture. 1967. *Black Power: The Politics of Liberation in America.* New York: Vintage Books.

Haraway, Donna. 1991. *Simians, Cyborgs and Women: The Reinvention of Nature.* New York: Routledge.

Hardy, Q. 2016. "Looking for a choice of voices in AI technology." *New York Times*, October 9. https://www.nytimes.com/2016/10/10/technology/looking-for-a-choice-of-voices-in-ai-technology.html.

Hargreaves, Roger, and Peter Hamilton. 2001. *Beautiful and the Damned: The Creation of Identity in Nineteenth-Century Photography*. Burlington, VT: Lund Humphries.

Hart, Kim. 2018. "Public wants big tech regulated." *Axios*, February 28. https://www.axios.com/axios-surveymonkey-public-wants-big-tech-regulated-5f60 af4b-4faa-4f45-bc45–018c5d2b360f.html.

Harvey, Aaron. 2016. "The list that could take your life." Huffington Post, September 27. https://www. huffingtonpost.com/entry/the-list-that-can-take-your-life_us_57eae82ce4b07f20daa0fd51.

Helm, Angela Bronner. 2016. "'3 black teens' Google search sparks outrage." *Root*, June 12, https://www. theroot.com/3-black-teens-google-search-sparks-out rage-1790855635.

Helmreich, Stefan. 1998. *Silicon Second Nature: Culturing Artificial Life in a Digital World*. Berkeley: University of California Press.

Hetey, Rebecca C., and Jennifer L. Eberhardt, 2018. "The numbers don't speak for themselves: Racial disparities and the persistence of inequality in the criminal justice system." *Current Directions in Psychological Science* 27, 183–7.

hooks, bell. 1992. *Black Looks: Race and Representation*. Boston, MA: South End Press.

hooks, bell. 2015. "Understanding patriarchy." No Borders: Louisville's Radical Lending Library. http:// imaginenoborders.org/pdf/zines/UnderstandingPatri archy.pdf.

Hopkinson, Nalo. 1998. *Brown Girl in the Ring*. New York: Warner Books.

Hossfeld, K. J. 1990. "'Their logic against them': Contradictions in sex, race, and class in Silicon Valley." In A. Nelson, T. Tu, & A. H. Hines (eds.),

Technicolor: Race, Technology and Everyday Life (pp. 34–63). New York: NYU Press.

Hovmand, Peter. 2014. *Community-Based System Dynamics*. New York: Springer.

Hoyle, Ben. 2018. "Tech-free schools for children of Silicon Valley." *Times*, February 10, https://www.the times.co.uk/article/tech-free-schools-for-children-of-silicon-valley-jbh637vwp.

Imarisha, Walidah, and adrienne maree brown. 2015. *Octavia's Brood: Science Fiction Stories from Social Justice Movements*. Oakland, CA: AK Press.

Irani, Lilly, and M. Six Silberman. 2016. "Stories we tell about labor: Turkopticon and the trouble with 'Design.'" UC San Diego. https://escholarship.org/uc/item/8nm273g3.

Jackson, John L. 2013. *Thin Description: Ethnography and the Hebrew Israelites of Jerusalem*. Cambridge, MA: Harvard University Press.

Jafari Naimi, Nassim, Lisa Nathan, and Ian Hargraves. 2015. "Values as hypotheses: Design, inquiry, and the service of values." *Design Issues* 31 (4), 91–104.

Jarmon, Renina. 2013. *Black Girls Are From the Future: Essays on Race, Digital Creativity and Pop Culture*. Washington, DC: Jarmon Media.

Jasanoff, Sheila (ed). 2004. *States of Knowledge: The Co-production of Science and the Social Order*. New York: Routledge.

Kahn, Jonathan. 2017. *Race on the Brain: What Implicit Bias Gets Wrong about the Struggle for Racial Justice*. New York: Columbia University Press.

Keane, Tom. 2018. "Federal agencies continue to advance capabilities with Azure Government." Azure Government Cloud, January 24. https://blogs.msdn.

microsoft.com/azuregov/2018/01/24/federal-agencies
-continue-to-advance-capabilities-with-azure-gove
rnment.

Keel, Terence. 2018. *Divine Variations: How Christian Thought Became Racial Science*. Palo Alto, CA: Stanford University Press.

Kilgore, James. 2014. "The grey area of electronic monitoring in the USA." *Crime Justice Matters* 95, 18–19. https://www.crimeandjustice.org.uk/publica tions/cjm/article/grey-area-electronic-monitoring-usa.

Kilgore, James. 2015. "Electronic monitoring is not the answer: Critical reflections on a flawed alternative." Center for Media Justice. https://centerformediajus tice.org/wp-content/uploads/2015/10/EM-Report-Kil gore-final-draft-10-4-15.pdf.

Kim, Pauline. 2017. "Auditing algorithms for discrimi-nation." *University of Pennsylvania Law Review* 166 (1), Article 10. https://papers.ssrn.com/sol3/papers. cfm?abstract_id=3093982.

King, Samantha. 2006. *Pink Ribbons, Inc.: Breast Cancer and the Politics of Philanthropy*. Minneapolis: University of Minnesota Press.

Kirchner, Lauren. 2015a. "When big data becomes bad data." ProPublica, September 2. https://www. propublica.org/article/when-big-data-becomes-bad-data.

Kirchner, Lauren. 2015b. "Will 'DNA phenotyping' lead to racial profiling by police?" *Pacific Standard*, February 26. https://psmag.com/news/will-dna-phe notyping-lead-to-racial-profiling-by-police.

Koenig, Barbara, Sandra Soo-Jin Lee, and Sarah S. Richardson (eds). 2008. *Revisiting Race in a Genomic Age*. New Brunswick, NJ: Rutgers University Press.

kracktivist. 2013. "#India – Warning – UID will create a digital caste system." Kractivist. https://www.kractiv ist.org/india-warning-uid-will-create-a-digital-caste-system-aadhaar-aadhar.

Krupar, Shiloh, and Nadine Ehlers. 2017. "'When treating patients like criminals makes sense': Medical hot spotting, race, and debt." In *Subprime Health: The American Health-Care System and Race-Based Medicine*, edited by Nadine Ehlers and Leslie Hinkson, 31–54. Minneapolis: University of Minnesota Press.

Kurzgesagt. 2016. "Genetic engineering will change everything forever: CRISPR." October 8. https://kur zgesagt.org/portfolio/crispr.

Lebowitz, Shana. 2018. "Silicon Valley parents are so panicked about kids' screen time they're having nan-nies sign 'no-phone contracts' and posting photos of rule-breakers online." Business Insider South Africa, November 13. https://www.businessinsider. co.za/silicon-valley-nannies-monitor-kids-screen-tim e-2018–10.

Leon, Ana Maria. 2016. "Spaces of co-liberation." e-Flux Architecture. https://www.e-flux.com/architect ure/dimensions-of-citizenship/178280/spaces-of-co-liberation.

Leong, Nancy. 2012. "Racial capitalism." *Harvard Law Review*, 126, 2151–226.

Levin, Sam. 2016. "A beauty contest was judged by AI and the robots didn't like dark skin." *Guardian*, September 8. https://www.theguardian.com/technol ogy/2016/sep/08/artificial-intelligence-beauty-conte st-doesnt-like-black-people.

Lewis, Amanda. 2004. "'What group?' Studying

Whites and Whiteness in the era of 'colorblindness.'" *Sociological Theory* 22 (4), 623–46.

Liao, Shannon. 2018. "Amazon warehouse workers skip bathroom breaks to keep their jobs, says report." The Verge, April 16. https://www.theverge.com/2018/4/16/17243026/amazon-warehouse-jobs-worker-conditions-bathroom-breaks.

Littman, Margaret. 2002. "Are marketers the new racial profilers?" Alternet, October 23, https://www.alternet.org/story/14370/are_marketers_the_new_racial_profilers.

Maltais, Michelle. 2017. "What's so wrong about White joggers in a Black neighborhood?" *Los Angeles Times*, March 15. https://www.latimes.com/local/la-me-leimert-park-joggers-discussion-20170315-htmlstory.html.

Marche, Stephen, 2012. "Is Facebook making us lonely?" *Atlantic*, May 15. https://www.theatlantic.com/magazine/archive/2012/05/is-facebook-making-us-lonely/308930.

Matney, Lucas. 2017. "Zuckerberg apologizes for his tone-deaf VR cartoon tour of Puerto Rico devastation." TechCrunch. https://techcrunch.com/2017/10/10/zuckerberg-apologizes-for-his-tone-deaf-vr-cartoon-tour-of-puerto-rico-devastation.

M'Charek, Amade. 2013. "Beyond fact or fiction: On the materiality of race in practice." *Cultural Anthropology* 28 (3): 420–42.

McWhorter, John. 2016. "'Racist' technology is a bug – not a crime." *Time*, September 12. http://time.com/4475627/is-technology-capable-of-being-racist.

Melamed, Jodi. 2015. "Racial capitalism." *Critical Ethnic Studies* 1 (1), 77–85.

References

Merriam-Webster Online. n.d. 'Glitch'. https://www.merriam-webster.com/dictionary/glitch.

Metz, Cade. 2013. "Facebook's deep learning guru reveals the secret of AI." *Wired*, December 12. https://www.wired.com/2013/12/facebook-yann-lecun-qa.

Milner, Yeshimabeit. 2018. "An open letter to Facebook from the Data for Black Lives movement." Medium Corporation, April 4. https://medium.com/@YESHICAN/an-open-letter-to-facebook-from-the-data-for-black-lives-movement-81e693c6b46c.

Mingus, Mia. 2011. "Moving toward ugly: A politic beyond desirability." Talk delivered at the symposium "Femme of Color," Oakland, CA, August 21. https://www.photographytalk.com/forum/photography-general-discussion/268790-is-this-a-double-exposure-or-a-ghost.

Monahan, Torin, and Neal A. Palmer. 2009. "The emerging politics of DHS fusion centers." *Security Dialogue* 40 (6), 616–36.

Moore, Malcolm. 2011. "Apple, HP and Dell among companies responsible for 'electronic sweatshops,' claims report." *Telegraph*, July 21. https://www.telegraph.co.uk/technology/apple/8652295/Apple-HP-and-Dell-among-companies-responsible-for-electronic-sweatshops-claims-report.html.

Morgan, Edmund S. 1975. *American Slavery, American Freedom: The Ordeal of Colonial Virginia*. New York: Norton.

Morgan, Eric J. 2006. "The world is watching: Polaroid and South Africa." *Enterprise & Society* 7, 520–49.

Morozov, Evgeny. 2009. "Texting toward utopia: Does the Internet spread democracy?" *Boston Review*,

March 1. http://bostonreview.net/evgeny-morozov-te
xting-toward-utopia-internet-democracy.

Morris, David Z. 2018. "China will block travel for those with bad 'social credit.'" *Fortune*, March 18. http://fortune.com/2018/03/18/china-travel-ban-soc ial-credit.

Muhammad, Khalil. 2011. *The Condemnation of Blackness: Race, Crime, and the Making of Modern Urban America*. Cambridge, MA: Harvard University Press.

Munger, Kevin. 2016. "Tweetment effects on the Tweeted: Experimentally reducing racist harass-ment." *Political Behavior* 39 (3), 629–49.

Murakawa, Naomi. 2014. *The First Civil Right: How Liberals Built Prison America*. Oxford: Oxford University Press.

Murray, Seb. 2018. "Will a robot recruiter be hiring you for your next job?" *Guardian*, February 2. https://www.theguardian.com/careers/2018/feb/02/will-a-ro bot-recruiter-be-hiring-you-for-your-next-job.

Nakamura, Lisa. 2002. *Cybertypes: Race, Ethnicity, and Identity on the Internet*. London: Routledge.

Nakamura, Lisa. 2008. *Digitizing Race: Visual Cultures of the Internet*. Minneapolis: University of Minnesota Press.

Nelson, Alondra. 2002. "Introduction: Future texts." *Social Text* 20 (2): 1–15.

Nelson, Alondra. 2013. *Body and Soul: The Black Panther Party and the Fight against Medical Discrimination*. Minneapolis: University of Minnesota Press.

Nelson, Alondra. 2016. *The Social Life of DNA: Race, Reparations, and Reconciliation after the Genome*. New York: Beacon Press.

References

Nguyen, Clinton. 2016. "China might use data to create a score for each citizen based on how trustworthy they are." Business Insider, October 26. https://www.businessinsider.com/china-social-credit-score-like-black-mirror-2016–10.

Noble, Safiya. 2018. *Algorithms of Oppression: How Search Engines Reinforce Racism*. New York: NYU Press.

Noble, Safiya, and Brendesha Tynes, eds. 2016. *The Intersectional Internet: Race, Sex, Class and Culture Online*. New York: Peter Lang.

Nopper, Tamara K. 2019. "Digital character in 'the scored society': FICO, social networks, and competing measurements of creditworthiness." In *Captivating Technology: Race, Carceral Technoscience, and Liberatory Imagination in Everyday Life*, edited by Ruha Benjamin, pp. 170–87. Durham, NC: Duke University Press.

N-Tech Lab. 2015. "Russian startup N-Tech.Lab upstaged Google in face recognition." PR Newswire, December 16. https://www.prnewswire.com/news-releases/russian-startup-n-techlab-upstaged-google-in-face-recognition-562635061.html.

Obasogie, Osagie K. 2014. *Blinded by Sight: Seeing Race through the Eyes of the Blind*. Palo Alto, CA: Stanford University Press.

Omi, Michael, and Howard Winant, eds. 1994. *Racial Formation in the United States: From the 1960s to the 1990s*, 2nd edn. New York: Routledge.

O'Neil, Cathy. 2016. *Weapons of Math Destruction: How Big Data Increases Inequality and Threatens Democracy*. New York: Crown.

Oremus, William. 2016. "What virtual reality is good

for." *Slate*, August 11. https://slate.com/technology/2016/08/the-only-good-reasons-to-use-virtual-reality-and-the-current-vr-renaissance-is-ignoring-them.html.

Panofsky, Aaron. 2014. *Misbehaving Science: Controversy and the Development of Behavior Genetics*. Chicago, IL: University of Chicago Press.

paperson, la. 2017. *A Third University is Possible*. Minneapolis: University of Minnesota Press.

Pasquale, Frank. 2014. *The Black Box Society: The Secret Algorithms That Control Money and Information*. Cambridge, MA: Harvard University Press.

Pearson, Jordan. 2016a. "It's our fault that AI thinks white names are more 'pleasant' than black names." Motherboard, August 26. https://motherboard.vice.com/en_us/article/z43qka/its-our-fault-that-ai-thinks-white-names-are-more-pleasant-than-black-names.

Pearson, Jordan. 2016b. "Why an AI-judged beauty contest picked nearly all white winners." Motherboard, September 5. https://motherboard.vice.com/en_us/article/78k7de/why-an-ai-judged-beauty-contest-picked-nearly-all-white-winners.

Perry, Imani. 2011. *More Beautiful and More Terrible: The Embrace and Transcendence of Racial Inequality in the United States*. New York: NYU Press.

Perry, Imani. 2018. *Vexy Thing: On Gender and Liberation*. Durham, NC: Duke University Press.

Philip, Kavita, Lilly Irani, and Paul Dourish. 2012. "Postcolonial computing: A tactical survey." *Science, Technology, and Human Values* 37 (1), 3–29.

Pitti, Stephen J. 2004. *The Devil in Silicon Valley: Northern California, Race, and Mexican Americans*. Princeton, NJ: Princeton University Press.

References

Plenke, Max. 2015a. "Google just misidentified 2 black people in the most racist way possible." Mic Network, June 30. https://mic.com/articles/121555/google-pho tos-misidentifies-african-americans-as-gorillas.

Plenke, Max. 2015b. "We figured out why some electronics don't work for black people." Mic Network, September 9. https://mic.com/articles/124899/the-reason-this-racist-soap-dispenser-doesn-t-work-on-bl ack-skin.

Pollock, Anne. 2012. *Medicating Race: Heart Disease and Durable Preoccupations with Difference.* Durham, NC: Duke University Press.

Poole, Deborah. 1997. *Vision, Race, and Modernity: A Visual Economy of the Andean Image World.* Princeton, NJ: Princeton University Press.

Ramirez, Catherine S. 2008. "Afrofuturism/ Chicanofuturism." *Azlan: A Journal of Chicano Studies* 33 (1), 185–94.

Reichardt, Jasia. 1978. *Robots: Fact, Fiction, and Prediction.* Middlesex: Penguin Books.

Richardson, George P. 2011. "Reflections on the foundations of system dynamics." *System Dynamics Review* 27 (3), 219–43.

Richardson, Kathleen. 2015. *An Anthropology of Robots and AI: Annihilation Anxiety and Machines.* New York: Routledge.

Richardson, Sarah, and Hallam Stevens, eds. 2015. *Postgenomics: Perspectives on Biology after the Genome.* Durham, NC: Duke University Press.

Ridley, Matt. 2015. "The myth of basic science." *Wall Street Journal*, October 23. https://www.wsj.com/ articles/the-myth-of-basic-science-1445613954.

Rietveld, Cornelius A., S. E. Medland, J. Derringer, et

al. 2013. "GWAS of 126,559 individuals identifies genetic variants associated with educational attainment." *Science* 1467–71. http://science.sciencemag.org/content/340/6139/1467.

Rivero, Daniel. 2016. "Kuwait's new DNA collection law is scarier than we ever imagined." Splinter News, August 24. https://splinternews.com/kuwaits-new-dna-collection-law-is-scarier-than-we-ever-1793861357.

Rivitz, Will. 2015. "The unfortunate, overlooked significance of Yik Yak." *Daily Princetonian*, November 30. http://www.dailyprincetonian.com/article/2015/11/the-unfortunate-overlooked-significance-of-yik-yak.

Roberts, Dorothy. 1998. *Killing the Black Body: Race, Reproduction, and the Meaning of Liberty*. New York: Vintage Books.

Roberts, Dorothy. 2012. *Fatal Invention: How Science, Politics, and Big Business Re-Create Race in the Twenty-First Century*. New York: The New Press.

Roberts, Siobhan. 2018. "The Yoda of Silicon Valley." *New York Times*, December 17. https://www.nytimes.com/2018/12/17/science/donald-knuth-computers-algorithms-programming.html.

Robertson, Adi. 2017. "VR was sold as an 'empathy machine' – but some artists are getting sick of it." The Verge, May 3. https://www.theverge.com/2017/5/3/15524404/tribeca-film-festival-2017-vr-empathy-machine-backlash.

Roediger, David. 2007. *Wages of Whiteness: Race and the Making of the American Working Class*. New York: Verso.

Rollins, Oliver. 2017. "Risky bodies: Race and the

science of crime." In *Living Racism: Through the Barrel of the Book*, edited by T. Rajack-Tally and D. Brooms, pp. 91–119. Lanham, MD: Lexington Books.

Rorty, Amelie O. 1962. "Slaves and machines." *Analysis* 22, 118–20.

Roth, Lorna. 2009. "Looking at Shirley, the ultimate norm: Colour balance, image technologies, and cognitive equity." *Canadian Journal of Communication* 34 (1), 111–36.

Rouse, Margaret. 2016. "What is robot?" SearchEnterpriseAI. https://searchenterpriseai.techtar get.com/definition/robot.

Roy, Arundhati. 2014. *Capitalism: A Ghost Story.* Chicago, IL: Haymarket Books.

Rusert, Britt. 2017. *Fugitive Science: Empiricism and Freedom in Early African American Culture.* New York: NYU Press.

Rusert, Britt, and Adrienne Brown. 2018. W. E. B. Du *Bois's Data Portraits: Visualizing Black America.* Princeton, NJ: Princeton University Press.

Russell, Andrew, and Lee Vinsel. 2016. "Innovation is overvalued. Maintenance often matters more." *Aeon Essays*, April 7. https://aeon.co/essays/innovation-is-overvalued-maintenance-often-matters-more.

Saleh, Maryam. 2018. "Chicago's promise: Caught in a gang dragnet and detained by ICE, an immigrant tests the limits of a sanctuary city." *Intercept*, January 28. https://theintercept.com/2018/01/28/chicago-gangs-immigration-ice.

Samatar, Sofia. 2015. "Skin feeling." *New Inquiry*, September 25. https://thenewinquiry.com/skin-feeling.

Sampson, Curt. 2009. "Parsing Roman numbers – beautifully." March 26. http://www.starling-software.

com/en/blog/my-beautiful-code/2009/03/26.parsing-roman-numbersmdashbeautifully.html.

Sankar, Pamela. 2010. "Forensic DNA phenotyping: Reinforcing race in law enforcement." Chapter 3 in *What's the Use of Race? Modern Governance and the Biology of Difference*, edited by Ian Whitmarsh and David S. Jones, pp. 49–62. Cambridge, MA: MIT Press.

Schalk, Sami. 2018. *Bodyminds Reimagined: (Dis) Ability, Race, and Gender in Black Women's Speculative Fiction*. Durham, NC: Duke University Press.

Scholz, Trebor, and Nathan Schneider, eds. 2016. *Ours to Hack and to Own: The Rise of Platform Cooperativsm: A New Vision for the Future of Work and a Fairer Internet*. New York: OR Books.

Schonbrun, Zach. 2017. "Tarnished by Charlottesville, Tiki Torch Company tries to move on." *New York Times*, August 20. https://www.nytimes.com/2017/08/20/business/media/charlottesville-tiki-torch-company.html.

Seamster, Louise, and Raphaël Charron-Chénier. 2017. "Predatory inclusion and education debt: Rethinking the racial wealth gap." *Social Currents* 4 (3), 199–207.

Sharpe, Christina E. 2014. "Black life, annotated." *New Inquiry*, August 8. https://thenewinquiry.com/black-life-annotated.

Sharpe, Christina E. 2016. *In the Wake: On Blackness and Being*. Durham, NC: Duke University Press.

Shih, Johanna. 2006. "Circumventing discrimination: Gender and ethnic strategies in Silicon Valley." *Gender & Society*, 20, 177–206.

Shultz, Mark. 2016. "Is this the face of UNC student

Faith Hedgepeth's killer?" *Newsobserver*, September 26. http://www.newsobserver.com/news/local/community/chapel-hill-news/article104310946.html.

Sieczkowski, Cavan. 2012. "Bic pens 'for her' get hilariously snarky Amazon reviews." Huffington Post, August 30, https://www.huffingtonpost.com/2012/08/30/bic-pen-for-her-amazon-reviews_n_1842991.html.

Silverstein, Jason. n.d. "Behold, the isotope." *GeneWatch*. http://www.councilforresponsiblegenetics.org/genewatch/GeneWatchPage.aspx?pageId=390&archive=yes.

Sinclair, Bruce, ed. 2004. *Technology and the African-American Experience: Needs and Opportunities for Study*. Cambridge, MA: MIT Press.

Sinclair, Kamal. 2018. "Making a new reality." Medium Corporation, August 27. https://makinganewreality.org/making-a-new-reality-summary-3fc8741595ef .

Sismondo, Sergio, and Jeremy A. Greene, eds. 2015. *The Pharmaceutical Studies Reader*. Oxford: Wiley Blackwell.

Skrla, Linda, James Joseph Scheurich, Juanita Garcia et al. 2004. "Equity audits: A practical leadership tool for developing equitable and excellent schools." *Educational Administration Quarterly* 40 (1), 133–61. http://journals.sagepub.com/doi/abs/10.1177/0013161X03259148.

Smedley, Audrey. 2007. "The history of the idea of race . . . and why it matters." Paper presented at the conference *Race, Human Variation and Disease: Consensus and Frontiers*, sponsored by the American Anthropological Association. http://www.understandingrace.org/resources/pdf/disease/smedley.pdf.

References

Smith, David. 2013. "'Racism' of early colour photography explored in art exhibition." *Guardian*, January 25. https://www.theguardian.com/artandde sign/2013/jan/25/racism-colour-photography-exhibi tion.

Snow, Jackie. 2018. "'We're in a diversity crisis': Founder of Black in AI on what's poisoning algorithms in our lives." *Technology Review*, February 14. https://www.technologyreview.com/s/610192/we re-in-a-diversity-crisis-black-in-ais-founder-on-whats -poisoning-the-algorithms-in-our.

Soep, Elisabeth. 2010. "Chimerical avatars and other identity experiments from Prof. Fox Harrell." Boing Boing, April 19. https://boingboing.net/2010/04/19/ chimerical-avatars-a.html.

Solon, Olivia. 2018. "They'll squash you like a bug: How Silicon Valley keeps a lid on leakers." *Guardian*, March 16. https://www.theguardian.com/technology/ 2018/mar/16/silicon-valley-internal-work-spying-sur veillance-leakers.

State Council. 2014. "Planning outline for the construction of a social credit system (2014–2020)." China Copyright and Media. https://chinacopyright andmedia.wordpress.com/2014/06/14/planning-out line-for-the-construction-of-a-social-credit-system-20 14–2020.

Stop LAPD Spying Coalition 2013. *"To Observe and Suspect": A People's Audit of the Los Angeles Police Department's Special Order 1*. https://stoplapdspying. org/wp-content/uploads/2013/04/PEOPLES-AUDIT- UPDATED-APRIL-2–2013-A.pdf.

Streitfeld, David. 2019. "Big tech may look troubled, but it's just getting started." *New York Times*, January

References

1. https://www.nytimes.com/2019/01/01/technology/big-tech-troubled-just-getting-started.html.

Sturken, Marita, and Lisa Cartwright. 2017. *Practices of Looking: An Introduction to Visual Culture.* Oxford: Oxford University Press.

Sweeney, Latanya. 2013. "Discrimination in online ad delivery: Google ads, black names and white names, racial discrimination, and click advertising." *ACM Queue* 11 (3), 10–29.

TallBear, Kim. 2013. *Native American DNA: Tribal Belonging and the False Promise of Genetic Science.* Minneapolis: University of Minnesota Press.

Tanz, Jason. 2016. "Soon we won't program computers: We'll train them like dogs." *Wired,* May 17. https://www.wired.com/2016/05/the-end-of-code.

Tarnoff, Ben. 2017. "Empathy – the latest gadget Silicon Valley wants to sell you." *Guardian*, October 25. https://www.theguardian.com/technology/2017/oct/25/empathy-virtual-reality-facebook-mark-zuckerberg-puerto-rico.

Taylor, Adam. 2016. "Kuwait plans to create a huge DNA database of residents and visitors: Scientists are appalled." *Washington Post*, September 14.

Taylor, Keeanga-Yamahtta, 2016. *From #Black LivesMatter to Black Liberation.* Chicago, IL: Haymarket Books.

Thomas, Sheree Renee, ed. 2000. *Dark Matter: A Century of Speculative Fiction from the African Diaspora.* New York: Warner Books.

Thompson, Nicholas. 2018a. "Jack Dorsey on Twitter's role in free speech and filter bubbles." *Wired*, October 16. https://www.wired.com/story/jack-dorsey-twitters-role-free-speech-filter-bubbles.

References

Thompson, Nicholas. 2018b. "When tech knows you better than you know yourself." *Wired*, October 4. https://www.wired.com/story/artificial-intelligence-yuval-noah-harari-tristan-harris.

Thompson, Nicholas, and Issa Lapowsky. 2018. "6 questions from the *New York Times*' Facebook bombshell." *Wired*, November 15. https://www.wired.com/story/6-questions-new-york-times-facebook-bombshell.

Toye, Frederick E.O. (Director). 2016, November 13. "Trompe L'Oeil" [Television series episode]. In Jonathan Nolan and Lisa Joy, *Westworld*. New York: HBO.

Travis, John. 2009. "Scientists decry 'flawed' and 'horrifying' nationality tests." ScienceInsider, http://news.sciencemag.org.

Truitt, Elly R. 2015. *Medieval Robots: Mechanism, Magic, Nature, and Art*. Philadelphia: University of Pennsylvania Press.

Tufekci, Zeynep. 2015. "Algorithmic harms beyond Facebook and Google: Emergent challenges of computational agency symposium essays." *Colorado Technology Law* 13, 203–18.

Tufekci, Zeynep. 2017. *Twitter and Tear Gas: The Power and Fragility of Networked Protest*. New Haven, CT: Yale University Press.

Tufekci, Zeynep. 2019. "It's the (democracy-poisoning) golden age of free speech." *Wired*, January 16. https://www.wired.com/story/free-speech-issue-tech-turmoil-new-censorship.

Turan, Kenneth. 2009 "Sleep Dealer." *Los Angeles Times*, April 17. http://articles.latimes.com/2009/apr/17/entertainment/et-sleep17.

References

Turse, Nick. 2016. "Pentagon video warns of 'unavoidable' dystopian future for world's biggest cities." The Intercept, October 13. https://theintercept.com/2016/10/13/pentagon-video-warns-of-unavoidable-dystopian-future-for-worlds-biggest-cities.

Tutton, R., C. Hauskeller, and S. Sturdy. 2014. "Suspect technologies: Forensic testing of asylum seekers at the UK border." *Ethnic and Racial Studies* 37, 738–52.

Unterhalter, Beryl. 1972. "The polaroid experiment in South Africa: A progress report." *Vanderbilt Journal of Transnational Law* 6, 109–20.

van Dijk, J. A. G. M. 2006. "Digital divide research, achievements and shortcomings." *Poetics* 34 (4–5), 221–35.

Vertesi, Janet. 2014. "My experiment opting out of big data made me look like a criminal." *Time*, May 1. http://time.com/83200/privacy-internet-big-data-opt-out.

Vinsel, Lee. 2017. "Design thinking is kind of like syphilis: It's contagious and rots your brains." Medium, December 6. https://medium.com/@sts_news/design-thinking-is-kind-of-like-syphilis-its-contagious-and-rots-your-brains-842ed078af29.

Vinsel, Lee. 2018. "Design thinking is a boondoggle." *Chronicle of Higher Education*, May 21. https://www.chronicle.com/article/Design-Thinking-Is-a/243472.

Wachter-Boettcher, Sara. 2017. *Technically Wrong: Sexist Apps, Biased Algorithms, and Other Threats of Toxic Tech*. New York: W. W. Norton.

Wacquant, Loïc. 2005. "Race as civic felony." *International Social Science Journal* 57 (183), 127–42.

Wacquant, Loïc. 2009. *Punishing the Poor: The*

Neoliberal Government of Insecurity. Durham, NC: Duke University Press.

Wacquant, Loïc. 2017. "Jim Crow as caste terrorism: From historical description to analytic model." Working paper prepared for the workshop "History, Culture & Society," Department of Sociology, Harvard University, Cambridge, April 7.

Wailoo, Keith, Alondra Nelson, and Catherine Lee, eds. 2012. *Genetics and the Unsettled Past: The Collision of DNA, Race, and History*. New Brunswick, NJ: Rutgers University Press.

Wang, Jackie. 2018. *Carceral Capitalism*. South Pasadena, CA: Semiotext(e).

Weheliye, Alexander. 2014. *Habius Viscus: Racializing Asssemblages, Biopolitics, and Black Feminist Theories of the Human*. Durham, NC: Duke University Press.

Weller, Chris. 2017. "Bill Gates and Steve Jobs raised their kids tech free – and it should've been a red flag." *Independent*, October 24. https://www.independent.co.uk/life-style/gadgets-and-tech/bill-gates-and-steve-jobs-raised-their-kids-techfree-and-it-shouldve-been-a-red-flag-a8017136.html

Wells, Liz, ed. 1996. *Photography: A Critical Introduction*. New York: Routledge.

Williams, Brennan. 2015. "Shonda Rhimes says she isn't 'diversifying' television, she's 'normalizing' it – there's a difference." Huffington Post, March 16. https://www.huffingtonpost.com/2015/03/16/shonda-rhimes-diversity-normalize-television_n_6878842.html.

Winner, Langdon. 1980. "Do artifacts have politics?" *Daedalus* 109, 121–36.

References

Womack, Ytasha L. 2015. *Afrofuturism: The World of Black Sci-Fi and Fantasy Culture*. Chicago, IL: Lawrence Hill Books.

Wynter, Sylvia. 2003. "Unsettling the coloniality of being/power/truth/freedom: Towards the human, after man, its overrepresentation: An argument." *New Centennial Review* 3 (3), 257–337.

Yang, Robert. 2017. "'If you walk in someone else's shoes, then you've taken their shoes': Empathy machines as appropriation machines." https://www.blog.radiator.debacle.us/2017/04/if-you-walk-in-someone-elses-shoes-then.html

Zercoe, Cole. 2017. "How virtual reality could transform law enforcement." PoliceOne.com, December 7. https://www.policeone.com/policing-in-the-video-age/articles/467266006-How-virtual-reality-could-transform-law-enforcement.

Zuberi, Tufuku. 2003. *Thicker Than Blood: How Racial Statistics Lie*. Minneapolis: University of Minnesota Press.

Index

Index

Index

Index

Index

Index

Index

Index

Index

Index

Index

Index